LOOP PARALLELIZATION

A Book Series On
LOOP TRANSFORMATIONS FOR RESTRUCTURING COMPILERS

Utpal Banerjee

Series Titles:

Loop Transformations for Restructuring Compilers: The Foundations

Loop Parallelization

LOOP PARALLELIZATION

Utpal Banerjee
Intel Corporation

Loop Transformations for Restructuring Compilers

KLUWER ACADEMIC PUBLISHERS
Boston / Dordrecht / London

Distributors for North America:
Kluwer Academic Publishers
101 Philip Drive
Assinippi Park
Norwell, Massachusetts 02061 USA

Distributors for all other countries:
Kluwer Academic Publishers Group
Distribution Centre
Post Office Box 322
3300 AH Dordrecht, THE NETHERLANDS

ISBN 978-1-4419-5141-0

Library of Congress Cataloging-in-Publication Data

A C.I.P. Catalogue record for this book is available
from the Library of Congress.

Contents

List of Figures

List of Tables

List of Notations

In the following, $\mathbf{i} = (i_1, i_2, \ldots, i_m)$ and $\mathbf{j} = (j_1, j_2, \ldots, j_m)$ are two vectors of size m, and $1 \leq \ell \leq m$.

Preface

The series *Loop Transformations for Restructuring Compilers* deals with transformations that change a nest of Fortran-like **do** loops automatically into a parallel form. Volume I in this series, subtitled *The Foundations*, provided the general mathematical background, discussed data dependence, and introduced some of the major transformations. This book is Volume II in the same series. It creates a detailed theory of iteration-level transformations.

We continue using the program model introduced in Volume I: a perfect nest of loops with stride 1, whose body is a sequence of assignment statements. We allow loop limits that are general enough so that a transformation applied to a loop nest in the selected class returns another loop nest in the same class. Iterations of the loop nest are considered to be atomic units, and we assume that any dependence between them is uniform. An iteration-level loop transformation simply defines a new execution order for the iterations. The transformed program is typically a mixed nest of **do** and **doall** loops, where a **doall** loop is a loop structure whose iterations are not ordered in any way. Each loop transformation comes from a one-to-one mapping of the index space of the loop nest under consideration. These mappings are shaped by the distance matrix of the loop nest, but are independent of its index space.

When searching for parallelism, we do not think of any particular computer architecture, but take the view that parallelism between iterations should be exposed to the fullest extent possible. We will distinguish between two types of parallelism: vertical and horizontal. Vertical parallelism refers to the situation where the dependence graph of the given loop nest **L** has been partitioned such that the members of the partition can be executed independently of one another. Horizontal parallelism refers to the situation where a number of iterations of **L** can be executed simultaneously (after their predecessors have finished). We display both kinds of parallelism by finding a loop nest equivalent to **L**, that has an outer ring of **doall** loops, then a **do** loop, and finally an inner core of **doall** loops.

Our notion of the equivalence of transformed programs is somewhat stronger than equivalence of observable results. In this work, we do not consider transformations that change the number or kind of fundamental operations in a loop body (e.g., replacing a loop performing a summation by a recurrence solver). Furthermore, we do not address ourselves to transformations whose legality requires knowledge of the algebraic properties of fundamental operations (e.g., using associativity to reverse a loop performing a summation). Although these types of transformations are sometimes employed in production compilers, they are not easily amenable to systematic treatment, and are beyond the scope of the present work.

The books in this series are directed towards graduate and advanced undergraduate students, and professional writers of restructuring compilers. The recommended background for Volume I consisted of some knowledge of programming languages and linear algebra, and familiarity with calculus and graph theory. For Volume II, we will assume in addition that the reader has studied the material in Volume I. The algorithms in this book are based on concepts and algorithms developed in the previous book. For convenience of the reader, a concise review of some of the concepts related to the program model, dependence, and loop transformation is given in Chapter 1. Chapters 2–4 describe the three basic classes of iteration-level transformations: loop permutations, unimodular transformations, and remainder transformations. The final chapter puts these transformaions in proper perspective in relation to vertical and horizontal parallelism inherent in a given program.

As was our custom in Volume I, we often leave out a step in an argument or the proof of a result. Sometimes, a missing step is indicated by a comment to the reader, for example, (why?) or (explain). Filling these gaps and supplying these proofs are very useful in building intuition into the subject. They should be taken seriously along with the numerous examples and exercises in the book. For the referencing of examples, exercises, etc., we have used a simple scheme: Exercise 2 refers to the second exercise in the current section; Exercise 3.1.2 refers to the second exercise in the first section of Chapter 3 of the current book; and Algorithm I-2.2 is Algorithm 2.2 in Volume I of the series.

The next step will be to generalize and supplement the material of this book. We will extend the program model to include imperfect nesting, non-unit strides, conditional statements, etc. We will also look inside an iteration to find potential parallelism at lower levels, and study programs more complex than a loop nest to find potential parallelism at a higher level. The dependence analysis of a perfect loop nest developed in Volume I is adequate for the handling of programs used in Volume II. A more general dependence analysis is needed if we generalize our program model. Dependence analysis and transformations (at different levels) of more general loops will be studied in future volumes of the series.

U.B.

Santa Clara, California

Acknowledgments

An earlier version of the manuscript was used as text for a fall '93 Computer Science course at the University of Illinois at Urbana-Champaign. Of those who attended, the following students gave written comments: David August, William Blume, Xiangfeng Chen, Mohammad Haghighat, Teresa Johnson, Venkata Krishnan, Antonio Lain, Celso Mendes, Hideki Saito, Bruce Stotts, and Jenn-Yuan Tsai. The comments from August, Johnson, and Saito were quite detailed. The interaction with the students and their suggestions for improvement were very useful to the author for preparation of the final version.

David August, Teresa Johnson, and Celso Mendes also read the final manuscript meticulously. They gave many suggestions and found many errors. Teresa Johnson suggested some problems. Celso Mendes gave the author a number of diagrams on which the figures for elementary transformations (in Chapters 2 and 3) are based. Mohammad Haghighat improved the efficiency of Algorithm 2.1 for finding permutation preventing direction vectors, by discarding unnecessary assignments. He also directed the author's attention to many interesting questions, and helped debug the manuscript. The author would like to thank all students who attended his class, and thank especially Celso, David, Mohammad, and Teresa for their devoted work.

The final manuscript was read by Suresh Rao, James Radigan, David Sehr, Kevin Smith, and K. Sridharan of Intel Corporation. David Sehr and K. Sridharan gave a number of comments. Nancy

Navarro (Intel) proofread the manuscript and took care of the printing arrangements. The author would like to express his gratitude to these colleagues. Finally, he would like to thank Dr. Richard Wirt for making it possible for him to continue writing this series of books at Intel.

Chapter 1

Background

1.1 Introduction

Our aim is to automatically rewrite a given loop nest in a form that allows parallel execution of independent iterations. We assume that the reader is familiar with the author's *Loop Transformations for Restructuring Compilers—The Foundations* which will be referred to as "Volume I" throughout this book. In Volume I, we laid the basic mathematical framework for a theory of loop transformations, defined dependence and related concepts, described some algorithms by which dependence can be detected in a large class of programs, and gave an introduction to some of the major loop transformations. In this book, we will study in detail the fundamental iteration-level transformations with the goal of loop parallelization in mind.

We continue to use as our model program a perfect nest of Fortran-like **do** loops whose body is a sequence of assignment statements. The stride of each loop is taken to be 1, and the limits of any loop L are allowed to be defined in terms of linear (affine) functions of index variables (of loops surrounding L) with rational coefficients. Iterations of the loop nest are considered to be atomic units, and it is assumed that any dependence between them is always uniform. This simplified model lets us concentrate on the intricacies of loop transformations without having to spend a great

deal of effort on technical difficulties. It also helps keep the mathe-
matics relatively simple. This model will be generalized to include
imperfectly nested loops, non-unit strides, conditional statements,
and non-uniform dependences in a future project.

For the sake of completeness, a review of some of the basic concepts from Volume I is given in Sections 1.2–1.4. This review is
quite condensed, however, and should not be used as a first-time
introduction to the subject. In Section 1.5, we briefly describe the
contents of the book and explain the goal of parallelization.

1.2   Program Model

Our model program is a perfect nest $\mathbf{L}$ of m **do** loops:

L_1 :   **do** $I_1 = p_1, q_1$
L_2 :   **do** $I_2 = p_2, q_2$

$\vdots$ $\vdots$

L_m :   **do** $I_m = p_m, q_m$
                      $H(I_1, I_2, \ldots, I_m)$
                  enddo

                $\vdots$

           enddo
        enddo

We will write $\mathbf{L} = (L_1, L_2, \ldots, L_m)$. The loop nest is called a *single*,
double, or *triple* loop if the value of m is 1, 2, or 3, respectively.
The *index variables* of the individual loops are $I_1, I_2, \ldots, I_m$, and
they form the *index vector* $\mathbf{I} = (I_1, I_2, \ldots, I_m)$ of $\mathbf{L}$. The *lower* and
upper limits of the loop L_r (i.e., the *lower* and *upper* bounds of the
index variable I_r) are p_r and q_r, respectively, $1 \leq r \leq m$. The
stride of each index variable is 1. The *body* of the loop nest is
$H(I_1, I_2, \ldots, I_m)$ or $H(\mathbf{I})$. We assume that $H(\mathbf{I})$ is a sequence of
assignment statements.

By a 'constant' we will mean a symbol whose value is known
at compile-time. We assume that p_1 and q_1 are integer constants.

The index variable I_1 of L_1, the outermost loop, starts with the value p_1 and goes up in steps of 1 to the maximum value of q_1. If $q_1 < p_1$, then the loop nest **L** is not executed. We assume that p_2 and q_2 are integer-valued functions of I_1. For each value i_1 of I_1 in the range $\{p_1, p_1 + 1, \ldots, q_1\}$, the index variable I_2 starts with the value $p_2(i_1)$ and goes up in steps of 1 to the maximum value of $q_2(i_1)$. If $q_2(i_1) < p_2(i_1)$, then the instance of the loop nest $(L_2, L_3, \ldots, L_m)$ corresponding to $I_1 = i_1$ is not executed. In general, for $1 \leq r \leq m$, the loop limits p_r and q_r are integer-valued functions of $I_1, I_2, \ldots, I_{r-1}$. For a set of possible values $i_1, i_2, \ldots, i_{r-1}$ of the index variables $I_1, I_2, \ldots, I_{r-1}$, respectively, the range of I_r is

$$\{p_r(i_1, i_2, \ldots, i_{r-1}), \ p_r(i_1, i_2, \ldots, i_{r-1}) + 1, \ldots, \ q_r(i_1, i_2, \ldots, i_{r-1})\}.$$

A set of possible values $i_1, i_2, \ldots, i_m$ of $I_1, I_2, \ldots, I_m$ determines a value $\mathbf{i} = (i_1, i_2, \ldots, i_m)$ of the index vector $\mathbf{I}$, which is also called an *index value* or an *index point* of the loop nest **L**. The set of all index points is the *index space* of **L**; it is denoted by $\mathcal{R}$. We have $\mathcal{R} \subset \mathbf{Z}^m$, where $\mathbf{Z}^m$ is the set of integer m-vectors (the Cartesian product of m copies of the set $\mathbf{Z}$ of integers). Another way to view it is to say that $\mathcal{R}$ is the set of all integer points in a subset of $\mathbf{R}^m$, where $\mathbf{R}^m$ is the set of real m-vectors (the Cartesian product of m copies of the real line $\mathbf{R}$). By a slight abuse of language, we will often refer to $\mathcal{R}$ as a certain subset of $\mathbf{R}^m$, even though $\mathcal{R}$ is only the set of integer points in that subset. For example, we may describe $\mathcal{R}$ as a parallelogram in the plane or as a cube in 3-space.

If the limits p_r and q_r are integer constants, the index space

$$\mathcal{R} = \{\mathbf{I} \in \mathbf{Z}^m : p_1 \leq I_1 \leq q_1, \ p_2 \leq I_2 \leq q_2, \ldots, \ p_m \leq I_m \leq q_m\}$$

is a rectangular parallelepiped, bounded by the $2m$ hyperplanes $I_r = p_r$ and $I_r = q_r$, $1 \leq r \leq m$. This is the simplest case; it is indicated by saying that the loop nest **L** is *rectangular*.

The next step is to allow p_r and q_r to be linear (affine) functions of $I_1, I_2, \ldots, I_{r-1}$ with integer coefficients. For $1 \leq r \leq m$, let

$$
\begin{aligned}
p_r(I_1, I_2, \ldots, I_{r-1}) &= p_{r0} + p_{r1}I_1 + p_{r2}I_2 + \cdots + p_{r(r-1)}I_{r-1} \\
q_r(I_1, I_2, \ldots, I_{r-1}) &= q_{r0} + q_{r1}I_1 + q_{r2}I_2 + \cdots + q_{r(r-1)}I_{r-1}.
\end{aligned}
$$

We can write the system of inequalities $p_r \leq I_r$ as

$$
\left.
\begin{array}{rcl}
p_{10} & \leq & I_1 \\
p_{20} & \leq & -p_{21}I_1 + I_2 \\
p_{30} & \leq & -p_{31}I_1 - p_{32}I_2 + I_3 \\
& \vdots & \\
p_{m0} & \leq & -p_{m1}I_1 - p_{m2}I_2 - \cdots - p_{m(m-1)}I_{m-1} + I_m,
\end{array}
\right\}
$$

or as $\mathbf{p}_0 \leq \mathbf{IP}$ where $\mathbf{p}_0 = (p_{10}, p_{20}, \ldots, p_{m0})$ and

$$
\mathbf{P} = \begin{pmatrix}
1 & -p_{21} & -p_{31} & \cdots & -p_{m1} \\
0 & 1 & -p_{32} & \cdots & -p_{m2} \\
0 & 0 & 1 & \cdots & -p_{m3} \\
\vdots & \vdots & \vdots & \ddots & \vdots \\
0 & 0 & 0 & \cdots & 1
\end{pmatrix}.
$$

Similarly, the inequalities $I_r \leq q_r$ can be put in the form $\mathbf{IQ} \leq \mathbf{q}_0$ where $\mathbf{q}_0 = (q_{10}, q_{20}, \ldots, q_{m0})$ and

$$
\mathbf{Q} = \begin{pmatrix}
1 & -q_{21} & -q_{31} & \cdots & -q_{m1} \\
0 & 1 & -q_{32} & \cdots & -q_{m2} \\
0 & 0 & 1 & \cdots & -q_{m3} \\
\vdots & \vdots & \vdots & \ddots & \vdots \\
0 & 0 & 0 & \cdots & 1
\end{pmatrix}.
$$

The m-vectors $\mathbf{p}_0$ and $\mathbf{q}_0$ are respectively the *lower* and *upper limit vectors* of $\mathbf{L}$, and the $m \times m$ upper triangular matrices $\mathbf{P}$ and $\mathbf{Q}$ are the *lower* and *upper limit matrices*. The index space $\mathcal{R}$ is the set of all integer m-vectors $\mathbf{I}$ that simultaneously satisfy the two sets of inequalities (called the *constraints* on $\mathbf{I}$):

$$
\left.
\begin{array}{rcl}
\mathbf{p}_0 & \leq & \mathbf{IP} \\
\mathbf{IQ} & \leq & \mathbf{q}_0.
\end{array}
\right\} \tag{1.1}
$$

The index space is now a polytope,[1] or rather, the set of all integer points of a polytope (Exercise 1). This polytope is a rectangular

---

[1]A *polytope* in $\mathbf{R}^m$ is a bounded set of the form $\{\mathbf{x} \in \mathbf{R}^m : \mathbf{xA} \leq \mathbf{c}\}$ for some real matrix $\mathbf{A}$ and real vector $\mathbf{c}$.

parallelepiped if $\mathbf{P}$ and $\mathbf{Q}$ are equal to the $m \times m$ identity matrix $\mathcal{I}_m$ (which is the rectangular loop nest case).

In the most general case we will consider, the loop limits are derived from sets of linear functions with rational coefficients. More precisely, p_r could be the ceiling of the maximum of a number of linear functions in $I_1, I_2, \ldots, I_{r-1}$, and q_r the floor of the minimum of a number of such functions, $1 \leq r \leq m$. Moreover, the coefficients in these functions are allowed to be rational numbers. The lower and upper limit vectors and matrices can be defined as before, but now they may have rational elements and more than m columns. The index space $\mathcal{R}$ is defined by a set of inequalities of the same form as (1.1), and it is still a polytope in $\mathbf{R}^m$. (See the following examples.) These generalized loop limits probably seem to be overly complex, but they cannot be avoided. A loop transformation may easily transform even a rectangular loop nest into one having an index space that can only be described in this general way (Exercise 1.4.4).

A loop nest is *regular* if the lower and upper limit matrices are equal. A rectangular nest is necessarily regular, since then $\mathbf{P}$ and $\mathbf{Q}$ are both equal to the identity matrix. Examples of different types of index spaces are given below.

Example 1.1 Consider the double loop $\mathbf{L}$:

$L_1:$ **do** $I_1 = 10, 25$
$L_2:$ **do** $I_2 = \lceil (I_1 + 5)/3 \rceil, I_1$
             $H(I_1, I_2)$
        enddo
     enddo

The index space $\mathcal{R}$ consists of all integer vectors (I_1, I_2) such that

$$\left.\begin{array}{ccccc} 10 & \leq & I_1 & \leq & 25 \\ (I_1 + 5)/3 & \leq & I_2 & \leq & I_1. \end{array}\right\} \qquad (1.2)$$

It is a trapezoid (Figure 1.1) bounded by the lines:

$$I_1 = 10, \ I_1 = 25, \ 3I_2 = I_1 + 5, \ I_2 = I_1.$$

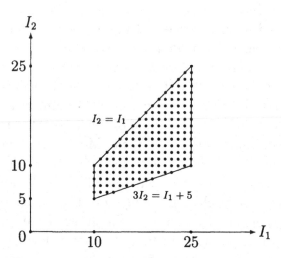

Figure 1.1: Index space of Example 1.1.

The inequalities in (1.2) giving the lower bounds of the index variables can be written as

$$\left. \begin{array}{rcccc} 10 & \leq & I_1 & & \\ \frac{5}{3} & \leq & -\frac{1}{3}I_1 & + & I_2 \end{array} \right\}$$

or in the matrix form as

$$\left(10, \ \tfrac{5}{3} \ \right) \leq (I_1, I_2) \begin{pmatrix} 1 & -\frac{1}{3} \\ 0 & 1 \end{pmatrix}. \tag{1.3}$$

Similarly, the inequalities in (1.2) giving the upper bounds on the index variables can be written as

$$\left. \begin{array}{rcccc} I_1 & & & \leq & 25 \\ -I_1 & + & I_2 & \leq & 0 \end{array} \right\}$$

or in the matrix form as

$$(I_1, I_2) \begin{pmatrix} 1 & -1 \\ 0 & 1 \end{pmatrix} \leq (25, 0). \tag{1.4}$$

From (1.3) and (1.4), we see that the lower limit vector $\mathbf{p}_0$, the lower limit matrix $\mathbf{P}$, the upper limit vector $\mathbf{q}_0$, and the upper limit matrix $\mathbf{Q}$ for the double loop $\mathbf{L}$ are as follows:

$$\mathbf{p}_0 = \left(10, \tfrac{5}{3}\right), \qquad \mathbf{q}_0 = (25, 0),$$

$$\mathbf{P} = \begin{pmatrix} 1 & -\tfrac{1}{3} \\ 0 & 1 \end{pmatrix}, \qquad \mathbf{Q} = \begin{pmatrix} 1 & -1 \\ 0 & 1 \end{pmatrix}.$$

This loop nest is not regular.

Example 1.2 Consider the double loop $\mathbf{L}$:

$L_1:$ **do** $I_1 = 0, 20$
$L_2:$ **do** $I_2 = \lceil \max(2I_1 - 5, 3I_1/2) \rceil, \lfloor \min(2I_1, 5 + 3I_1/2) \rfloor$
             $H(I_1, I_2)$
          enddo
     enddo

The index space $\mathcal{R}$ consists of all integer vectors (I_1, I_2) such that

$$\left. \begin{array}{ccc} 0 \leq & I_1 & \leq 20 \\ \max(2I_1 - 5, 3I_1/2) \leq & I_2 & \leq \min(2I_1, 5 + 3I_1/2). \end{array} \right\} \quad (1.5)$$

It is a parallelogram (Figure 1.2) bounded by the lines:

$$I_2 = 2I_1, \ I_2 = 2I_1 - 5, \ 2I_2 = 3I_1, \ 2I_2 = 3I_1 + 10.$$

The inequalities in (1.5) giving the lower bounds of the index variables can be written as

$$\left. \begin{array}{rcrcl} 0 & \leq & & & I_1 \\ -5 & \leq & -2I_1 & + & I_2 \\ 0 & \leq & -\tfrac{3}{2}I_1 & + & I_2 \end{array} \right\}$$

or in the matrix form as

$$(0, -5, 0) \leq (I_1, I_2) \begin{pmatrix} 1 & -2 & -\tfrac{3}{2} \\ 0 & 1 & 1 \end{pmatrix}. \quad (1.6)$$

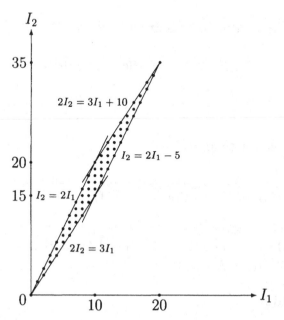

Figure 1.2: Index space of Example 1.2.

Similarly, the inequalities in (1.5) giving the upper bounds on the index variables can be written as

$$\left.\begin{array}{rcl} I_1 & \leq & 20 \\ -2I_1 + I_2 & \leq & 0 \\ -\frac{3}{2}I_1 + I_2 & \leq & 5 \end{array}\right\}$$

or in the matrix form as

$$(I_1, I_2) \begin{pmatrix} 1 & -2 & -\frac{3}{2} \\ 0 & 1 & 1 \end{pmatrix} \leq (20, 0, 5). \tag{1.7}$$

From (1.6) and (1.7), we see that the lower limit vector $\mathbf{p_0}$, the lower limit matrix $\mathbf{P}$, the upper limit vector $\mathbf{q_0}$, and the upper limit matrix $\mathbf{Q}$ for the double loop $\mathbf{L}$ are as follows:

$$\mathbf{p_0} = (0, -5, 0), \qquad\qquad \mathbf{q_0} = (20, 0, 5),$$

$$\mathbf{P} = \begin{pmatrix} 1 & -2 & -\frac{3}{2} \\ 0 & 1 & 1 \end{pmatrix}, \qquad \mathbf{Q} = \begin{pmatrix} 1 & -2 & -\frac{3}{2} \\ 0 & 1 & 1 \end{pmatrix}.$$

Since $\mathbf{P} = \mathbf{Q}$, the loop nest $\mathbf{L}$ is regular. (Can you simplify $\mathbf{p}_0$, $\mathbf{P}$, $\mathbf{q}_0$, $\mathbf{Q}$ by discarding redundant inequalities?)

EXERCISES 1.2

1. Prove that the index space of the loop nest $\mathbf{L}$ is the set of integer points of a polytope.

2. Find $\mathbf{p}_0, \mathbf{q}_0, \mathbf{P}, \mathbf{Q}$ for a double loop with the following loop limits:

    (a) $p_1 = 10$, $q_1 = 100$, $p_2 = 2I_1$, $q_2 = 2I_1 + 20$;

    (b) $p_1 = 0$, $q_1 = 200$, $p_2 = 0$, $q_2 = 300 - \frac{3}{2}I_1$.

    Draw the index space. Point out if the loop nest is rectangular or regular.

3. Find $\mathbf{p}_0, \mathbf{q}_0, \mathbf{P}, \mathbf{Q}$ for a triple loop with the following loop limits:

    (a) $p_1 = 0$, $q_1 = 100$, $p_2 = \lceil I_1/2 \rceil$, $q_2 = \min(200, 4I_1)$, $p_3 = I_1 + I_2$, $q_3 = 200$;

    (b) $p_1 = 0$, $q_1 = 200$, $p_2 = 0$, $q_2 = \lfloor \frac{4}{5}I_1 \rfloor$, $p_3 = \lceil I_2/4 \rceil$, $q_3 = \min(100, 2I_2, I_1 - I_2)$.

    Point out if the loop nest is rectangular or regular.

1.3   Dependence

An *iteration* of the loop nest $\mathbf{L}$ is an instance $H(\mathbf{i})$ of the body $H(\mathbf{I})$ of $\mathbf{L}$ defined by an index value $\mathbf{i}$. The iterations of $\mathbf{L}$ are executed sequentially in the increasing (lexicographic) order[2] of values of the index vector $\mathbf{I}$, that is, $H(\mathbf{i})$ is executed before $H(\mathbf{j})$ if $\mathbf{i} \prec \mathbf{j}$.

Let $1 \leq r \leq m$. We may sometimes write $L_r(I_1, I_2, \ldots, I_{r-1})$ instead of L_r to emphasize the dependency of this loop on the index variables of loops surrounding it. The notation for a nest of loops $(L_r, L_{r+1}, \ldots, L_m)$ can be extended similarly.

The program $\mathbf{L} = (L_1, L_2, \ldots, L_m)$ is thought of as a nest of m loops when we are transforming all the loops in one step. It may also

---

[2]Lexicographic order: For $\mathbf{i} = (i_1, i_2)$ and $\mathbf{j} = (j_1, j_2)$, $\mathbf{i} \prec \mathbf{j}$ means either $i_1 < j_1$, or $i_1 = j_1$ and $i_2 < j_2$. The definition of this relation is easily extended to vectors of any given size. See Section I-1.3.

be thought of as a single loop L_1 with index variable I_1. The body of L_1 is taken to be either the loop nest $(L_2, L_3, \ldots, L_m)(I_1)$ with index vector $(I_2, I_3, \ldots, I_m)$, or the loop $L_2(I_1)$ with index variable I_2. The iterations of L_1 are the instances of its body for different values of I_1. They can be expressed as instances of the loop nest $(L_2, L_3, \ldots, L_m)(I_1)$, or as instances of the loop $L_2(I_1)$. In general, for $1 \le r \le m$, we can think of $\mathbf{L}$ as a nest of r loops $(L_1, L_2, \ldots, L_r)$ with a suitable body.

An iteration of a loop nest $(L_1, L_2, \ldots, L_r)$, $1 \le r < m$, represents a sequence of iterations of the loop nest $\mathbf{L}$. Unless otherwise indicated, the word 'iteration' will mean an iteration $H(\mathbf{i})$ of $\mathbf{L}$.

Example 1.3 Consider the loop nest $\mathbf{L}$:

$$
\begin{aligned}
&L_1: &&\textbf{do } I_1 = 1, 3 \\
&L_2(I_1): &&\quad \textbf{do } I_2 = I_1, 2 \\
&L_3(I_1, I_2): &&\qquad \textbf{do } I_3 = I_1, I_1 + I_2 \\
& && \qquad\quad H(I_1, I_2, I_3) \\
& && \qquad \textbf{enddo} \\
& && \quad \textbf{enddo} \\
& && \textbf{enddo}
\end{aligned}
$$

The body of L_1 is the loop $L_2(I_1)$:

$$
\begin{aligned}
&L_2(I_1): &&\textbf{do } I_2 = I_1, 2 \\
&L_3(I_1, I_2): &&\quad \textbf{do } I_3 = I_1, I_1 + I_2 \\
& && \quad\; H(I_1, I_2, I_3) \\
& && \quad \textbf{enddo} \\
& && \textbf{enddo}
\end{aligned}
$$

The iterations of L_1 are the instances $L_2(1), L_2(2), L_2(3)$ of the loop $L_2(I_1)$:

$$
\begin{aligned}
&L_2(1): &&\textbf{do } I_2 = 1, 2 \\
&L_3(1, I_2): &&\quad \textbf{do } I_3 = 1, 1 + I_2 \\
& && \quad\; H(1, I_2, I_3) \\
& && \quad \textbf{enddo} \\
& && \textbf{enddo}
\end{aligned}
$$

		$L_3(1,1)$	$H(1,1,1)$
			$H(1,1,2)$
	$L_2(1)$		$H(1,2,1)$
		$L_3(1,2)$	$H(1,2,2)$
L_1			$H(1,2,3)$
			$H(2,2,2)$
	$L_2(2)$	$L_3(2,2)$	$H(2,2,3)$
			$H(2,2,4)$
	$L_2(3)$	$\emptyset$	

Table 1.1: Iterations of individual loops (Example 1.3).

$L_2(2)$:   **do** $I_2 = 2, 2$
$L_3(2, I_2)$:   **do** $I_3 = 2, 2 + I_2$
                  $H(2, I_2, I_3)$
           enddo
      enddo

$L_2(3)$: Not executed.

The iterations of $L_2(1)$ are $L_3(1,1)$ and $L_3(1,2)$, and the only iteration of $L_2(2)$ is $L_3(2,2)$:

$L_3(1,1)$:   **do** $I_3 = 1, 2$
             $H(1, 1, I_3)$
          enddo

$L_3(1,2)$:   **do** $I_3 = 1, 3$
             $H(1, 2, I_3)$
          enddo

$L_3(2,2)$:   **do** $I_3 = 2, 4$
             $H(2, 2, I_3)$
          enddo

The iterations of **L** are shown in Table 1.1, grouped into iterations of the individual loops; they are arranged in their sequential order of execution.

The loop transformations considered in this book treat the iterations of **L** as indivisible units. The theory of such transformations is based on the concept of dependence between distinct iterations. An iteration $H(\mathbf{j})$ *depends* on a different iteration $H(\mathbf{i})$, if the following conditions are satisfied:

1. $H(\mathbf{i})$ is executed before $H(\mathbf{j})$ in **L**, that is, $\mathbf{i} \prec \mathbf{j}$;

2. There is a memory location that is referenced (read or written) by both iterations, and at least one of the two references is a 'write';

3. That memory location is not written by any iteration $H(\mathbf{k})$ that comes between $H(\mathbf{i})$ and $H(\mathbf{j})$ (i.e., such that $\mathbf{i} \prec \mathbf{k} \prec \mathbf{j}$).

The *iteration dependence graph* of **L** is the graph of the dependence relation in the set of iterations of **L**. Thus, it is a digraph whose vertices represent the iterations of **L**, and there is an edge directed from a vertex u to a vertex v iff the iteration corresponding to v depends on the iteration corresponding to u. To draw the iteration dependence graph, we usually take a picture of the index space of **L**, identify the index points with their corresponding iterations, and then draw an arrow from an index point $\mathbf{i}$ to an index point $\mathbf{j}$ whenever the iteration $H(\mathbf{j})$ depends on the iteration $H(\mathbf{i})$. Since it is the only type of dependence graph we will consider in this book, the iteration dependence graph will be often referred to simply as the dependence graph.

There are no cycles in an iteration dependence graph. An iteration $H(\mathbf{j})$ is *indirectly dependent* (or *depends indirectly*) on another iteration $H(\mathbf{i})$ if there is a directed path from $H(\mathbf{i})$ to $H(\mathbf{j})$ in the dependence graph. The relation of indirect dependence is irreflexive and transitive, and therefore it defines a partial order. (Indirect dependence is the strict relation corresponding to this partial order.)

Two distinct iterations are *weakly connected* if there is an undirected path joining them. The relation of weak connectedness is an equivalence relation. The equivalence classes of this relation are called the *weakly connected components* of the dependence graph. The partition of the dependence graph into its weakly connected components will be referred to as the *weak partition*. Dependence implies indirect dependence which, in turn, implies weak connectedness.

If an iteration $H(\mathbf{j})$ depends on an iteration $H(\mathbf{i})$, then the difference $\mathbf{d} = \mathbf{j} - \mathbf{i}$ between the two index values is called a *dependence distance vector* for the loop nest $\mathbf{L}$. Since $\mathbf{i} \prec \mathbf{j}$ by definition, we have $\mathbf{d} \succ \mathbf{0}$, that is, a distance vector is always positive.[3]

Let N denote the number of distinct (dependence) distance vectors for $\mathbf{L}$, and let D denote the set of those vectors. It is often convenient to operate on the distance vectors arranged as a matrix. The *distance matrix* for $\mathbf{L}$ is an $N \times m$ matrix whose rows are made up of the vectors in D in any order; it is unique up to a permutation of rows. The distance matrix is also referred to as the *dependence matrix* and it is denoted by $\mathcal{D}$.

A distance vector $\mathbf{d}$ is *uniform* if for each index point $\mathbf{i}$ such that $\mathbf{i} + \mathbf{d}$ is also an index point, the iteration $H(\mathbf{i} + \mathbf{d})$ depends on the iteration $H(\mathbf{i})$. Unless otherwise indicated, we will assume that all distance vectors for $\mathbf{L}$ are uniform.

The *sign* of a vector is the vector of signs of its elements. Thus, if $\mathbf{d} = (2, -3, 0)$, then

$$\mathbf{sig}(\mathbf{d}) = (\mathrm{sig}(2), \mathrm{sig}(-3), \mathrm{sig}(0)) = (1, -1, 0).$$

A *dependence direction vector* for $\mathbf{L}$ is the sign $\boldsymbol{\sigma}$ of a distance vector for $\mathbf{L}$. Obviously, two or more distance vectors may yield the same direction vector. The *direction matrix* for $\mathbf{L}$ is an $N' \times m$ matrix, where $N' \leq N$, whose rows are made up of all the distinct direction vectors for $\mathbf{L}$ arranged in any order. The direction matrix is unique up to a permutation of rows; it is denoted by $\boldsymbol{\Delta}$.

If d_ℓ is the first nonzero element of a vector $\mathbf{d} = (d_1, d_2, \ldots, d_m)$ from the left, then it is the *leading element* of $\mathbf{d}$ and ℓ is the *level*

---

[3]Here 'positive' means lexicographically positive. A vector with all positive elements is certainly (lexicographically) positive, but a (lexicographically) positive vector may have one or more negative elements, e.g., $(0, 2, -11, 0)$.

of $\mathbf{d}$. The level of a positive vector $\mathbf{d}$ is ℓ iff $\mathbf{d} \succ_\ell \mathbf{0}$.[4] A *dependence level* for $\mathbf{L}$ is the level of a distance vector for $\mathbf{L}$. If ℓ is a dependence level, then we say that there is a dependence in $\mathbf{L}$ at level ℓ, or that the loop L_ℓ *carries* a dependence. There are m possible dependence levels: $1, 2, \ldots, m$.

Example 1.4 Let $H(I_1, I_2)$ denote the body of the loop nest:

L_1 :   **do** $I_1 = 0, 4$
L_2 :   **do** $I_2 = 0, 4$
                    $X(I_1 + 1, I_2 + 2) = Y(I_1, I_2) + 1$
                    $Y(I_1 + 2, I_2 + 1) = X(I_1, I_2) + 1$
                enddo
            enddo

There are two distance vectors: $(1, 2)$ and $(2, 1)$, both uniform. They form the rows of the distance matrix which can be taken to be

$$\begin{pmatrix} 1 & 2 \\ 2 & 1 \end{pmatrix}.$$

The only direction vector is $(1, 1)$. There is a dependence at level 1, but not at level 2. Thus, L_1 carries a dependence, but not L_2. There are 5 weakly connected components:

$$\mathcal{H}_1 = \{H(0,0), H(0,3), H(1,2), H(2,1), H(3,0), H(2,4), H(3,3), H(4,2)\}$$
$$\mathcal{H}_2 = \{H(0,1), H(1,0), H(1,3), H(2,2), H(3,1), H(3,4), H(4,3)\}$$
$$\mathcal{H}_3 = \{H(0,2), H(1,1), H(2,0), H(1,4), H(2,3), H(3,2), H(4,1), H(4,4)\}$$
$$\mathcal{H}_4 = \{H(0,4)\}$$
$$\mathcal{H}_5 = \{H(4,0)\}.$$

The dependence graph is shown in Figure 1.3(a), and the first three components are shown in Figures 1.3(b)–(d).

---

[4]If $\mathbf{a} = (a_1, a_2, a_3)$ and $\mathbf{b} = (b_1, b_2, b_3)$, then $\mathbf{a} \succ_2 \mathbf{b}$ (equivalently, $\mathbf{b} \prec_2 \mathbf{a}$) means $a_1 = b_1$ and $a_2 > b_2$. For a general definition, see Section I-1.3.

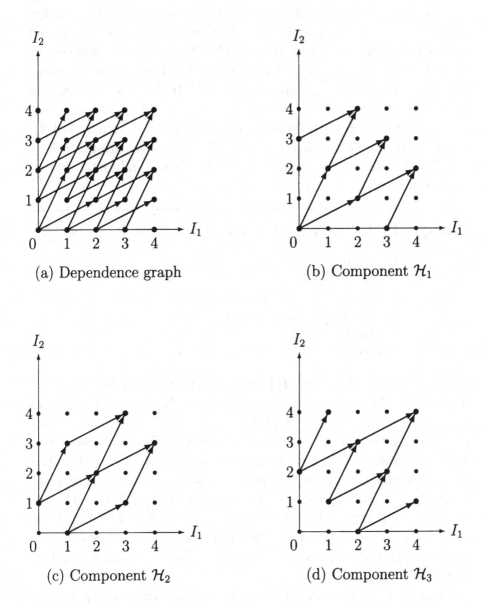

Figure 1.3: Dependence graph of Example 1.4 and the major weakly connected components.

Note that there would be only three components if the index space were all of the plane. We can connect any iteration by an undirected path to one of $H(0,0), H(0,1), H(0,2)$ by sufficiently enlarging the index space. For example, there would be an undirected path joining iterations $H(0,4)$ and $H(0,1)$, if only we had an iteration $H(2,5)$.

The iteration $H(4,4)$ does not depend on the iteration $H(0,2)$, but $H(4,4)$ depends *indirectly* on $H(0,2)$. The iterations $H(1,4)$ and $H(3,2)$ are weakly connected, but one is not indirectly dependent on the other.

Example 1.5 Let $H(I_1, I_2)$ denote the body of the loop nest:

$L_1:$ **do** $I_1 = 0, 4$
$L_2:$ **do** $I_2 = 0, I_1$
               $X(I_1, I_2) = Y(I_1 + 4, I_2) + 1$
               $Y(I_1, I_2 + 4) = X(2I_1, I_2 + 1) + 1$
           enddo
       enddo

We see that the iteration $H(1,0)$ reads the memory location represented by the array element $X(2,1)$, and that the same location is written by the iteration $H(2,1)$. Since $H(2,1)$ is executed after $H(1,0)$ and there is no iteration in between that also references $X(2,1)$, it follows that $H(2,1)$ depends on $H(1,0)$. Thus, $(1,1)$ is a dependence distance vector. It is not uniform, since there are index points (i_1, i_2) and $(i_1 + 1, i_2 + 1)$ such that $H(i_1 + 1, i_2 + 1)$ does not depend on $H(i_1, i_2)$. (For example, take $(2,0)$ and $(3,1)$.) Similarly, it can be seen by enumeration that there is one other distance vector, namely $(2,1)$, also not uniform. The dependence graph is shown in Figure 1.4.

Note that the elements of the array Y do not cause a dependence since the index space is not large enough to hold two index points of the form (i_1, i_2) and $(i_1 + 4, i_2 - 4)$. If it were, there would have been a uniform distance vector $(4, -4)$ in the loop nest.

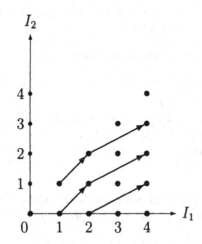

Figure 1.4: Dependence graph of Example 1.5.

EXERCISES 1.3

1. For the program:

L_1 :   **do** $I_1 = 2, 4$
$L_2(I_1)$:   **do** $I_2 = I_1, 2I_1$
$L_3(I_1, I_2)$:   **do** $I_3 = I_1, I_2$
                    $H(I_1, I_2, I_3)$
             enddo
         enddo
     enddo

find the iterations of $L_1, (L_1, L_2), (L_1, L_2, L_3), L_2(3), L_3(4, 5)$. (Indicate loops by their labels.)

2. Consider the triple loop:

do $I_1 = 1, 50$
     do $I_2 = 1, 100$
         do $I_3 = I_2, I_1$
            $X(I_1, I_2, I_3) = X(I_1 - 2, I_2 + 3, I_3 - 4) + X(I_1, I_2 - 3, I_3 + 4) +$
                $X(I_1 - 2, I_2 - 3, I_3 + 4) + X(I_1 + 2, I_2 - 3, I_3 + 1)$
         enddo
     enddo
enddo

Find the distance and direction matrices, and the dependence levels. Which loops carry a dependence?

3. Draw the dependence graph of the double loop:

$L_1:$ **do** $I_1 = 0, 6$
$L_2:$ **do** $I_2 = 0, I_1$
$$X(I_1 + 1, I_2 - 2) = Y(I_1, I_2) + 1$$
$$Y(I_1 + 1, I_2) = X(I_1, I_2) + 1$$
        enddo
     enddo

Find the weakly connected components and show them in separate figures. Find two iterations $H(i_1, i_2)$ and $H(j_1, j_2)$ such that

(a) $H(j_1, j_2)$ depends on $H(i_1, i_2)$;

(b) $H(j_1, j_2)$ does not depend on $H(i_1, i_2)$, but depends indirectly;

(c) $H(j_1, j_2)$ does not depend indirectly on $H(i_1, i_2)$, but the two iterations are weakly connected.

4. Consider a nest $\mathbf{L} = (L_1, L_2, L_3, L_4)$. Discuss the relationships between the following statements (e.g., x and y are equivalent, x implies z, etc.):

(a) 3 is a dependence level for $\mathbf{L}$.

(b) There is a dependence in $\mathbf{L}$ at level 3.

(c) L_3 carries a dependence.

(d) There is at least one distance vector in $\mathbf{L}$ of the form $(0, 0, d_3, d_4)$ with $d_3 > 0$.

(e) Column 3 of the distance matrix $\mathcal{D}$ of $\mathbf{L}$ is not a zero vector.

(f) There is a direction vector in $\mathbf{L}$ of the form $(0, 0, 1, *)$.

(g) $\mathbf{L}$ has the direction vectors $(0, 0, 1, 1)$ and $(0, 0, 1, -1)$.

(h) Column 3 of the direction matrix $\mathbf{\Delta}$ of $\mathbf{L}$ is not a zero vector.

5. Write down the negations of all statements in Exercise 4 except (g). Discuss the implications between these statements.

6. Show that a loop L_ℓ in a nest $\mathbf{L}$ carries a dependence, iff there are iterations $H(\mathbf{i})$ and $H(\mathbf{j})$ such that $\mathbf{i} \prec_\ell \mathbf{j}$ and $H(\mathbf{j})$ depends on $H(\mathbf{i})$.

1.4 Loop Transformation

An *execution order* for the set of iterations $\{H(\mathbf{I}) : \mathbf{I} \in \mathcal{R}\}$ of $\mathbf{L}$ is any partial order in that set. We started with an execution order implied by the semantics of $\mathbf{L}$. It is a total order defined by the condition that $H(\mathbf{i})$ be executed before $H(\mathbf{j})$ if $\mathbf{i} \prec \mathbf{j}$. The whole idea of transforming the loop nest $\mathbf{L}$ (as understood in this book) is to find a suitable new execution order for its iterations. A new execution order is *valid* if it guarantees that an iteration $H(\mathbf{i})$ will be executed before an iteration $H(\mathbf{j})$ whenever $H(\mathbf{j})$ depends on $H(\mathbf{i})$ in $\mathbf{L}$. It follows that in a valid execution order, an iteration $H(\mathbf{i})$ will be executed before an iteration $H(\mathbf{j})$ whenever $H(\mathbf{j})$ depends *indirectly* on $H(\mathbf{i})$ in $\mathbf{L}$. Thus, a valid execution order is any partial order that includes the partial order defined by indirect dependence.

In a total execution order, two distinct iterations are always comparable, and hence one must be executed before the other; there is no scope here for simultaneous execution of two or more iterations. In a partial execution order, two iterations may or may not be comparable, and if not, they can be executed simultaneously (after their predecessors have finished). Thus, a partial execution order for the iterations of $\mathbf{L}$ is necessary if we want to execute $\mathbf{L}$ efficiently on a multiprocessor. However, we are restricted to *valid* execution orders only, to guarantee that the meaning of the program will remain unchanged. Indirect dependence itself defines a valid execution order which is the best from the point of view of parallelization. If the goal is not parallelization, then finding a new (valid) *total* execution order for the iterations of $\mathbf{L}$ may be necessary.

An *iteration-level loop transformation* is a mechanism that defines a new execution order for the iterations of $\mathbf{L}$. The *transformed program* for $\mathbf{L}$ consists of the same iterations with the new execution order. The transformation is *valid* and the transformed program is *equivalent* to $\mathbf{L}$ if the new execution order is valid.

To formally express a program with a partial execution order for its iterations, program constructs other than a nest of **do** loops are needed. For our purpose, it would be sufficient to define a nest of

do and **doall** loops, to be called a *mixed* loop nest. In a **do** loop, there is a strict sequential ordering of the iterations. In a **doall** loop, the iterations are not ordered at all. In a mixed loop nest, two iterations are ordered if they belong to two distinct iterations of (an instance of) a **do** loop in the nest (see Section I-6.1).

For a mixed loop nest, the index vector, index values, index space, and body are defined exactly as in the case of a nest of **do** loops. Consider a mixed nest $\mathbf{L} = (L_1, L_2, \ldots, L_m)$ with index vector $\mathbf{I}$ and body $H(\mathbf{I})$. The execution order of iterations of $\mathbf{L}$ is defined as follows:

> *An iteration $H(\mathbf{i})$ of $\mathbf{L}$ is executed before another itera-*
> *tion $H(\mathbf{j})$, if there is a **do** loop L_r in the nest and $\mathbf{i} \prec_r \mathbf{j}$.*

For two distinct index values $\mathbf{i}$ and $\mathbf{j}$, we have either $\mathbf{i} \prec \mathbf{j}$ or $\mathbf{j} \prec \mathbf{i}$. Suppose $\mathbf{i} \prec \mathbf{j}$. Then, there is a unique r in $1 \leq r \leq m$ such that $\mathbf{i} \prec_r \mathbf{j}$. If L_r is a **doall** loop, then the iterations $H(\mathbf{i})$ and $H(\mathbf{j})$ are not comparable; if L_r is a **do** loop, then they are and $H(\mathbf{i})$ is executed before $H(\mathbf{j})$.

Example 1.6 Consider the mixed loop nest $\mathbf{L}$:

$L_1:$ **doall** $I_1 = 1, 2$
$L_2(I_1):$ **do** $I_2 = 1, 3$
$L_3(I_1, I_2):$ **doall** $I_3 = 1, 2$
                        $H(I_1, I_2, I_3)$
                enddoall
            enddo
        enddoall

The execution orders for the iterations of individual loops are shown (informally) in Figure 1.5, and the digraph representing the execution order for the iterations of the loop nest $\mathbf{L}$ is given in Figure 1.6. (We have used the abbreviation H_{111} for $H(1, 1, 1)$, and similar notations for the other iterations.)

L_1

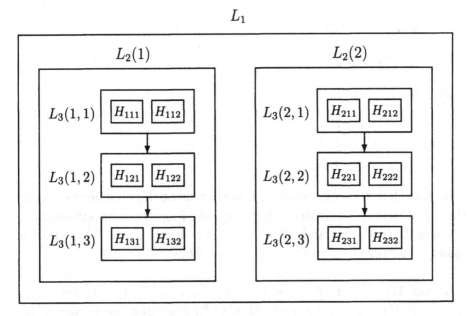

Figure 1.5: Iterations of individual loops (Example 1.6).

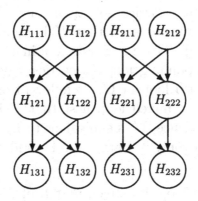

Figure 1.6: Execution order for iterations of **L** (Example 1.6).

The **doall** loop *corresponding* to a **do** loop:

$$L: \quad \textbf{do } I = p, q$$
$$\qquad H(I)$$
$$\quad \textbf{enddo}$$

is denoted by:

$$\overline{L}: \quad \textbf{doall } I = p, q$$
$$\qquad H(I)$$
$$\quad \textbf{enddoall}$$

It is clear that $\overline{L}$ is equivalent to L iff there is no dependence between the iterations of L.[5] Stated differently, the loop transformation that changes L into $\overline{L}$ is valid, iff L carries no dependence. This idea is easily generalized to apply to a nest of loops:

Lemma 1.1 *Consider a nest* $\textbf{L} = (L_1, L_2, \ldots, L_m)$ *of* **do** *loops. Let* $\textbf{L}'$ *denote the mixed loop nest obtained by changing some loops of* $\textbf{L}$ *into their corresponding* **doall** *loops. Then* $\textbf{L}'$ *is equivalent to* $\textbf{L}$, *iff none of the changed loops carries a dependence in* $\textbf{L}$.

PROOF. The 'if' Part: Assume that each **doall** loop in $\textbf{L}'$ came from a loop in $\textbf{L}$ that carries no dependence. Let $H(\textbf{i})$ and $H(\textbf{j})$ denote any two iterations such that $H(\textbf{j})$ depends on $H(\textbf{i})$ in $\textbf{L}$. Then, we have $\textbf{i} \prec \textbf{j}$. There is a unique r in $1 \leq r \leq m$ such that $\textbf{i} \prec_r \textbf{j}$. The corresponding loop L_r carries a dependence in $\textbf{L}$, so that L_r remains a **do** loop in $\textbf{L}'$. It follows from the definition of execution order for a mixed loop nest that $H(\textbf{i})$ will be executed before $H(\textbf{i})$ in $\textbf{L}'$. Hence, $\textbf{L}'$ is equivalent to $\textbf{L}$.

The proof of the 'only if' Part is similar and is left to the reader. □

Let L_r denote a loop in a given nest $\textbf{L}$ of **do** loops. It is sometimes convenient to say that L_r 'can execute in parallel' to mean

---

[5]The execution order of the **doall** loop $\overline{L}$ is empty. It can include the partial order defined by indirect dependence in L iff that partial order is also empty.

that the mixed loop nest $\mathbf{L'}$ obtained by changing L_r into its corresponding **doall** loop is equivalent to $\mathbf{L}$. Thus, the following statements all mean the same thing:

- L_r can execute in parallel.

- L_r can be changed into its corresponding **doall** loop.

- The mixed loop nest obtained by changing L_r into its corresponding **doall** loop is equivalent to $\mathbf{L}$.

- The loop transformation of $\mathbf{L}$ that changes L_r into its corresponding **doall** loop is valid.

By Lemma 1.1, these statements are true iff L_r carries no dependence.

One can trivially extend the discussion in the above paragraph to a set of loops in $\mathbf{L}$. Note that a set of loops can execute in parallel iff the loops can execute in parallel separately.

Example 1.7 In the program

$$
\begin{aligned}
&L_1: &&\textbf{do } I_1 = 0, 4 \\
&L_2: &&\quad \textbf{do } I_2 = 0, 4 \\
&&&\qquad X(I_1 + 1, I_2 + 2) = Y(I_1, I_2) + 1 \\
&&&\qquad Y(I_1 + 2, I_2 + 1) = X(I_1, I_2) + 1 \\
&&&\quad \textbf{enddo} \\
&&&\textbf{enddo}
\end{aligned}
$$

of Example 1.4, there is a dependence carried by the outer loop L_1, but there is no dependence carried by the inner loop L_2. Hence, L_2 can be changed into the corresponding **doall** loop, that is, the double loop

$$
\begin{aligned}
&L_1: &&\textbf{do } I_1 = 0, 4 \\
&\overline{L}_2: &&\quad \textbf{doall } I_2 = 0, 4 \\
&&&\qquad X(I_1 + 1, I_2 + 2) = Y(I_1, I_2) + 1 \\
&&&\qquad Y(I_1 + 2, I_2 + 1) = X(I_1, I_2) + 1 \\
&&&\quad \textbf{enddoall} \\
&&&\textbf{enddo}
\end{aligned}
$$

is equivalent to (L_1, L_2). On the other hand, the loop nest obtained from the given program by changing L_1 into its corresponding **doall** loop $\overline{L}_1$ will not be equivalent to (L_1, L_2).

If we interchange the two loops in (L_1, L_2), we get the double loop:

L_2 :   **do** $I_2 = 0, 4$
L_1 :   **do** $I_1 = 0, 4$
                        $X(I_1 + 1, I_2 + 2) = Y(I_1, I_2) + 1$
                        $Y(I_1 + 2, I_2 + 1) = X(I_1, I_2) + 1$
                    enddo
                enddo

In terms of Figure 1.3(a), the iterations of (L_2, L_1) are executed in consecutive rows from bottom up, while the iterations of (L_1, L_2) are executed in consecutive columns from left to right. (The iterations are the same.) It is clear that if an iteration $H(j_1, j_2)$ depends on an iteration $H(i_1, i_2)$ in (L_1, L_2), then $H(i_1, i_2)$ will be executed before $H(j_1, j_2)$ in (L_2, L_1). Thus, the nest (L_2, L_1) is equivalent to the nest (L_1, L_2), and the loop transformation of interchange is valid in this case. (This transformation will be discussed in the next chapter.) The current inner loop, L_1, can execute in parallel.

EXERCISES 1.4

1. Draw diagrams like Figures 1.5 and 1.6 for the execution order of iterations of the mixed loop nest:

   L_1 :   **do** $I_1 = 1, 2$
   $L_2(I_1)$:   **doall** $I_2 = 1, I_1 + 1$
   $L_3(I_1, I_2)$:   **do** $I_3 = I_1, I_2 + 1$
                            $H(I_1, I_2, I_3)$
                        enddo
                    enddoall
                enddo

2. Suppose we have interchanged the two loops in the program of Example 1.4, and replaced the I_1-loop in the transformed program by its corresponding **doall** loop. Explain why the final program is or is not equivalent to (L_1, L_2).

3. Take the program of Exercise 1.3.3. Can we execute either **do** loop in parallel? Can we interchange the two loops (to get an equivalent program)?

4. Show that the transformation

$$(K_1, K_2) = (I_1, I_2) \begin{pmatrix} 2 & -3 \\ -1 & 2 \end{pmatrix}$$

changes the rectangular loop nest

    do $K_1 = 0, 5$
        do $K_2 = 0, 10$
            $H(K_1, K_2)$
        enddo
    enddo

into the regular loop nest of Example 1.2. (Hint: Find a description of the index space in terms of I_1 and I_2.)

5. Let $\mathbf{L}_1$ and $\mathbf{L}_2$ denote two nests of **do** loops with the same set of iterations. How are two iterations $H(\mathbf{i})$ and $H(\mathbf{j})$ related in $\mathbf{L}_2$, if in $\mathbf{L}_1$

    (a) $H(\mathbf{j})$ depends on $H(\mathbf{i})$;

    (b) $H(\mathbf{j})$ depends indirectly on $H(\mathbf{i})$;

    (c) $H(\mathbf{i})$ and $H(\mathbf{j})$ are weakly connected?

Give simple examples to illustrate the various possibilities in each case.

6. In the previous exercise, prove that $\mathbf{L}_2$ is equivalent to $\mathbf{L}_1$ iff the following condition holds: An iteration $H(\mathbf{j})$ depends on an iteration $H(\mathbf{i})$ in $\mathbf{L}_2$ iff $H(\mathbf{j})$ depends on $H(\mathbf{i})$ in $\mathbf{L}_1$.

7. Let $\mathcal{L}$ denote a set of nests of **do** loops such that each nest has the same set of iterations. (The number of loops in a nest may vary.) Define a relation $\sim$ in $\mathcal{L}$ by requiring that for any two nests $\mathbf{L}_1$ and $\mathbf{L}_2$ in $\mathcal{L}$, we have $\mathbf{L}_1 \sim \mathbf{L}_2$ if $\mathbf{L}_2$ is equivalent to $\mathbf{L}_1$. Prove that $\sim$ is an equivalence relation.

1.5   Loop Parallelization

Let **L** denote a nest of m **do** loops of the type considered in this
chapter. Let **I** denote the index vector, $H(\mathbf{I})$ the body, and $\mathcal{R}$ the
index space of **L**. Assume that the dependence information for **L** has
been computed. Our aim is to find analytically a mixed loop nest
L′ equivalent to **L**, that makes explicit the parallelism between the
iterations of **L**. We will distinguish between two types of parallelism:
vertical and horizontal [PoBa87].

Vertical parallelism refers to the situation where the dependence
graph of **L** has been partitioned such that the members of the partition can be executed independently of one another. A necessary
condition for this is that there be no undirected path joining any two
iterations of **L** that lie in two distinct members of the partition. A
partition of the dependence graph is called *vertical* if it satisfies this
condition. The ideal vertical partition is the weak partition whose
members are the weakly connected components. A mixed loop nest
L′ with an outer ring of **doall** loops represents a vertical partition,
where the members of the partition are given by the iterations of
that outer **doall** nest, and the execution order of iterations of **L**
within a given member is determined by the other loops in **L′**.

Horizontal parallelism refers to the situation where a number of
iterations of **L** can be executed simultaneously (after their predecessors have finished). To achieve this kind of parallelism, we need to
break up the dependence graph of **L** into a sequence of antichains
such that an iteration in a given antichain cannot depend on an
iteration in a succeeding antichain. A partition of the dependence
graph is called *horizontal* if it satisfies this condition. The ideal
horizontal partition is the one where the antichains in the sequence
are all maximal (Section I-1.2).[6] A mixed loop nest **L′** with an outer
ring of **do** loops surrounding an inner core of **doall** loops represents

---

[6]Two horizontal partitions with the same minimum number of antichains
may be considered to be equally ideal from the point of view of parallelization.
This minimum would be the maximum number of iterations that form a chain
in the dependence graph (see Theorem I-1.1).

a horizontal partition, where the antichains are given by the iterations of the outer **do** nest, and the individual iterations of **L** in an antichain are given by the iterations of the inner **doall** nest.

To get both types of parallelism, we first find a vertical partition of the dependence graph, and then find a horizontal partition of each member of the vertical partition. The final result is represented as a mixed loop nest **L′** (equivalent to **L**) that consists of an outer ring of **doall** loops, then a **do** loop, and finally an inner core of **doall** loops. Let $H(\mathbf{i})$ and $H(\mathbf{j})$ denote any two distinct iterations. If $H(\mathbf{j})$ depends on $H(\mathbf{i})$ in **L**, then $H(\mathbf{j})$ will necessarily execute after $H(\mathbf{i})$ in **L′**. Ideally, the converse should also be true, so that the execution order of **L′** would force $H(\mathbf{j})$ to execute after $H(\mathbf{i})$ iff $H(\mathbf{j})$ depends on $H(\mathbf{i})$ in **L**. This ideal is difficult to achieve mainly because to do so, one must give a very prominent role to the extent and shape of the index space $\mathcal{R}$ of **L** in the algorithms. We find a loop nest **L′** by constructing a suitable one-to-one mapping of $\mathcal{R}$, using a formula determined by the dependence structure of **L**, and not by $\mathcal{R}$.[7] This keeps the analysis relatively simple, and even then we come rather close to the ideal situation helped by the assumed uniform nature of the distance vectors.

We will consider three basic types of mappings of the index space, leading to three kinds of loop transformations:

1. Loop Permutation: A mapping $\mathbf{I} \mapsto \mathbf{I}\mathcal{P}$ of $\mathcal{R}$ into $\mathbf{Z}^m$, where $\mathcal{P}$ is an $m \times m$ permutation matrix;

2. Unimodular Transformation: A mapping $\mathbf{I} \mapsto \mathbf{I}\mathbf{U}$ of $\mathcal{R}$ into $\mathbf{Z}^m$, where $\mathbf{U}$ is an $m \times m$ unimodular matrix;

3. Remainder Transformation: A mapping $\mathbf{I} \mapsto (\mathbf{Y}; \mathbf{K})$ of $\mathcal{R}$ into $\mathbf{Z}^{m+\rho}$, where $\mathbf{Y}$ is an m-vector, $\mathbf{K}$ is a ρ-vector, $\mathbf{I} = \mathbf{Y} + \mathbf{K}\mathbf{S}$, and $\mathbf{S}$ is a $\rho \times m$ echelon matrix with rank ρ derived from the distance matrix $\mathcal{D}$ of **L**.[8]

---

[7]To compute the ranges of the new variables introduced, the description of $\mathcal{R}$ must be taken into account.

[8]There are other conditions; we will discuss the details in Chapter 4.

Since a permutation matrix is unimodular, a loop permutation is a special case of a unimodular transformation.

Each transformation finds a nest of **do** loops equivalent to **L**. In that transformed program, some loops do not carry any dependence and therefore they can be changed into the corresponding **doall** loops. In general, each transformation can be used to find a mixed loop nest (equivalent to **L**) with outermost or innermost **doall** loops to display vertical or horizontal parallelism, respectively. The transformations can be applied successively to find both kinds of parallelism in a given program.

The loop transformation algorithms in this book are based on the basic algorithms developed in Volume I. It is strongly suggested that the reader review those algorithms at this point. It is also a good idea to read the section on floor and ceiling functions (Section 1.2.4) in [Knut73]. We will assume that the dependence information for **L** has already been computed. Bodies of loop nests used in examples and exercises will be such that the distance or direction vectors can be found by inspection. They can be formally computed by one of the algorithms in Chapter 5 of Volume I.

Chapter 2

Loop Permutations

2.1 Introduction

As explained in Section 1.4, an iteration-level loop transformation of the model loop nest **L** simply changes the given sequential (i.e., total) execution order of its iterations. Suppose the new execution order is also to be sequential. We can get a whole class of new sequential orders by permuting the loops. Originally, the points of the index space $\mathcal{R}$ of **L** were to be traced in the increasing (lexicographic) order of the index vector $(I_1, I_2, \ldots, I_m)$. Each permutation π of the set $\{1, 2, \ldots, m\}$ defines a new execution order of the iterations, where the index points are traced in the increasing (lexicographic) order of the vector $(I_{\pi(1)}, I_{\pi(2)}, \ldots, I_{\pi(m)})$. The corresponding loop transformation is called a *loop permutation*. After a valid loop permutation, it may be possible to replace one or more **do** loops by their corresponding **doall** loops.

Given a particular loop permutation, the first question is: "Is the transformation valid?" After a loop permutation has been shown to be valid, we would like to know next how it changes the form and the dependence structure of the given program. The main underlying issue is the role of loop permutation in construction of horizontal and vertical partitions of the dependence graph to capture horizontal and vertical parallelism in the given loop nest.

Loop permutations form a special class of unimodular transformations, the topic of the next chapter. They merit a separate treatment, however, since they are cheaper to implement than a general unimodular transformation, and often satisfy architecture-specific optimization goals. We study the mechanics of loop permutations, but do not try to relate them to architectural features.

The simplest and most commonly used type of loop permutation is loop interchange. Loop interchange has been studied in detail by Michael Wolfe ([Wolf82], [Wolf86b], [Wolf89]), and by Randy Allen & Ken Kennedy ([Alle83], [AlKe84]). Loop permutations in general along with some specific types are discussed by the author in [Bane90], on which this chapter is based.

In Section 2.2, we study when a loop permutation is valid and how it changes the dependence structure of the program. Section 2.3 gives an algorithm to find all direction vectors that will 'prevent' a given permutation. This section also provides compact forms for sets of direction vectors that prevent certain common permutations. Parallelization by loop permutation is described in Section 2.4. To avoid the overshadowing of important issues by the technical process of loop limit computation, we will use rectangular loop nests as examples in most sections. Limit computation will be illustrated separately in Section 2.5. Finally, in Section 2.6, we will state some optimization problems related to loop permutation.

We often represent a permutation of the variables in the index vector $\mathbf{I} = (I_1, I_2, \ldots, I_m)$ as the result $\mathbf{I}\mathcal{P}$ of the application of a permutation matrix $\mathcal{P}$ to the vector $\mathbf{I}$. A permutation π of the set $\{1, 2, \ldots, m\}$ uniquely determines an $m \times m$ permutation matrix $\mathcal{P}$, which is obtained by rearranging the columns of the identity matrix $\mathcal{I}_m$ in the order: col $\pi(1)$, col $\pi(2), \ldots$, col $\pi(m)$. Thus, for $1 \leq r \leq m$, column r of $\mathcal{P}$ has its unique 1 in row $\pi(r)$. We will use the compact notation:

$$\mathcal{P} = \begin{bmatrix} 1 & 2 & \cdots & m \\ \pi(1) & \pi(2) & \cdots & \pi(m) \end{bmatrix}$$

for a permutation matrix, introduced in Section I-2.5. Since the first row in this notation is redundant, sometimes we abbreviate it to $\mathcal{P} = [\,\pi(1) \quad \pi(2) \quad \cdots \quad \pi(m)\,]$ if no confusion is possible. For an example, note that if

$$\mathcal{P} = [\,2 \quad 3 \quad 1\,] \equiv \begin{bmatrix} 1 & 2 & 3 \\ 2 & 3 & 1 \end{bmatrix} \equiv \begin{pmatrix} 0 & 0 & 1 \\ 1 & 0 & 0 \\ 0 & 1 & 0 \end{pmatrix}$$

then we have $(I_1, I_2, I_3)\mathcal{P} = (I_2, I_3, I_1)$, $(I_2, I_3, I_1)\mathcal{P} = (I_3, I_1, I_2)$, and $(-5, 3, 0)\mathcal{P} = (3, 0, -5)$.

Example 2.1 Take any rectangular double loop **L**:

$L_1 :$ **do** $I_1 = p_1, q_1$
$L_2 :$ **do** $I_2 = p_2, q_2$
           $H(I_1, I_2)$
       enddo
    enddo

The index space of (L_1, L_2) is shown in Figure 2.1. In geometrical terms, the iterations are executed as follows: process from left to right the columns $I_1 = p_1, I_1 = p_1 + 1, \ldots, I_1 = q_1$, and execute the iterations on any given column from bottom up.

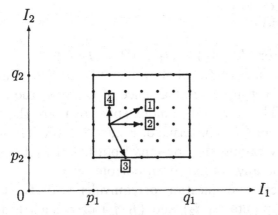

Figure 2.1: Index space of **L** in Example 2.1.

There are only two 2×2 permutation matrices: the identity matrix $\mathcal{I}_2$ and the interchange matrix

$$\mathcal{P} = \begin{pmatrix} 0 & 1 \\ 1 & 0 \end{pmatrix}.$$

Consider the loop permutation (interchange) of $\mathbf{L}$ defined by $\mathcal{P}$. In the transformed program, $\mathbf{L}_\mathcal{P}$, the iterations are executed in the increasing order of $(I_1, I_2)\mathcal{P} = (I_2, I_1)$. That means we process the horizontal rows $I_2 = p_2, I_2 = p_2 + 1, \ldots, I_2 = q_2$ (in the index space of Figure 2.1) from bottom up, and execute the iterations on any row from left to right. The ranges of I_1 and I_2 are independent of each other, and they remain unchanged. We can represent $\mathbf{L}_\mathcal{P}$ as

L_2 :   **do** $I_2 = p_2, q_2$
L_1 :   **do** $I_1 = p_1, q_1$
            $H(I_1, I_2)$
         enddo
      enddo

or as

$L_{\mathcal{P}1}$:   **do** $K_1 = p_2, q_2$
$L_{\mathcal{P}2}$:   **do** $K_2 = p_1, q_1$
            $H(K_2, K_1)$
         enddo
      enddo

with index vector $(K_1, K_2) = (I_1, I_2)\mathcal{P} = (I_2, I_1)$.

The index space of $\mathbf{L}_\mathcal{P}$ is shown in Figure 2.2. This space is obtained by reflecting the index space of $\mathbf{L}$ across the line $I_1 = I_2$ in Figure 2.1. The rows of the index space of $\mathbf{L}$ are the columns of the index space of $\mathbf{L}_\mathcal{P}$. (In terms of Figure 2.2, the iterations in $\mathbf{L}_\mathcal{P}$ are executed by taking the columns from left to right, and taking the iterations on any column from bottom up.)

Consider next the question of equivalence of $\mathbf{L}_\mathcal{P}$ to $\mathbf{L}$. Take any two index points (i_1, i_2) and (j_1, j_2) of $\mathbf{L}$ such that the iteration $H(j_1, j_2)$ depends on the iteration $H(i_1, i_2)$. Then we have

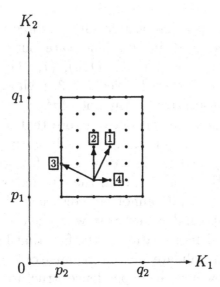

Figure 2.2: Index space of $\mathbf{L}_{\mathcal{P}}$ in Example 2.1.

$(i_1, i_2) \prec (j_1, j_2)$, since $H(i_1, i_2)$ must execute before $H(j_1, j_2)$ in $\mathbf{L}$. The condition for the equivalence of $\mathbf{L}_{\mathcal{P}}$ to $\mathbf{L}$ requires that $H(i_1, i_2)$ execute before $H(j_1, j_2)$ also in $\mathbf{L}_{\mathcal{P}}$, that is, $(i_2, i_1) \prec (j_2, j_1)$. The only situation where $(i_1, i_2) \prec (j_1, j_2)$ holds and $(i_2, i_1) \prec (j_2, j_1)$ does not is when $i_1 < j_1$ and $i_2 > j_2$. Thus, interchange of the loops in $\mathbf{L}$ is invalid iff there is an iteration $H(j_1, j_2)$ depending on an iteration $H(i_1, i_2)$ such that $i_1 < j_1$ and $i_2 > j_2$.

The condition obtained in the previous paragraph can be stated in different ways. Let (d_1, d_2) denote the distance vector corresponding to the dependence of $H(j_1, j_2)$ on $H(i_1, i_2)$. Then, we have $(d_1, d_2) = (j_1 - i_1, j_2 - i_2)$. In terms of distance vectors, interchange of the loops in $\mathbf{L}$ is invalid iff there is a distance vector (d_1, d_2) such that $d_1 > 0$ and $d_2 < 0$. Next, the direction vector corresponding to (d_1, d_2) is $(\text{sig}(d_1), \text{sig}(d_2))$. In terms of direction vectors, interchange of the loops in $\mathbf{L}$ is invalid iff the direction vector $(1, -1)$ is present in $\mathbf{L}$. Thus, whether or not loop interchange is valid can be determined from a knowledge of direction vectors alone.

Now look at the problem graphically. A direction vector of dependence is positive, by definition. There are four positive direction vectors in two dimensions: $(1,1)$, $(1,0)$, $(1,-1)$, $(0,1)$. In Figure 2.1, we show four vectors labeled $1, 2, 3, 4$ whose signs are these direction vectors, respectively. Any one of these four vectors could be a distance vector of dependence. (Note that a distance vector cannot point from right to left, or vertically down.) In Figure 2.2, we show what happened to the four vectors after loop interchange. Vector 3 now has the sign $(-1,1)$ in the new index space. Since it points from right to left, it cannot be a distance vector for the program $\mathbf{L}_{\mathcal{P}}$. This problem does not arise with the other three vectors. This is a graphical demonstration of the fact that having the direction vector $(1,-1)$ invalidates the interchange of loops in $\mathbf{L}$. Figures 2.1 and 2.2 also show how the dependence structure of the loop nest $\mathbf{L}$ is changed under a valid loop interchange (see Exercise 1).

EXERCISES 2.1

1. In Example 2.1, describe which of the four distance vectors 1–4 of Figure 2.1 may be present so that one or both loops of $\mathbf{L}$ can execute in parallel (consider three separate cases). Repeat for the nest $\mathbf{L}_{\mathcal{P}}$ assuming a valid interchange. Can you derive some conclusions as to why loop interchange may be a useful tool for parallelization?

2.2   Basic Concepts

Our model program is the loop nest $\mathbf{L} = (L_1, L_2, \dots, L_m)$:

L_1 :   **do** $I_1 = p_1, q_1$
L_2 :   **do** $I_2 = p_2, q_2$
$\vdots$ $\vdots$
L_m :   **do** $I_m = p_m, q_m$
                  $H(I_1, I_2, \dots, I_m)$
                enddo
                  $\vdots$
          enddo
      enddo

An iteration $H(\mathbf{i})$ is executed before another iteration $H(\mathbf{j})$ in $\mathbf{L}$ iff $\mathbf{i} \prec \mathbf{j}$. Take any $m \times m$ permutation matrix $\mathcal{P}$. Let $\mathbf{L}_{\mathcal{P}}$ denote the program consisting of the iterations of $\mathbf{L}$, such that an iteration $H(\mathbf{i})$ is executed before another iteration $H(\mathbf{j})$ in $\mathbf{L}_{\mathcal{P}}$ iff $\mathbf{i}\mathcal{P} \prec \mathbf{j}\mathcal{P}$. The program $\mathbf{L}_{\mathcal{P}}$ is the *transformed program defined by* $\mathcal{P}$, and the transformation $\mathbf{L} \mapsto \mathbf{L}_{\mathcal{P}}$ is the *(loop) permutation of* $\mathbf{L}$ *defined by* $\mathcal{P}$. In a loop permutation, the index variables retain their identity; only their ordering is changed. We retain the labels for the individual loops, remembering that their limits may change. If $\mathcal{P} = [\pi(1) \ \ \pi(2) \ \ \cdots \ \ \pi(m)]$, then the transformation $\mathbf{L} \mapsto \mathbf{L}_{\mathcal{P}}$ can be written as

$$(L_1, L_2, \ldots, L_m) \mapsto (L_{\pi(1)}, L_{\pi(2)}, \ldots, L_{\pi(m)}).$$

Theorem 2.1 *The permutation of a loop nest* $\mathbf{L}$ *defined by a permutation matrix* $\mathcal{P}$ *is valid iff* $\mathbf{d}\mathcal{P} \succ \mathbf{0}$ *for each distance vector* $\mathbf{d}$.

PROOF. The 'if' Part: Assume that $\mathbf{d}\mathcal{P} \succ \mathbf{0}$ for each distance vector $\mathbf{d}$ of $\mathbf{L}$. Let $H(\mathbf{i})$ and $H(\mathbf{j})$ denote any two iterations of $\mathbf{L}$ such that $H(\mathbf{j})$ depends on $H(\mathbf{i})$. The difference $\mathbf{j} - \mathbf{i}$ is some distance vector $\mathbf{d}$. We have

$$\mathbf{j}\mathcal{P} - \mathbf{i}\mathcal{P} = (\mathbf{j} - \mathbf{i})\mathcal{P} = \mathbf{d}\mathcal{P} \succ \mathbf{0}$$

so that $\mathbf{i}\mathcal{P} \prec \mathbf{j}\mathcal{P}$. This means $H(\mathbf{i})$ will be executed before $H(\mathbf{j})$ in $\mathbf{L}_{\mathcal{P}}$, and hence the transformed program $\mathbf{L}_{\mathcal{P}}$ is equivalent to $\mathbf{L}$.

The 'only if' Part: Assume that $\mathbf{L}_{\mathcal{P}}$ is equivalent to $\mathbf{L}$. Given any distance vector $\mathbf{d}$ of $\mathbf{L}$, there is at least one pair of iterations $H(\mathbf{i}), H(\mathbf{j})$ such that $H(\mathbf{j})$ depends on $H(\mathbf{i})$ and $\mathbf{j} - \mathbf{i} = \mathbf{d}$. Since $H(\mathbf{i})$ must be executed before $H(\mathbf{j})$ in $\mathbf{L}_{\mathcal{P}}$, we have $\mathbf{i}\mathcal{P} \prec \mathbf{j}\mathcal{P}$. This implies $\mathbf{d}\mathcal{P} = \mathbf{j}\mathcal{P} - \mathbf{i}\mathcal{P} \succ \mathbf{0}$. □

Corollary 1 *If the permutation of* $\mathbf{L}$ *defined by the matrix* $\mathcal{P}$ *is valid, then the distance matrix of the transformed program* $\mathbf{L}_{\mathcal{P}}$ *is* $\mathcal{D}\mathcal{P}$ *where* $\mathcal{D}$ *is the distance matrix of* $\mathbf{L}$.

PROOF. The proof is left as an exercise. □

One very important feature of loop permutations is that their validity can be determined from a knowledge of direction vectors alone. This is quite useful since the number of direction vectors is never more (and often less) than the number of distance vectors, and direction vectors may be easier to compute and store than distance vectors. The reason direction vectors can be used for loop permutations is that a permutation matrix changes the components of a vector $\mathbf{x}$ and the components of the sign vector $\mathbf{sig}(\mathbf{x})$ in 'the same way.' For example, if $\mathbf{x} = (3, -2, 0)$ and $\mathcal{P} = \begin{bmatrix} 3 & 2 & 1 \end{bmatrix}$, then $\mathbf{x}\mathcal{P} = (0, -2, 3)$. Now $\mathbf{sig}(\mathbf{x}) = (1, -1, 0)$, so that we have $\mathbf{sig}(\mathbf{x})\mathcal{P} = (0, -1, 1)$. The fact that $\mathbf{x}\mathcal{P}$ is negative can be deduced from a knowledge of $\mathbf{x}$ by computing $\mathbf{x}\mathcal{P}$, or from a knowledge of $\mathbf{sig}(\mathbf{x})$ by computing $\mathbf{sig}(\mathbf{x})\mathcal{P}$. A formal proof follows:

Theorem 2.2 *The permutation of a loop nest* $\mathbf{L}$ *defined by a permutation matrix* $\mathcal{P}$ *is valid iff* $\boldsymbol{\sigma}\mathcal{P} \succ \mathbf{0}$ *for each direction vector* $\boldsymbol{\sigma}$ *of* $\mathbf{L}$.

PROOF. The proof rests on the fact that

$$\mathbf{sig}(\mathbf{d}\mathcal{P}) = \mathbf{sig}(\mathbf{d}) \cdot \mathcal{P}$$

for each m-vector $\mathbf{d}$ and each $m \times m$ permutation matrix $\mathcal{P}$. Let $\mathbf{d} = (d_1, d_2, \ldots, d_m)$, and let π denote the permutation of the set $\{1, 2, \ldots, m\}$ corresponding to the matrix $\mathcal{P}$. We have

$$
\begin{aligned}
\mathbf{sig}(\mathbf{d}\mathcal{P}) &= \mathbf{sig}((d_1, d_2, \ldots, d_m) \cdot \mathcal{P}) \\
&= \mathbf{sig}\left(d_{\pi(1)}, d_{\pi(2)}, \ldots, d_{\pi(m)}\right) \\
&= \left(\mathrm{sig}(d_{\pi(1)}), \mathrm{sig}(d_{\pi(2)}), \ldots, \mathrm{sig}(d_{\pi(m)})\right) \\
&= (\mathrm{sig}(d_1), \mathrm{sig}(d_2), \ldots, \mathrm{sig}(d_m)) \cdot \mathcal{P} \\
&= \mathbf{sig}(\mathbf{d}) \cdot \mathcal{P}.
\end{aligned}
$$

Thus, if $\mathbf{d}$ is a distance vector of $\mathbf{L}$ and $\boldsymbol{\sigma}$ its corresponding direction vector, then we have $\mathbf{sig}(\mathbf{d}\mathcal{P}) = \boldsymbol{\sigma}\mathcal{P}$. This means $\mathbf{d}\mathcal{P}$ is positive iff $\boldsymbol{\sigma}\mathcal{P}$ is positive. The proof then follows from Theorem 2.1. □

Corollary 1 *If the permutation of* **L** *defined by the matrix* $\mathcal{P}$ *is valid, then the direction matrix of the transformed program* $\mathbf{L}_{\mathcal{P}}$ *is* $\Delta \mathcal{P}$ *where* Δ *is the direction matrix of* **L**.

PROOF. The proof is left as an exercise. $\quad\square$

There is no simple formula to describe how a dependence level is changed by a loop permutation. Some results on level change for particular permutations are given in the next section. A useful thing to know is that if a loop carries no dependence in **L**, then it will still not carry a dependence after certain valid loop permutations:

Theorem 2.3 *Let* $1 \le p < m$. *Consider a valid loop permutation that does not change the loops* $L_1, L_2, \ldots, L_{p-1}$. *If* L_p *does not carry a dependence in the nest* **L**, *then it will not carry a dependence in the transformed program.*

PROOF. The loop L_p carries a dependence iff there is a direction vector of the form $(0, 0, \ldots, 0, 1, *, \ldots, *)$ with its leading 1 in the pth place. There are two possibilities: either the direction matrix Δ has a 1 in column p, or it does not. If this column has no 1 now, it cannot acquire a 1 if it is moved. In this case, L_p does not carry a dependence now, and obviously will not carry one after any loop permutation. Assume then that column p of Δ does have a 1. Since by hypothesis, L_p carries no dependence in **L**, each 1 in column p of Δ is 'covered' by a 1 in a column q with $q < p$. In general, a 1 in column p could become the leading 1 of the corresponding direction vector after a valid loop permutation. However, that possibility is ruled out if we restrict ourselves to permutations that do not change loops L_1–L_{p-1}, which is our hypothesis. $\quad\square$

We will consider three special kinds of loop permutations: interchange, left and right circulations. Let $1 \le p < q \le m$. *Interchange of the two loops* L_p *and* L_q is defined by the permutation of $\{1, 2, \ldots, m\}$ that maps p to q, q to p, and leaves every other element unchanged. The corresponding permutation matrix is the interchange matrix:

$$\begin{bmatrix} 1 & \cdots & p-1 & p & p+1 & \cdots & q-1 & q & q+1 & \cdots & m \\ 1 & \cdots & p-1 & q & p+1 & \cdots & q-1 & p & q+1 & \cdots & m \end{bmatrix}.$$

Left circulation of the loops L_p through L_q is defined by the permutation of $\{1, 2, \ldots, m\}$ that 'rotates' the sequence $p, p+1, \ldots, q$ by one step to the left, and leaves every other element unchanged. The corresponding permutation matrix is

$$\begin{bmatrix} 1 & \cdots & p-1 & p & p+1 & \cdots & q-1 & q & q+1 & \cdots & m \\ 1 & \cdots & p-1 & p+1 & p+2 & \cdots & q & p & q+1 & \cdots & m \end{bmatrix}.$$

Similarly, the *right circulation* of the loops L_p through L_q is the inverse transformation defined by the permutation matrix:

$$\begin{bmatrix} 1 & \cdots & p-1 & p & p+1 & \cdots & q-1 & q & q+1 & \cdots & m \\ 1 & \cdots & p-1 & q & p & \cdots & q-2 & q-1 & q+1 & \cdots & m \end{bmatrix}.$$

Example 2.2 Consider a nest $\mathbf{L} = (L_1, L_2, L_3, L_4)$ with the direction matrix:

$$\boldsymbol{\Delta} = \begin{pmatrix} 0 & 1 & 1 & -1 \\ 0 & 0 & 0 & 1 \\ 1 & 0 & -1 & 0 \end{pmatrix}.$$

The permutation $(L_1, L_2, L_3, L_4) \mapsto (L_1, L_4, L_3, L_2)$ interchanges loops L_2 and L_4. It is not valid, since it changes the direction vector $(0, 1, 1, -1)$ into $(0, -1, 1, 1)$, which is negative.

The permutation $(L_1, L_2, L_3, L_4) \mapsto (L_1, L_3, L_4, L_2)$ is the left circulation of loops L_2 through L_4. It is valid, and it changes the direction matrix $\boldsymbol{\Delta}$ into

$$\begin{pmatrix} 0 & 1 & -1 & 1 \\ 0 & 0 & 1 & 0 \\ 1 & -1 & 0 & 0 \end{pmatrix}$$

which is the direction matrix of the transformed program. The dependence levels in the transformed program are 1, 2, 3, while the levels in the original program were 1, 2, 4.

The permutation $(L_1, L_2, L_3, L_4) \mapsto (L_1, L_4, L_2, L_3)$ is the right circulation of loops L_2 through L_4. It is not valid, since it changes the direction vector $(0, 1, 1, -1)$ into $(0, -1, 1, 1)$ which is negative.

The loop L_3 carries no dependence in **L**. The interchange of loops L_3 and L_4 in **L** is valid, and it does not affect the first two loops. It creates the loop nest (L_1, L_2, L_4, L_3) with the direction matrix:

$$\begin{pmatrix} 0 & 1 & -1 & 1 \\ 0 & 0 & 1 & 0 \\ 1 & 0 & 0 & -1 \end{pmatrix}.$$

Note that L_3 (which is now the innermost loop) still carries no dependence in the transformed program. Compare this with the fact that L_3 carries a dependence in the nest (L_1, L_3, L_4, L_2), which is the transformed program of the left circulation considered above.

The $m \times m$ identity matrix $\mathcal{I}$ is a permutation matrix, and it is clear that $\mathbf{L}_\mathcal{I} = \mathbf{L}$. The facts stated in the following theorem are also easy to derive:

Theorem 2.4 *Let* $\mathcal{P}$ *and* $\mathcal{Q}$ *denote two* $m \times m$ *permutation matrices. For a nest* **L** *of* m *loops, we have*

(a) $(\mathbf{L}_\mathcal{P})_\mathcal{Q} = \mathbf{L}_{\mathcal{P}\mathcal{Q}}$

(b) $(\mathbf{L}_\mathcal{P})_{\mathcal{P}^{-1}} = \mathbf{L}$.

EXERCISES 2.2

1. The direction matrix $\boldsymbol{\Delta}$ of a nest (L_1, L_2, L_3, L_4) is given below. Find the levels of dependence. Identify all valid loop interchanges. Decide if the left and right circulations of loops L_2 through L_4 are valid. List all loops that can be made the outermost (innermost) loop by a valid permutation. Show the new direction matrix and new dependence levels after each valid loop permutation that you find.

(a) $\boldsymbol{\Delta} = \begin{pmatrix} 1 & -1 & 0 & 1 \\ 0 & 1 & 1 & -1 \\ 1 & 0 & 0 & -1 \end{pmatrix}$

(b) $\boldsymbol{\Delta} = \begin{pmatrix} 1 & -1 & 0 & 0 \\ 0 & 1 & -1 & 0 \\ 0 & 0 & 1 & -1 \end{pmatrix}$

(c) $\boldsymbol{\Delta} = \begin{pmatrix} 1 & 1 & -1 & 0 \\ 1 & 0 & -1 & 1 \\ 0 & 1 & 1 & -1 \end{pmatrix}$.

2. Let $\mathcal{L}$ denote the set of all perfect nests $\mathbf{L}$ of a given length m (of the type considered in this book). Each $m \times m$ permutation matrix $\mathcal{P}$ defines a mapping $\mathcal{T}_\mathcal{P} : \mathbf{L} \mapsto \mathbf{L}_\mathcal{P}$ on $\mathcal{L}$. Prove that these mappings form a group under the product: $\mathcal{T}_\mathcal{P} \circ \mathcal{T}_\mathcal{Q} = \mathcal{T}_{\mathcal{P}\mathcal{Q}}$.

3. (See Section I-2.5.) The effect of a given loop permutation on $\mathbf{L}$ can be realized by applying to it a sequence of loop interchanges. (We may even assume that each interchange involves two adjacent loops.) Thus, the validity of a loop permutation can be determined by checking if each loop interchange in the defining sequence yields an equivalent program. Explain the difficulties of this approach, if any. Give examples.

2.3 Preventing Permutations

To test the validity of the loop permutation defined by a given permutation matrix $\mathcal{P}$ when the direction matrix $\boldsymbol{\Delta}$ is known, we simply compute the product $\boldsymbol{\Delta}\mathcal{P}$ and see if its rows are positive. Suppose now that the direction matrix is not known, and that we compute direction vectors only as needed. The validity of a given loop permutation can be determined by checking the existence of direction vectors that are made negative by the application of the corresponding matrix. If a direction vector has only 0's and 1's, then no permutation matrix can make it negative. Even when a direction vector has one or more -1's, some permutations will make it negative and some will not. For example, if $\boldsymbol{\sigma} = (1, -1, 0, 1)$, then the interchange of the first two loops will make $\boldsymbol{\sigma}$ negative, but the interchange of the first and the fourth loops will not. Hence, existence of the direction vector $(1, -1, 0, 1)$ should be checked if the interchange of the first two loops is being contemplated, but not if we are trying to interchange the first and the fourth loops.

Formally, a direction vector $\boldsymbol{\sigma}$ *prevents* the loop permutation defined by a permutation matrix $\mathcal{P}$ if $\boldsymbol{\sigma} \succ \mathbf{0}$ and $\boldsymbol{\sigma}\mathcal{P} \prec \mathbf{0}$. We will find all direction vectors that prevent a given permutation, and express them in compact and disjoint direction vector forms. (See Section I-1.3 for notation.) Example 2.3 explains this method:

Example 2.3 Consider a nest of four loops and the loop permutation defined by the matrix:

$$\mathcal{P} = \begin{bmatrix} 1 & 2 & 3 & 4 \\ 3 & 1 & 4 & 2 \end{bmatrix}.$$

If $\boldsymbol{\sigma} = (\sigma_1, \sigma_2, \sigma_3, \sigma_4)$, then we have $\boldsymbol{\sigma}\mathcal{P} = (\sigma_3, \sigma_1, \sigma_4, \sigma_2)$. We want all direction vectors $\boldsymbol{\sigma}$ such that $\boldsymbol{\sigma} \succ \mathbf{0}$ and $\boldsymbol{\sigma}\mathcal{P} \prec \mathbf{0}$. Any negative 4-vector has one of the four disjoint forms:

$$(-1, *, *, *), (0, -1, *, *), (0, 0, -1, *), (0, 0, 0, -1).$$

We will restrict or eliminate these forms using the condition $\boldsymbol{\sigma} \succ \mathbf{0}$. The fourth form is eliminated right away since no positive direction vector can be turned into it by any permutation.

If $(\sigma_3, \sigma_1, \sigma_4, \sigma_2)$ has the form $(-1, *, *, *)$, then $(\sigma_1, \sigma_2, \sigma_3, \sigma_4)$ has the form $(*, *, -1, *)$. All positive direction vectors of this type must belong to one of the two forms: $(1, *, -1, *)$, $(0, 1, -1, *)$.

If $(\sigma_3, \sigma_1, \sigma_4, \sigma_2)$ has the form $(0, -1, *, *)$, then $(\sigma_1, \sigma_2, \sigma_3, \sigma_4)$ has the form $(-1, *, 0, *)$, which is always negative. Therefore, this form can be completely ruled out.

If $(\sigma_3, \sigma_1, \sigma_4, \sigma_2)$ has the form $(0, 0, -1, *)$, then $(\sigma_1, \sigma_2, \sigma_3, \sigma_4)$ is of the form $(0, *, 0, -1)$. The only positive direction vector included in this form is $(0, 1, 0, -1)$.

Thus, all direction vectors that prevent the loop permutation defined by the given permutation matrix $\mathcal{P}$ are given by three disjoint forms: $(1, *, -1, *), (0, 1, -1, *), (0, 1, 0, -1)$.

We will present results on forms of direction vectors that prevent certain simple permutations such as interchanges and circulations, and then give an algorithm to find direction vector forms for any given permutation. All results in the first part are derived from the following lemma:

Lemma 2.5 *Let* $1 \leq p < q \leq m$. *Let* π *denote a permutation of the set* $\{1, 2, \ldots, m\}$ *that does not change the elements 1 through* $p - 1$ *nor the elements* $q + 1$ *through* m. *A direction vector* $\sigma = (\sigma_1, \sigma_2, \ldots, \sigma_m)$ *will prevent the permutation of the loops* $L_1, L_2, \ldots, L_m$ *defined by* π, *iff it is of the form*

$$(0, 0, \ldots, 0, \sigma_p, \sigma_{p+1}, \ldots, \sigma_q, *, *, \ldots, *)$$

where $(\sigma_p, \sigma_{p+1}, \ldots, \sigma_q) \succ 0$ *and* $(\sigma_{\pi(p)}, \sigma_{\pi(p+1)}, \ldots, \sigma_{\pi(q)}) \prec 0$.

PROOF. Let $\mathcal{P}$ denote the permutation matrix corresponding to π. Suppose that σ prevents the loop permutation defined by $\mathcal{P}$. Then we have $\sigma \succ 0$ and $\sigma\mathcal{P} \prec 0$. By hypothesis, π only rearranges $p, p+1, \ldots, q$ among themselves, and we have

$$\sigma\mathcal{P} = (\sigma_1, \sigma_2, \ldots, \sigma_{p-1}, \sigma_{\pi(p)}, \sigma_{\pi(p+1)}, \ldots, \sigma_{\pi(q)}, \sigma_{q+1}, \ldots, \sigma_m).$$

The initial segment $(\sigma_1, \sigma_2, \ldots, \sigma_{p-1})$ must be zero, since $\sigma\mathcal{P}$ would be positive if it were positive, and σ would be negative if it were negative. Then, σ and $\sigma\mathcal{P}$ have the forms:

$$\sigma = (0, 0, \ldots, 0, \sigma_p, \sigma_{p+1}, \ldots, \sigma_q, \sigma_{q+1}, \ldots, \sigma_m)$$
$$\sigma\mathcal{P} = (0, 0, \ldots, 0, \sigma_{\pi(p)}, \sigma_{\pi(p+1)}, \ldots, \sigma_{\pi(q)}, \sigma_{q+1}, \ldots, \sigma_m).$$

The middle segment $(\sigma_p, \sigma_{p+1}, \ldots, \sigma_q)$ of σ must be positive, since σ would be negative if it were negative, and σ would be equal to $\sigma\mathcal{P}$ if it were zero. Similarly, we can show that the middle segment of $\sigma\mathcal{P}$ must be negative. Thus, σ has the form described in the lemma.

The proof that a direction vector having the given form will prevent the loop permutation is trivial. □

Corollary 1 *Let $1 \le p < q \le m$. If the loops $L_p, L_{p+1}, \ldots, L_{q-1}$ carry no dependence, then the loops $L_p, L_{p+1}, \ldots, L_q$ can be permuted arbitrarily among themselves. (The loops L_1–L_{p-1} and L_{q+1}–L_m are kept fixed.)*

PROOF. Take any permutation of $\{p, p+1, \ldots, q\}$. Extend it uniquely to a permutation π of $\{1, 2, \ldots, m\}$ by requiring that π not change the elements 1 through $(p-1)$ and $(q+1)$ through m. To prevent the loop permutation defined by π, we need a direction vector of the form in Lemma 2.5. But a direction vector of the form

$$(0, 0, \ldots, 0, \sigma_p, \sigma_{p+1}, \ldots, \sigma_q, *, *, \ldots, *)$$

with $(\sigma_p, \sigma_{p+1}, \ldots, \sigma_q) \succ \mathbf{0}$ implies dependence at one of the levels $p, p+1, \ldots, q$. If there is no dependence at levels p through $(q-1)$, then the only possibility left is dependence at level q which means $(\sigma_p, \sigma_{p+1}, \ldots, \sigma_q) = (0, 0, \ldots, 0, 1)$. This violates the condition $(\sigma_{\pi(p)}, \sigma_{\pi(p+1)}, \ldots, \sigma_{\pi(q)}) \prec \mathbf{0}$, since $(\sigma_{\pi(p)}, \sigma_{\pi(p+1)}, \ldots, \sigma_{\pi(q)})$ is a rearrangement of $(0, 0, \ldots, 0, 1)$. Thus, there is no direction vector that would prevent the loop permutation defined by π. $\square$

The case $q = p + 1$ in the above corollary states that if there is no dependence at level p, then the loops L_p and L_{p+1} can be interchanged. The following theorem gives a general necessary and sufficient condition under which this interchange is valid.

Theorem 2.6 *Let $1 \le p < m$. The loops L_p and L_{p+1} in the loop nest $(L_1, L_2, \ldots, L_m)$ can be interchanged iff there is no direction vector of the form*

$$(\underbrace{0, 0, \ldots, 0}_{p-1}, 1, -1, *, *, \ldots, *).$$

PROOF. Taking $q = p + 1$ in Lemma 2.5, we see that a direction vector $\boldsymbol{\sigma} = (\sigma_1, \sigma_2, \ldots, \sigma_m)$ will prevent this loop interchange iff it has the form

$$(0, 0, \ldots, 0, \sigma_p, \sigma_{p+1}, *, *, \ldots, *)$$

where $(\sigma_p, \sigma_{p+1}) \succ 0$ and $(\sigma_{p+1}, \sigma_p) \prec 0$. Of the 9 possible values of (σ_p, σ_{p+1}), the only one that satisfies these two conditions is $(\sigma_p, \sigma_{p+1}) = (1, -1)$.   □

Corollary 1 *Suppose that interchange of the adjacent loops L_p and L_{p+1} is valid. A dependence at level u before the interchange becomes a dependence at level v after the interchange, where*

$$v = \begin{cases} u & \text{if } 1 \leq u < p \\ p \text{ or } p+1 & \text{if } u = p \\ p & \text{if } u = p+1 \\ u & \text{if } p+1 < u \leq m. \end{cases}$$

PROOF. Dependence at level u is due to one or more direction vectors of the form $(0, 0, \ldots, 0, 1, *, *, \ldots, *)$ with $(u - 1)$ leading zeros.

If $1 \leq u < p$ or $p + 1 < u \leq m$, then the interchange of loops L_p and L_{p+1} does not change the first u elements of this direction vector form. Hence, a dependence at such a level u will still be a dependence at the same level after the interchange.

Dependence at level p is due to one or more direction vectors of the form $(0, 0, \ldots, 0, 1, *, *, \ldots, *)$ with $(p - 1)$ leading zeros. We can rule out the form $(0, 0, \ldots, 0, 1, -1, *, \ldots, *)$ since we assume that the interchange of loops L_p and L_{p+1} is valid. Dependence at level p due to a direction vector of the form $(0, 0, \ldots, 0, 1, 1, *, \ldots, *)$ remains a dependence at level p after the interchange, while that due to a direction vector of the form $(0, 0, \ldots, 0, 1, 0, *, \ldots, *)$ becomes a dependence at level $(p + 1)$.

It is now easy to see that a dependence at level $(p + 1)$ becomes a dependence at level p after the loop interchange.   □

Consider next the interchange of two arbitrary loops. By Corollary 1 to Lemma 2.5, if there is no dependence at levels p through $q - 1$, then the loops L_p and L_q can be interchanged. This is only a sufficient condition, however. There is a necessary and sufficient condition for the validity of this interchange; see Exercises 4 and 6 for the extensions of Theorem 2.6 and its corollary.

It is often useful to know if we can legally move a given loop in $\mathbf{L}$ to a certain position in the nest, without making any other changes. Let $1 \leq p < q \leq m$. Left circulation of loops L_p through L_q moves L_p inward to the qth position, while right circulation of the same loops moves L_q outward to the pth position.

Theorem 2.7 *Let $1 \leq p < q \leq m$. Left circulation of loops L_p through L_q is valid iff there is no direction vector of the form*

$$(\underbrace{0, 0, \ldots, 0}_{p-1}, 1, \sigma_{p+1}, \sigma_{p+2}, \ldots, \sigma_q, *, *, \ldots, *)$$

where $(\sigma_{p+1}, \sigma_{p+2}, \ldots, \sigma_q) \prec 0$.

PROOF. Left circulation of loops L_p through L_q is defined by the following permutation matrix:

$$\begin{bmatrix} 1 & \cdots & p-1 & p & p+1 & \cdots & q-1 & q & q+1 & \cdots & m \\ 1 & \cdots & p-1 & p+1 & p+2 & \cdots & q & p & q+1 & \cdots & m \end{bmatrix}.$$

By Lemma 2.5, a direction vector $(\sigma_1, \sigma_2, \ldots, \sigma_m)$ will prevent this transformation iff it is of the form

$$(0, 0, \ldots, 0, \sigma_p, \sigma_{p+1}, \ldots, \sigma_q, *, *, \ldots, *)$$

where $(\sigma_p, \sigma_{p+1}, \ldots, \sigma_q) \succ 0$ and $(\sigma_{p+1}, \sigma_{p+2}, \ldots, \sigma_q, \sigma_p) \prec 0$. These two conditions rule out the values $\sigma_p = -1$ and $\sigma_p = 0$, leaving $\sigma_p = 1$ as the only choice. Then, to make $(\sigma_{p+1}, \sigma_{p+2}, \ldots, \sigma_q, \sigma_p)$ negative, we must have $(\sigma_{p+1}, \sigma_{p+2}, \ldots, \sigma_q)$ negative. □

Corollary 1 *Let $1 \leq p < m$. If there is no dependence at level p, then the loop L_p can be moved farther inward (by left circulation of loops L_p–L_q) to any position $q > p$.*

PROOF. If there is no dependence at level p, then there is no direction vector of the form

$$(\underbrace{0, 0, \ldots, 0}_{p-1}, 1, *, *, \ldots, *),$$

and hence no direction vector of the form given in Theorem 2.7. □

Theorem 2.8 *Let $1 \leq p < q \leq m$. Right circulation of loops L_p through L_q) is valid iff there is no direction vector of the form*

$$(\underbrace{0, 0, \ldots, 0}_{p-1}, \sigma_p, \sigma_{p+1}, \sigma_{p+2}, \ldots, \sigma_{q-1}, -1, *, *, \ldots, *)$$

where $(\sigma_p, \sigma_{p+1}, \ldots, \sigma_{q-1}) \succ 0$.

PROOF. The proof is similar to that of Theorem 2.7.   □

If there is no dependence at level q, then the loop L_q can be moved inward, but not necessarily outward (why?). Thus, Theorem 2.8 does not have the corollary which would correspond to the corollary to Theorem 2.7. We have instead:

Corollary 1 *Let $1 < q \leq m$. If column q of the direction matrix has only 0's and 1's, then the loop L_q can be moved farther outward (by right circulation of loops L_p-L_q) to any position $p < q$.*

PROOF. Right circulation of loops L_p-L_q is valid, since the direction vector form of Theorem 2.8 that prevents it is ruled out.   □

We now present an algorithm that can compute all direction vectors that prevent any given loop permutation. After stating the algorithm, we will apply it to recompute the forms of Example 2.3.

Algorithm 2.1 Given an $m \times m$ permutation matrix

$$\mathcal{P} = \begin{bmatrix} 1 & 2 & \cdots & m \\ \pi(1) & \pi(2) & \cdots & \pi(m) \end{bmatrix},$$

this algorithm finds all direction vectors $\boldsymbol{\sigma} = (\sigma_1, \sigma_2, \ldots, \sigma_m)$ that prevent the loop permutation of the nest **L**, defined by $\mathcal{P}$. The direction vectors are presented as a set of disjoint direction vector forms consisting of $1, 0, -1, *$. We will use a temporary direction vector $(\mu_1, \mu_2, \ldots, \mu_m)$.

set $(\sigma_1, \sigma_2, \ldots, \sigma_m) \leftarrow (*, *, \ldots, *)$
do $k = 1, m - 1, 1$
    if $\pi(k) > 1$, **then**
        set $\sigma_{\pi(k)} \leftarrow -1$
        set $(\mu_1, \mu_2, \ldots, \mu_{\pi(k)-1}) \leftarrow (\sigma_1, \sigma_2, \ldots, \sigma_{\pi(k)-1})$
        while $(\mu_1, \mu_2, \ldots, \mu_{\pi(k)-1}) \neq \mathbf{0}$
            find the smallest $t < \pi(k)$ such that $\mu_t = *$
            set $\mu_t \leftarrow 1$
            store $(\mu_1, \mu_2, \ldots, \mu_{\pi(k)-1}, \sigma_{\pi(k)}, \ldots, \sigma_m)$
            set $\mu_t \leftarrow 0$
        endwhile
    endif
    set $\sigma_{\pi(k)} \leftarrow 0$
enddo   □

Note that in the **while** loop, we can always start with a value of t which is one more than the value in the previous iteration, if any. The direction vector forms generated by Algorithm 2.1 are disjoint, that is, each direction vector preventing the given permutation belongs to a unique form (prove). The direction vector forms for interchanges and circulations given in this section can be derived from this algorithm.

Let us repeat Example 2.3 and this time we will use Algorithm 2.1:

Example 2.4 We will show the detailed steps when Algorithm 2.1 is applied to find direction vectors that prevent the loop permutation defined by the matrix:

$$\mathcal{P} = \begin{bmatrix} 1 & 2 & 3 & 4 \\ 3 & 1 & 4 & 2 \end{bmatrix}$$

of Example 2.3. Here we have $m = 4$ and

$$\pi(1) = 3, \pi(2) = 1, \pi(3) = 4, \pi(4) = 2.$$

$(\sigma_1, \sigma_2, \sigma_3, \sigma_4) \leftarrow (*, *, *, *)$

$k \leftarrow 1$ $[\pi(k) = \pi(1) = 3]$

    $\sigma_3 \leftarrow -1$ $[\boldsymbol{\sigma} = (*, *, -1, *)]$

    $(\mu_1, \mu_2) \leftarrow (\sigma_1, \sigma_2)$ $[(\mu_1, \mu_2) = (*, *)]$

        $t \leftarrow 1$

        $\mu_1 \leftarrow 1$ $[(\mu_1, \mu_2) = (1, *)]$

        store $(1, *, -1, *)$

        $\mu_1 \leftarrow 0$ $[(\mu_1, \mu_2) = (0, *)]$

        $t \leftarrow 2$

        $\mu_2 \leftarrow 1$ $[(\mu_1, \mu_2) = (0, 1)]$

        store $(0, 1, -1, *)$

        $\mu_2 \leftarrow 0$ $[\,(\mu_1, \mu_2) = (0, 0)]$

    $\sigma_3 \leftarrow 0$ $[\boldsymbol{\sigma} = (*, *, 0, *)]$

$k \leftarrow 2$ $[\pi(k) = \pi(2) = 1]$

    $\sigma_1 \leftarrow 0$ $[\boldsymbol{\sigma} = (0, *, 0, *)]$

$k \leftarrow 3$ $[\pi(k) = \pi(3) = 4]$

    $\sigma_4 \leftarrow -1$ $[\boldsymbol{\sigma} = (0, *, 0, -1)]$

    $(\mu_1, \mu_2, \mu_3) \leftarrow (\sigma_1, \sigma_2, \sigma_3)$ $[(\mu_1, \mu_2, \mu_3) = (0, *, 0)]$

        $t \leftarrow 2$

        $\mu_2 \leftarrow 1$ $[(\mu_1, \mu_2, \mu_3) = (0, 1, 0)]$

        store $(0, 1, 0, -1)$

        $\mu_2 \leftarrow 0$ $[(\mu_1, \mu_2, \mu_3) = (0, 0, 0)]$

    $\sigma_4 \leftarrow 0$ $[\boldsymbol{\sigma} = (0, *, 0, 0)]$

EXERCISES 2.3

1. Show by an example that the converse of Corollary 1 to Lemma 2.5 is not necessarily true (i.e., the condition that there be no dependence at levels p through $q - 1$ is sufficient but not necessary for the validity of arbitrary permutations of the loops L_p through L_q).

2. Let $1 \leq p < q \leq m$. Assume that the loops $L_p, L_{p+1}, \ldots, L_{q-1}$ carry no dependence in $\mathbf{L}$. Prove that they will still carry no dependence after an arbitrary permutation of the loops $L_p, L_{p+1}, \ldots, L_q$ that keeps loops L_1–L_{p-1} and L_{q+1}–L_m fixed. Prove also that if there is no dependence at levels $p, p + 1, \ldots, q$ in $\mathbf{L}$, then there will still be no dependence at these levels after such a loop permutation. Give examples to illustrate the two situations.

3. Let $1 \leq p < m$. Suppose the interchange of the adjacent loops L_p and L_{p+1} is valid. If there is dependence at a level v in the transformed program, find the possible levels in the loop nest before the interchange.

4. Let $1 \leq p < q \leq m$. Prove that a direction vector $\sigma = (\sigma_1, \sigma_2, \ldots, \sigma_m)$ will prevent interchange of the loops L_p and L_q in the loop nest $\mathbf{L}$ iff σ has one of the following forms:

    (a) $(\underbrace{0, 0, \ldots, 0, 1}_{p-1}, \underbrace{*, *, \ldots, *}_{q-p-1}, \underbrace{-1, *, *, \ldots, *}_{m-q})$;

    (b) $(0, 0, \ldots, 0, 1, \sigma_{p+1}, \sigma_{p+2}, \ldots, \sigma_{q-1}, 0, *, *, \ldots, *)$

    where $(\sigma_{p+1}, \sigma_{p+2}, \ldots, \sigma_{q-1}) \prec 0$;

    (c) $(0, 0, \ldots, 0, 0, \sigma_{p+1}, \sigma_{p+2}, \ldots, \sigma_{q-1}, -1, *, *, \ldots, *)$

    where $(\sigma_{p+1}, \sigma_{p+2}, \ldots, \sigma_{q-1}) \succ 0$.

5. Using only $1, 0, -1$ and $*$, construct a minimal set of disjoint direction vector forms that account for all the direction vectors in the previous exercise. How many such direction vector forms are there?

6. Suppose that the interchange of the loops L_p and L_q is valid. Show that a dependence at a level u before the interchange becomes a dependence at level v after the interchange, where

$$
v = \begin{cases}
u & \text{if } 1 \leq u < p \\
\text{one of } p, p+1, \ldots, q & \text{if } u = p \\
u \text{ or } p & \text{if } p < u < q \\
p & \text{if } u = q \\
u & \text{if } q < u \leq m.
\end{cases}
$$

7. Let $1 \leq p < q \leq m$. Suppose the interchange of the loops L_p and L_q is valid. If there is dependence at a level v in the transformed program, find the possible levels in the loop nest before the interchange.

8. Let $1 < q \leq m$. Assume there is no dependence at level q. Show by examples that it may or may not be possible to move the loop L_q farther outward.

9. Using results of this section, find necessary and/or sufficient conditions under which a loop can be made the innermost loop by a valid loop permutation. Do the same for the outermost loop.

10. Using only $1, 0, -1$ and $*$, construct a minimal set of disjoint direction vector forms that account for all the direction vectors in Theorem 2.7. How many such direction vector forms are there?

11. Let $1 \leq p < q \leq m$. Suppose that left circulation of the loops L_p through L_q is valid. If there is dependence at a level u in the program before circulation, find the corresponding dependence level v after circulation.

12. Let $1 \leq p < t < q \leq m$. Prove that if left circulation of loops L_p through L_q is valid, then left circulation of loops L_p through L_t is also valid.

13. Using only $1, 0, -1$ and $*$, construct a minimal set of disjoint direction vector forms that account for all the direction vectors in Theorem 2.8. How many such direction vector forms are there?

14. Let $1 \leq p < q \leq m$. Suppose that right circulation of the loops L_p through L_q is valid. If there is dependence at a level u in the program before circulation, find the corresponding dependence level v after circulation.

15. Let $1 \leq p < t < q \leq m$. Prove that if right circulation of loops L_p through L_q is valid, then right circulation of loops L_t through L_q is also valid.

16. Consider a nest $(L_1, L_2, L_3, L_4, L_5)$ of 5 loops. Using the results of this section, find the direction vectors that prevent the following loop permutations:

    (a) Interchange of loops L_3 and L_4;

    (b) Interchange of loops L_2 and L_4;

    (c) Left circulation of loops: L_1, L_2, L_3;

    (d) Right circulation of loops: L_2, L_3, L_4, L_5.

17. Explain why the upper limit of k is $m - 1$ (and not m) in Algorithm 2.1.

18. For a given $m \times m$ permutation matrix $\mathcal{P}$, let $\Theta(\mathcal{P})$ denote the number of disjoint direction vector forms (found by Algorithm 2.1) that will prevent the loop permutation defined by $\mathcal{P}$. Find $\Theta(\mathcal{P})$ where $\mathcal{P}$ is the following matrix:

   (a) $\mathcal{I}_m$

   (b) $\begin{pmatrix} 1 & 2 & \cdots & m \\ m & m-1 & \cdots & 1 \end{pmatrix}$.

19. Show that $0 \leq \Theta(\mathcal{P}) \leq m(m-1)/2$ for a general $\mathcal{P}$.

20. Prove that $\Theta(\mathcal{P}) = \sum_{k=1}^{m} \theta_k$, where θ_k is the number of integers t such that $t > k$ and $\pi(t) < \pi(k)$.

21. Apply Algorithm 2.1 to find all direction vectors that prevent the permutation of a nest of 5 loops, defined by the following permutation matrix:

   (a) $\mathcal{P} = \begin{bmatrix} 1 & 2 & 3 & 4 & 5 \\ 5 & 4 & 3 & 2 & 1 \end{bmatrix}$

   (b) $\mathcal{P} = \begin{bmatrix} 1 & 2 & 3 & 4 & 5 \\ 4 & 5 & 1 & 2 & 3 \end{bmatrix}$

   (c) $\mathcal{P} = \begin{bmatrix} 1 & 2 & 3 & 4 & 5 \\ 2 & 1 & 4 & 3 & 5 \end{bmatrix}$

   (d) $\mathcal{P} = \begin{bmatrix} 1 & 2 & 3 & 4 & 5 \\ 3 & 2 & 4 & 5 & 1 \end{bmatrix}$.

2.4 Parallelization by Permutation

By Lemma 1.1, a loop L_r in a nest $\mathbf{L}$ can execute in parallel (i.e., can be changed into its corresponding **doall** loop) iff L_r carries no dependence. In this section, we study permutations $\mathcal{P}$ that reorder the loops of $\mathbf{L}$ in such a way that one or more outermost (innermost) loops in the transformed program $\mathbf{L}_{\mathcal{P}}$ can execute in parallel. The idea is to identify a set of loops that can be moved legally outward (inward) over other loops to form a ring of outermost (innermost) loops that carry no dependence. We have to remember two major points:

1. After a loop permutation, a loop that carried no dependence in $\mathbf{L}$ may carry one in $\mathbf{L}_{\mathcal{P}}$, while a loop that carried a dependence in $\mathbf{L}$ may not carry one in $\mathbf{L}_{\mathcal{P}}$.

2. If a loop carries no dependence, then it may be moved inward
to any position (Corollary 1 to Theorem 2.7), but we may or
may not be able to move it outward.

Example 2.5 Consider a nest of four loops $\mathbf{L} = (L_1, L_2, L_3, L_4)$
with the direction matrix:

$$\Delta = \begin{pmatrix} 1 & 1 & 0 & 1 \\ 0 & 1 & 0 & 1 \\ 1 & -1 & 0 & 1 \end{pmatrix}.$$

Note that L_3 carries no dependence, and that it will never carry a
dependence after a valid permutation. We can make it the outermost loop by right circulation of loops L_1–L_3 (Corollary 1 to Theorem 2.8); we can also make it the innermost loop by interchanging
L_3 and L_4 (Theorem 2.6). The loop L_4 carries no dependence in
$\mathbf{L}$, but L_1 does. We can make L_4 the outermost loop and L_1 the
innermost loop, by interchanging L_1 and L_4. After the interchange,
L_4 will carry a dependence, but not L_1. Finally, L_2 carries a dependence in $\mathbf{L}$. It cannot be made the outermost loop, but we can make
it the innermost loop by left circulation of L_2–L_4. It will carry no
dependence after getting moved to the innermost position.

Outer loop parallelization is easily characterized in terms of the
zero columns of the direction matrix:

Theorem 2.9 *Let Δ denote the direction matrix of a loop nest $\mathbf{L}$.
There exists a valid loop permutation $\mathbf{L} \mapsto \mathbf{L}_\mathcal{P}$ such that one or
more outermost loops in $\mathbf{L}_\mathcal{P}$ can execute in parallel, iff Δ has a
zero column.*

PROOF. The 'if' Part: Assume Δ has at least one zero column. Let
q denote the smallest integer such that column q of Δ is equal to
the zero vector. By Corollary 1 to Theorem 2.8, we can move the
loop L_q of $\mathbf{L}$ to the outermost position. Then the outermost loop,

L_q, in the transformed program carries no dependence (why?), and therefore can execute in parallel (Lemma 1.1).

The 'only if' Part: Assume that there is a valid loop permutation $\mathbf{L} \mapsto \mathbf{L_P}$, such that one or more outermost loops of $\mathbf{L_P}$ can execute in parallel. The direction matrix of the loop nest $\mathbf{L_P}$ is $\mathbf{\Delta P}$. Column 1 of this matrix does not have a -1 since all rows have to be positive (Theorem 2.1). It does not have a 1 either, since the outermost loop of $\mathbf{L_P}$ can execute in parallel and therefore cannot carry a dependence (Lemma 1.1). Thus, column 1 of $\mathbf{\Delta P}$ is equal to the zero vector, so that the original direction matrix $\mathbf{\Delta}$ has a zero column. □

If $\mathbf{\Delta}$ has two zero columns q and p with $q < p$, then we can make L_q the outermost loop and L_p the second outermost loop; three or more zero columns can be handled similarly. (The zero columns can be handled in any arbitrary order. We took this particular order to minimize the effort of loop limit computation.) The whole process can be completed by a single permutation. It is easy to show the validity of this loop permutation that moves loops of $\mathbf{L}$ with corresponding zero columns in $\mathbf{\Delta}$ outward over other loops. The following corollary is now clear:

Corollary 1 *The maximum number of outermost* **doall** *loops we can get by a loop permutation is equal to the number of zero columns of the direction matrix* $\mathbf{\Delta}$.

Next, consider inner loop parallelization by loop permutation. The general question is the following: Is there a valid loop permutation $\mathbf{L} \mapsto \mathbf{L_P}$ such that one or more innermost loops of $\mathbf{L_P}$ carry no dependence? There is no simple characterization; we give a sufficient condition under which such a permutation exists:

Theorem 2.10 *There exists a valid loop permutation* $\mathbf{L} \mapsto \mathbf{L_P}$ *such that one or more innermost loops in* $\mathbf{L_P}$ *can execute in parallel, if there is a loop in* $\mathbf{L}$ *that carries no dependence.*

PROOF. Suppose some loop L_p in **L** carries no dependence. By Corollary 1 to Theorem 2.7, we can move L_p to the innermost position by left circulation of loops L_p–L_m. The new innermost loop, L_p, still carries no dependence (Theorem 2.3), and hence it can execute in parallel (Lemma 1.1).   □

Suppose there are two or more loops carrying no dependence. They can be moved inward one by one, and be changed into their corresponding **doall** loops. In fact, we need only use a single permutation. It is easy to prove the validity of the permutation that moves all such loops inward over other loops.

Example 2.6 To see that the condition of the theorem is not necessary, consider a triple loop **L** $= (L_1, L_2, L_3)$ whose direction matrix is

$$\mathbf{\Delta} = \begin{pmatrix} 0 & 1 & 1 \\ 0 & 0 & 1 \\ 1 & 0 & -1 \end{pmatrix}.$$

Each of the three loops carries a dependence in **L**. Interchange of L_2 and L_3 is valid, and the direction matrix of the nest (L_1, L_3, L_2) is

$$\begin{pmatrix} 0 & 1 & 1 \\ 0 & 1 & 0 \\ 1 & -1 & 0 \end{pmatrix}.$$

The innermost loop, L_2, of the transformed program carries no dependence and hence it can execute in parallel.

EXERCISES 2.4

1. Let $1 < p < m$. State if the loop L_p in **L** can be made the innermost loop always/sometimes/never by a valid loop permutation, if column p of $\mathbf{\Delta}$ has only

   (a) 0's

   (b) 0's and 1's

   (c) 0's and -1's

   (d) 1's

   (e) −1's

   (f) 1's and −1's.

   After becoming the innermost loop, can L_r execute in parallel?
   Repeat for 'outermost' loop.

2. The direction matrix Δ of a nest (L_1, L_2, L_3, L_4) is given below. By
   using loop permutations, find all equivalent loop nests that have at least
   one **doall** loop:

   (a) $\Delta = \begin{pmatrix} 1 & 1 & 0 & 1 \\ 0 & 0 & 0 & 1 \\ 1 & -1 & 0 & 1 \end{pmatrix}$

   (b) $\Delta = \begin{pmatrix} 1 & 0 & 0 & 1 \\ 0 & 1 & 0 & 1 \\ 0 & 0 & 1 & 0 \end{pmatrix}$

   (c) $\Delta = \begin{pmatrix} 1 & 1 & 1 & -1 \\ 0 & 0 & 0 & 1 \\ 1 & 1 & -1 & 0 \end{pmatrix}$.

3. In the previous exercise, assume that the loop nest is rectangular and
   that the loop limits are as follows:

   $$L_1 : 1, 100; \quad L_2 : 1, 1000; \quad L_3 : 1, 10; \quad L_4 : 1, 500.$$

   Assume also that each iteration of the nest takes one unit of time for
   execution. Find the shortest possible execution time for the given loop
   nest in each case, by checking all the equivalent programs that you have
   found.

2.5   Computation of Loop Limits

The index space of **L** consists of all integer vectors in a polytope in
$\mathbf{R}^m$; it can be expressed as the set of integer m-vectors **I** such that

$$\left. \begin{array}{c} \mathbf{p}_0 \;\le\; \mathbf{IP} \\ \mathbf{IQ} \;\le\; \mathbf{q}_0 \end{array} \right\} \tag{2.1}$$

where $\mathbf{p}_0$ is the lower limit vector, $\mathbf{q}_0$ the upper limit vector, **P** the
lower limit matrix, and **Q** the upper limit matrix of **L**.

Consider the transformation of **L** into the loop nest **L$_\mathcal{P}$** by an $m \times m$ permutation matrix $\mathcal{P}$. Let π denote the permutation of the set $\{1, 2, \ldots, m\}$ corresponding to $\mathcal{P}$. Then, the new index vector **K** is given by

$$\mathbf{K} = (I_{\pi(1)}, I_{\pi(2)}, \ldots, I_{\pi(m)}).$$

Using Fourier's elimination method (Algorithm I-3.2), eliminate from the system (2.1) the variables

$$K_m = I_{\pi(m)}, \; K_{m-1} = I_{\pi(m-1)}, \ldots, \; K_1 = I_{\pi(1)}$$

in this order. We will have a set of $2m$ integer-valued functions $\alpha_r(K_1, \ldots, K_{r-1})$ and $\beta_r(K_1, \ldots, K_{r-1})$, $1 \le r \le m$, such that the index space is described by the set of inequalities:

$$\left.\begin{array}{ccccc}
\alpha_1 & \le & K_1 & \le & \beta_1 \\
\alpha_2(K_1) & \le & K_2 & \le & \beta_2(K_1) \\
& & \vdots & & \\
\alpha_m(K_1, K_2, \ldots, K_{m-1}) & \le & K_m & \le & \beta_m(K_1, K_2, \ldots, K_{m-1}).
\end{array}\right\}$$

These functions are the loop limits of the transformed program **L$_\mathcal{P}$**. If the nest **L** is rectangular, then so is the transformed nest **L$_\mathcal{P}$**. In this case, no detailed computation is needed; the limits of $K_r = I_{\pi(r)}$ will simply be $p_{\pi(r)}$ and $q_{\pi(r)}$, $1 \le r \le m$. We will illustrate the method of limit computation by several examples:

Example 2.7 Consider the triangular[1] double loop:

$L_1:$ **do** $I_1 = 10, 50$
$L_2:$ **do** $I_2 = 10, I_1$
             $H(I_1, I_2)$
          enddo
       enddo

---

[1]We call it a triangular double loop, because its index space is the set of all integer points in a triangle.

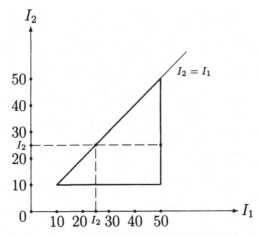

Figure 2.3: Index space of (L_1, L_2) in Example 2.7.

Its index space is shown in Figure 2.3. After loop interchange, we have a double loop whose index vector is (I_2, I_1). We now need to describe the triangular region in Figure 2.3 by two new sets of inequalities: In the first set, I_2 goes from a constant to a constant, and in the second, I_1 goes from a function of I_2 to a function of I_2. From the picture, it is clear that I_2 runs from 10 to 50, and that for a given I_2, we have $I_2 \leq I_1 \leq 50$. Hence, loop interchange will transform the given program into the triangular double loop:

L_2 :   **do** $I_2 = 10, 50$
L_1 :   **do** $I_1 = I_2, 50$
                $H(I_1, I_2)$
            enddo
        enddo

Note that we could get the new loop limits by eliminating first I_1 and then I_2 from the inequalities giving the old loop bounds:

$$10 \leq I_1 \leq 50$$
$$10 \leq I_2 \leq I_1.$$

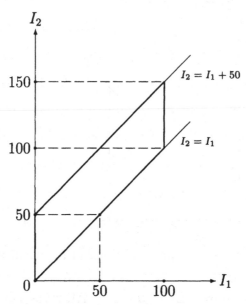

Figure 2.4: Index space of (L_1, L_2) in Example 2.8.

Example 2.8 In this example, we have a regular double loop:

L_1 :   **do** $I_1 = 0, 100$
L_2 :   **do** $I_2 = I_1, I_1 + 50$
                $H(I_1, I_2)$
         enddo
    enddo

whose index space is the parallelogram shown in Figure 2.4. This parallelogram is described by the inequalities:

$$\left. \begin{array}{rcccl} 0 & \leq & I_1 & \leq & 100 \\ I_1 & \leq & I_2 & \leq & I_1 + 50. \end{array} \right\} \qquad (2.2)$$

Note that I_2 ranges from 0 to 150. It is clear from the figure that the values of I_1 for different values of I_2 are as follows:

if $\quad 0 \leq I_2 \leq 50,\quad$ then $\qquad 0 \leq I_1 \leq I_2$
if $\quad 50 \leq I_2 \leq 100,\quad$ then $\quad I_2 - 50 \leq I_1 \leq I_2$
if $\quad 100 \leq I_2 \leq 150,\quad$ then $\quad I_2 - 50 \leq I_1 \leq 100.$

This table can be summed up in one line:

$$\max(0, I_2 - 50) \le I_1 \le \min(100, I_2).$$

This alternative description can also be derived by applying Fourier's method to the set of inequalities (2.2). We have

$$\begin{aligned} 0 &\le I_1 \le 100 \\ I_2 - 50 &\le I_1 \le I_2 \end{aligned}$$

so that

$$\max(0, I_2 - 50) \le I_1 \le \min(100, I_2).$$

Elimination of I_1 now gives us $0 \le I_2 \le 150$. The form of the loop nest after loop interchange is

L_2 :   **do** $I_2 = 0, 150$
L_1 :   **do** $I_1 = \max(0, I_2 - 50), \min(100, I_2)$
                $H(I_1, I_2)$
            enddo
        enddo

Example 2.9 To illustrate better the algebraic method of limit computation, we consider a loop nest with more complicated limits:

L_1 :   **do** $I_1 = 0, 100$
L_2 :   **do** $I_2 = \lceil I_1/2 \rceil, \min(200, 4I_1)$
L_3 :   **do** $I_3 = I_1 + I_2, 200$
                    $H(I_1, I_2, I_3)$
                enddo
            enddo
        enddo

Suppose we want to interchange the loops L_1 and L_3, so that the index vector will change from (I_1, I_2, I_3) to (I_3, I_2, I_1). The index space of the nest, which is currently described by a set of inequalities of the form

$$\begin{aligned} p_1 &\le I_1 \le q_1 \\ p_2(I_1) &\le I_2 \le q_2(I_1) \\ p_3(I_1, I_2) &\le I_3 \le q_3(I_1, I_2), \end{aligned}$$

needs to have a new description of the form

$$\begin{aligned}
p_1' &\le I_3 \le q_1' \\
p_2'(I_3) &\le I_2 \le q_2'(I_3) \\
p_3'(I_3, I_2) &\le I_1 \le q_3'(I_3, I_2).
\end{aligned}$$

To get this new description, we will apply Fourier Elimination (Algorithm I-3.2) to the current system and eliminate the variables in the order: I_1, I_2, I_3. It would be rather tedious to show the detailed steps of the algorithm; instead, we will sketch an outline of the overall process.

The index space of the loop nest (L_1, L_2, L_3) consists of all integer vectors (I_1, I_2, I_3) such that

$$\left.\begin{aligned}
0 &\le I_1 \\
I_1 &\le 100 \\
I_1/2 &\le I_2 \\
I_2 &\le 200 \\
I_2 &\le 4I_1 \\
I_1 + I_2 &\le I_3 \\
I_3 &\le 200.
\end{aligned}\right\} \tag{2.3}$$

Collect all inequalities involving I_1 and express each of them in a form that gives a lower or upper bound for I_1:

$$\left.\begin{aligned}
0 &\le I_1 \\
I_1 &\le 100 \\
I_1 &\le 2I_2 \\
I_2/4 &\le I_1 \\
I_1 &\le I_3 - I_2.
\end{aligned}\right\}$$

Collecting the lower and upper bounds, we get the range of I_1 in terms of I_2 and I_3:

$$\lceil \max(0, I_2/4) \rceil \le I_1 \le \min(100, 2I_2, I_3 - I_2). \tag{2.4}$$

Comparing each lower bound of I_1 with each upper bound, we eliminate I_1 and get the following inequalities:

$$\begin{aligned}
0 &\le 100, & 0 &\le 2I_2, & 0 &\le I_3 - I_2 \\
I_2/4 &\le 100, & I_2/4 &\le 2I_2, & I_2/4 &\le I_3 - I_2.
\end{aligned}$$

Now, take the inequalities that involve I_2 and write each in a form that gives a lower or upper bound to I_2. Express in the same way each inequality in the system (2.3) that involves I_2 but not I_1. The resulting system (after simplification) is

$$\left.\begin{array}{rcl} & I_2 & \leq & 200 \\ 0 \leq & I_2 & & \\ & I_2 & \leq & I_3 \\ & I_2 & \leq & 400 \\ & I_2 & \leq & 4I_3/5. \end{array}\right\}$$

This gives the range for I_2:

$$0 \leq I_2 \leq \lfloor \min(200, I_3, 400, 4I_3/5) \rfloor. \tag{2.5}$$

Comparing the lower bound of I_2 with each bound, we get only one nonredundant inequality: $0 \leq I_3$. Remember that in the original system (2.3), we still have one inequality involving I_3 alone that has not been used: $I_3 \leq 200$. The range for I_3 is then:

$$0 \leq I_3 \leq 200. \tag{2.6}$$

By dropping redundant terms in (2.4)–(2.6), we get limits for the loops L_3, L_2, L_1 in the loop nest after permutation. (Algorithm I-3.2 does not make these simplifications.) The permuted loop nest has the form:

L_3 :   **do** $I_3 = 0, 200$

L_2 :   **do** $I_2 = 0, \lfloor 4I_3/5 \rfloor$

L_1 :   **do** $I_1 = \lceil I_2/4 \rceil, \min(100, 2I_2, I_3 - I_2)$

          $H(I_1, I_2, I_3)$

             enddo

          enddo

       enddo

EXERCISES 2.5

1. A loop permutation changes a rectangular loop nest into a rectangular loop nest. What about a regular loop nest?

2. Find the new loop limits (analytically) when loops are interchanged in the following double loops:

    (a) L_1 :   **do** $I_1 = 1, 100$
        L_2 :   **do** $I_2 = I_1, 100$
                    $H(I_1, I_2)$
                enddo
            enddo

    (b) L_1 :   **do** $I_1 = 1, 100$
        L_2 :   **do** $I_2 = I_1, 2I_1 + 50$
                    $H(I_1, I_2)$
                enddo
            enddo

3. Consider the triple loop:

    L_1 :   **do** $I_1 = 1, 100$
    L_2 :   **do** $I_2 = I_1, I_1 + 50$
    L_3 :   **do** $I_3 = \max(I_2 - I_1, 30), \min(I_1 + I_2, 100)$
                    $H(I_1, I_2, I_3)$
                enddo
            enddo
        enddo

    Find the loop limits for the following loop nests:

    (a) (L_2, L_1, L_3)

    (b) (L_1, L_3, L_2)

    (c) (L_2, L_3, L_1).

2.6   Optimization Problems

There is only one nontrivial permutation for a double loop: the interchange of the two loops. It is valid iff there is no direction vector of the form $(1, -1)$. There are five nontrivial permutations for a triple loop. The details of which direction vectors prevent them and how they change dependence levels are given in Tables 2.1–2.3 at the end of this chapter.

For a general loop nest, we have presented a number of tools to handle the possible loop permutations. Some related optimization problems that we have not discussed are stated below:

1. Suppose the direction matrix of a loop nest **L** is known. Design an efficient algorithm to find the class of all valid loop permutations.

2. Suppose that the direction vectors of **L** are not known, but can be computed. Design an efficient algorithm to find the set of all valid loop permutations with a minimum amount of direction vector computation.

3. Suppose the direction matrix of **L** is known. Find a loop permutation $\mathbf{L} \mapsto \mathbf{L}_{\mathcal{P}}$ such that

   (a) One or more innermost loops of $\mathbf{L}_{\mathcal{P}}$ can execute in parallel; and

   (b) The number of iterations of the outer nest of loops that cannot execute in parallel is minimized.

Permutation	Preventing Direction Vectors
[1 3 2]	$(0, 1, -1)$
[2 1 3]	$(1, -1, *)$
[2 3 1]	$(1, -1, *), (1, 0, -1)$
[3 1 2]	$(1, *, -1), (0, 1, -1)$
[3 2 1]	$(1, *, -1), (0, 1, -1), (1, -1, 0)$

Table 2.1: Permutations and direction vectors in a triple Loop.

Permutation	Old Level	New Level
	1	1
[1 3 2]	2	2, 3
	3	2
	1	1, 2
[2 1 3]	2	1
	3	3
	1	1, 2, 3
[2 3 1]	2	1
	3	2
	1	1, 2
[3 1 2]	2	1, 3
	3	1
	1	1, 2, 3
[3 2 1]	2	1, 2
	3	1

Table 2.2: Level change under a permutation in a triple Loop.

Direction	Old	New Level under Permutation				
Vector	Level	[1 3 2]	[2 1 3]	[2 3 1]	[3 1 2]	[3 2 1]
$(1,1,1)$	1	1	1	1	1	1
$(1,1,0)$	1	1	1	1	2	2
$(1,1,-1)$	1	1	1	1	invalid	invalid
$(1,0,1)$	1	1	2	2	1	1
$(1,0,0)$	1	1	2	3	2	3
$(1,0,-1)$	1	1	2	invalid	invalid	invalid
$(1,-1,1)$	1	1	invalid	invalid	1	1
$(1,-1,0)$	1	1	invalid	invalid	2	invalid
$(1,-1,-1)$	1	1	invalid	invalid	invalid	invalid
$(0,1,1)$	2	2	1	1	1	1
$(0,1,0)$	2	3	1	1	3	2
$(0,1,-1)$	2	invalid	1	1	invalid	invalid
$(0,0,1)$	3	2	3	2	1	1

Table 2.3: Direction vectors, permutations, and change in dependence levels in a triple loop.

Chapter 3

Unimodular Transformations

3.1 Introduction

While studying loop permutations in the previous chapter, we saw that their usefulness in getting **doall** loops was somewhat limited. In this chapter, we consider a class of loop transformations that includes loop permutations as a proper subset, and is better suited for parallelization. A loop permutation is defined by a permutation matrix; a unimodular transformation is a loop transformation defined by a unimodular matrix. (Remember that permutation matrices are unimodular.)

In the given program L, an iteration $H(\mathbf{i})$ is executed before an iteration $H(\mathbf{j})$ iff $\mathbf{i} \prec \mathbf{j}$. An $m \times m$ unimodular matrix $\mathbf{U}$ defines a new execution order where $H(\mathbf{i})$ is executed before $H(\mathbf{j})$ iff $\mathbf{i}\mathbf{U} \prec \mathbf{j}\mathbf{U}$. The new order is also total (i.e., sequential) since for two distinct index points $\mathbf{i}$ and $\mathbf{j}$, we always have either $\mathbf{i}\mathbf{U} \prec \mathbf{j}\mathbf{U}$ or $\mathbf{j}\mathbf{U} \prec \mathbf{i}\mathbf{U}$.[1]

---

[1]The case $\mathbf{i}\mathbf{U} = \mathbf{j}\mathbf{U}$ is ruled out since that would imply $\mathbf{i} = \mathbf{j}$ as $\mathbf{U}$ is nonsingular. Thus, the property that $\det(\mathbf{U}) \neq 0$ is necessary to make the new order a total order. The stronger condition $\det(\mathbf{U}) = \pm 1$ (so that $\mathbf{U}^{-1}$ is an integer matrix) guarantees that the index space is mapped onto the set of all integer points in a polytope included in $\mathbf{R}^m$.

To test the validity of a general unimodular transformation, we
need to know the distance vectors of **L**. Direction vectors would not
suffice here as they did in the case of loop permutations. After a
valid transformation, if a loop in the transformed program carries no
dependence, then it can execute in parallel (i.e., can be changed into
its **doall** version). We will study when a unimodular transformation
is valid, how it changes the form and dependence structure of the
given program, and how to find equivalent loop nests with **doall**
loops using unimodular transformations.

Research on unimodular transformations goes back to Leslie
Lamport's paper in 1974 [Lamp74], although he did not use this
term or even matrices. This chapter is an extension of the author's
work on unimodular transformations of double loops [Bane91]. Research in this area has been done by Michael Wolfe [Wolf86a],
François Irigoin & Rémi Triolet [IrTr89], Michael Dowling [Dowl90],
Michael Wolf & Monica Lam ([WoLa91a], [WoLa91b]), and others.

In Section 3.2, we discuss the formal definition of a unimodular
transformation and the condition for its validity. Elementary transformations, which are the building blocks of a general unimodular
transformation, are described in Section 3.3. Use of a unimodular
transformation in finding innermost and outermost **doall** loops is
covered in Sections 3.4 and 3.5, respectively. Finally, Section 3.6
discusses the problem of computing loop limits in the transformed
program.

Example 3.1 Consider the double loop **L**:

L_1 :   **do** $I_1 = 0, 3$
L_2 :   **do** $I_2 = 0, 3$
    S : $A(I_1, I_2) = A(I_1 - 1, I_2) + A(I_1, I_2 - 1)$
            enddo
        enddo

The index space $\mathcal{R}$ of **L** is given by

$$\mathcal{R} = \{(I_1, I_2) : 0 \leq I_1 \leq 3, 0 \leq I_2 \leq 3\}.$$

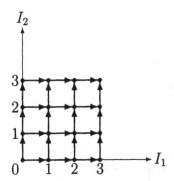

Figure 3.1: Dependence graph for Example 3.1.

There are two distance vectors in **L**: $(1,0)$ and $(0,1)$. The index space and the dependence graph are shown in Figure 3.1.

The outer loop L_1 cannot execute in parallel since there is dependence at level 1. The inner loop L_2 cannot execute in parallel since there is dependence at level 2. In terms of Figure 3.1, we cannot process the columns of iterations in parallel, nor can we process the iterations on a given column in parallel. Loop interchange is valid here since the direction vector $(1, -1)$ is absent. But interchange is not going to help us find **doall** loops, since the transformed program would also have dependence at both levels.

To find parallelism among the iterations, we group them in a slightly different way. Consider the packet of 7 parallel lines with equations:

$$I_1 + I_2 = c \quad (0 \le c \le 6)$$

shown in Figure 3.2. Note that if an iteration $H(j_1, j_2)$ depends on an iteration $H(i_1, i_2)$, then there is a c in $0 \le c < 6$ such that (i_1, i_2) lies on the line $I_1 + I_2 = c$ and (j_1, j_2) on the line $I_1 + I_2 = c + 1$. Hence, the dependence constraints will be satisfied if we trace the index points in the following order: Take the lines $I_1 + I_2 = c$ in the order from $c = 0$ to $c = 6$, and trace the points on each given line from bottom up.[2] These lines constitute a 'wave' through the

---

[2]The points on a given line can be traced in any order. We have chosen 'bottom up' for the sake of definiteness.

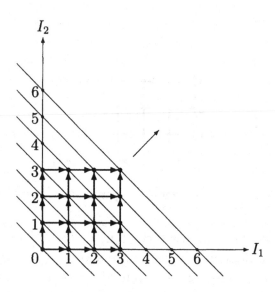

Figure 3.2: A wave through the index space of Example 3.1.

index space in the direction $(1, 1)$.

The tracing order described in the previous paragraph can be realized by introducing two new variables: $K_1 = I_1 + I_2$ and $K_2 = I_2$. For a given value of K_1, we get one of the lines $I_1 + I_2 = c$. Then, different values of K_2 give the index points on that line. The bounds on the new variables can be found as follows. Since

$$(I_1, I_2) = (K_1 - K_2, K_2),$$

the constraints on I_1 and I_2 give the inequalities:

$$\left.\begin{array}{rcrcl} 0 & \leq & K_1 - K_2 & \leq & 3 \\ 0 & \leq & K_2 & \leq & 3 \end{array}\right\}$$

which lead to the ranges:

$$\left.\begin{array}{rcccl} 0 & \leq & K_1 & \leq & 6 \\ \max(0, K_1 - 3) & \leq & K_2 & \leq & \min(3, K_1) \end{array}\right\}$$

by Fourier's method (Algorithm I-3.2). Thus, the given program is equivalent to the double loop $\mathbf{L_U}$:

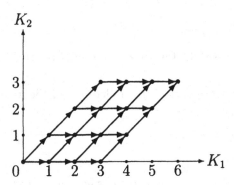

Figure 3.3: Index space of $\mathbf{L_U}$.

do $K_1 = 0, 6$
  do $K_2 = \max(0, K_1 - 3), \min(3, K_1)$
    $A(K_1 - K_2, K_2) = A(K_1 - K_2 - 1, K_2) + A(K_1 - K_2, K_2 - 1)$
  enddo
enddo

where the new body is obtained from S by replacing I_1 with $K_1 - K_2$ and I_2 with K_2. The index space of $\mathbf{L_U}$ is shown in Figure 3.3. Note that there is no dependence at level 2 in the new loop nest, since there is no dependence between iterations when the value of K_1 is fixed. (The parallel lines of Figure 3.2 have been transformed into the vertical lines $K_1 = c$ of Figure 3.3.) Hence, the inner loop of $\mathbf{L_U}$ can execute in parallel: it can be changed into a **doall** loop.

The index vectors of $\mathbf{L_U}$ and $\mathbf{L}$ are related via the equation:

$$(K_1, K_2) = (I_1, I_2) \cdot \mathbf{U}$$

where

$$\mathbf{U} = \begin{pmatrix} 1 & 0 \\ 1 & 1 \end{pmatrix}.$$

The matrix $\mathbf{U}$ is unimodular. We will show later how to find such a matrix $\mathbf{U}$ analytically, so that the given loop nest $\mathbf{L}$ can be transformed automatically into a program $\mathbf{L_U}$ whose inner loop can execute in parallel. This matrix is not unique; see the exercises.

EXERCISES 3.1

For all exercises below, take the loop nest $\mathbf{L} = (L_1, L_2)$ of Example 3.1 as the given program.

1. Keeping intact the packet of parallel lines of Figure 3.2 and K_1, change K_2 as follows:

   (a) $K_2 = I_1 + 2I_2$

   (b) $K_2 = I_1$.

   In each case, find a nest of two loops equivalent to (L_1, L_2) in which the inner loop can execute in parallel. Show the matrix $\mathbf{U}$, and draw the index space of the transformed program (as done in Figure 3.3).

2. Keep the lines of Figure 3.2 and $K_2 = I_2$, but change K_1 as follows:

   (a) $K_1 = 2I_1 + 2I_2 = (I_1, I_2)\begin{pmatrix} 2 \\ 2 \end{pmatrix}$

   (b) $K_1 = -I_1 - I_2 = (I_1, I_2)\begin{pmatrix} -1 \\ -1 \end{pmatrix}$.

   Both vectors $(2, 2)$ and $(-1, -1)$ are perpendicular to the lines $I_1 + I_2 = c$, but the gcd of the elements of $(2, 2)$ is not 1, and $(-1, -1)$ does not make an acute angle with the distance vectors $(1, 0)$ and $(0, 1)$. The matrix $\mathbf{U}$ connecting (I_1, I_2) and (K_1, K_2) is unimodular in the second case only. In each case, draw the transformed index space, and find a nest of two loops equivalent to (L_1, L_2) such that the inner loop can execute in parallel. What is the distinguishing feature of the two transformed programs?

3. Repeat Example 3.1 after choosing a packet of parallel lines given by equations of the form:

   (a) $I_1 + 2I_2 = c$

   (b) $2I_1 + I_2 = c$.

4. Find a set of necessary and sufficient conditions on constants p and q, such that a system of parallel lines of the form $pI_1 + qI_2 = c$ can be used in Example 3.1 to produce a double loop equivalent to (L_1, L_2) in which the inner loop can execute in parallel.

5. Consider the transformation:

$$(K_1, K_2) = (I_1, I_2) \cdot \begin{pmatrix} 2 & 4 \\ 3 & 5 \end{pmatrix}$$

where the matrix is not unimodular, although it is nonsingular. In the $K_1 K_2$-plane, plot the points that correspond to the 16 index points of **L**. Can you write a double loop of the form:

> **do** $K_1 = \cdots$
>> **do** $K_2 = \cdots$
>>
>> $\vdots$
>>
>> **enddo**
>
> **enddo**

equivalent to **L**?

6. Repeat the previous exercise with the transformation:

$$(K_1, K_2) = (I_1, I_2) \cdot \begin{pmatrix} 2 & 4 \\ 1 & 2 \end{pmatrix}$$

where the matrix now is singular.

3.2 Basic Concepts

Our model program is the loop nest $\mathbf{L} = (L_1, L_2, \ldots, L_m)$:

$L_1:$ **do** $I_1 = p_1, q_1$
$L_2:$ **do** $I_2 = p_2, q_2$

$\vdots$ $\vdots$

$L_m:$ **do** $I_m = p_m, q_m$
           $H(I_1, I_2, \ldots, I_m)$
         enddo

        $\vdots$

      enddo
    enddo

An iteration $H(\mathbf{i})$ is executed before another iteration $H(\mathbf{j})$ in **L** iff $\mathbf{i} \prec \mathbf{j}$. Take any $m \times m$ unimodular matrix **U**. Let $\mathbf{L_U}$ denote the program consisting of the iterations of **L**, such that an iteration $H(\mathbf{i})$ is executed before another iteration $H(\mathbf{j})$ in $\mathbf{L_U}$ iff $\mathbf{iU} \prec \mathbf{jU}$. We will show in Section 3.6 that $\mathbf{L_U}$ can be written as a nest of m loops with an index vector $\mathbf{K} = (K_1, K_2, \ldots, K_m)$ defined by

$\mathbf{K} = \mathbf{IU}$. The body of the new program is $H(\mathbf{KU}^{-1})$ which will be written as $H_{\mathbf{U}}(\mathbf{K})$. The program $\mathbf{L}_{\mathbf{U}}$ is the *transformed program* defined by $\mathbf{U}$, and the transformation $\mathbf{L} \mapsto \mathbf{L}_{\mathbf{U}}$ is the *unimodular transformation of* $\mathbf{L}$ *defined by* $\mathbf{U}$.

It is clear that $\mathbf{L}_{\mathcal{I}} = \mathbf{L}$ where $\mathcal{I}$ is the $m \times m$ identity matrix. The statements of the following theorem are also easy to derive:

Theorem 3.1 *Let* $\mathbf{U}$ *and* $\mathbf{V}$ *denote two* $m \times m$ *unimodular matrices. Then*

(a) $(\mathbf{L}_{\mathbf{U}})_{\mathbf{V}} = \mathbf{L}_{\mathbf{UV}}$

(b) $(\mathbf{L}_{\mathbf{U}})_{\mathbf{U}^{-1}} = \mathbf{L}.$

Next, we characterize valid unimodular transformations in terms of how they change the distance matrix of the program.

Theorem 3.2 *The unimodular transformation of a loop nest* $\mathbf{L}$ *defined by a (unimodular) matrix* $\mathbf{U}$ *is valid iff* $\mathbf{dU} \succ \mathbf{0}$ *for each distance vector* $\mathbf{d}$ *of* $\mathbf{L}$.

PROOF. The proof is similar to the proof of Theorem 2.1. □

Corollary 1 *If the unimodular transformation of* $\mathbf{L}$ *defined by a matrix* $\mathbf{U}$ *is valid, then the distance matrix of the transformed program* $\mathbf{L}_{\mathbf{U}}$ *is* $\mathcal{D}\mathbf{U}$ *where* $\mathcal{D}$ *is the distance matrix of* $\mathbf{L}$.

PROOF. Let $\mathbf{d}$ denote any distance vector of $\mathbf{L}$. Then, there are index values $\mathbf{i}$ and $\mathbf{j}$ such that the iteration $H(\mathbf{j})$ depends on the iteration $H(\mathbf{i})$, and $\mathbf{j} - \mathbf{i} = \mathbf{d}$. Let $\mathbf{k} = \mathbf{iU}$ and $\mathbf{l} = \mathbf{jU}$. The iterations $H(\mathbf{i})$ and $H(\mathbf{j})$ become iterations $H_{\mathbf{U}}(\mathbf{k})$ and $H_{\mathbf{U}}(\mathbf{l})$ in $\mathbf{L}_{\mathbf{U}}$ (same iterations, but different labels). Since the transformation is valid, $H_{\mathbf{U}}(\mathbf{l})$ depends on $H_{\mathbf{U}}(\mathbf{k})$ in $\mathbf{L}_{\mathbf{U}}$, so that a distance vector for $\mathbf{L}_{\mathbf{U}}$ is

$$\mathbf{l} - \mathbf{k} = \mathbf{jU} - \mathbf{iU} = (\mathbf{j} - \mathbf{i})\mathbf{U} = \mathbf{dU}.$$

Since an iteration depends on another iteration in $\mathbf{L}_{\mathbf{U}}$ iff the same dependence was there in the original nest $\mathbf{L}$, all distance vectors of $\mathbf{L}_{\mathbf{U}}$ are accounted for in this way. □

Details of loop limit computation will be discussed in Section 3.6. We will end this section with a few general observations on the new limits. Since $\mathbf{K} = \mathbf{IU}$, we have $K_r = \mathbf{I} \cdot \mathbf{u}^r = \mathbf{u}^r \cdot \mathbf{I}$ where $\mathbf{u}^r$ denotes column r of $\mathbf{U}$, $1 \le r \le m$. The extreme values of K_r are then $\min_{\mathbf{I} \in \mathcal{R}}(\mathbf{u}^r \cdot \mathbf{I})$ and $\max_{\mathbf{I} \in \mathcal{R}}(\mathbf{u}^r \cdot \mathbf{I})$, where $\mathcal{R}$ is the index space of $\mathbf{L}$. Note that these are the extreme values of K_r for the whole loop nest. In general, they do not tell us what the range of K_r is for a given set of values of $K_1, K_2, \ldots, K_{r-1}$. For the outermost loop, however, these formulas do give the lower and upper limits. It is sometimes useful to have an expression for the iteration count of this loop, and we state that expression below for future reference:

Theorem 3.3 *The number of iterations of the outermost loop in the program* $\mathbf{L_U}$ *after a valid unimodular transformation* $\mathbf{L} \mapsto \mathbf{L_U}$ *is*

$$\max_{\mathbf{I} \in \mathcal{R}}(\mathbf{u}^1 \cdot \mathbf{I}) - \min_{\mathbf{I} \in \mathcal{R}}(\mathbf{u}^1 \cdot \mathbf{I}) + 1.$$

Note that this number may include some iterations of the outermost loop that will not execute. The expression may be hard to compute depending on the shape of the index space. We have a simpified form when the given loop nest is rectangular:

Corollary 1 *Let* $\mathbf{L} = (L_1, L_2, \ldots, L_m)$ *denote a rectangular loop nest where the lower and upper limits of* L_r *are* p_r *and* q_r, *respectively,* $1 \le r \le m$. *If a unimodular matrix* $\mathbf{U} = (u_{rt})$ *defines a valid transformation* $\mathbf{L} \mapsto \mathbf{L_U}$, *then the number of iterations of the outermost loop of* $\mathbf{L_U}$ *is*

$$\sum_{r=1}^{m}(q_r - p_r)|u_{r1}| + 1.$$

PROOF. The index vectors $\mathbf{K}$ of $\mathbf{L_U}$ and $\mathbf{I}$ of $\mathbf{L}$ are connected by the equation: $\mathbf{K} = \mathbf{IU}$. In particular, we have

$$K_1 = I_1 u_{11} + I_2 u_{21} + \cdots + I_m u_{m1}.$$

Since $p_r \leq I_r \leq q_r$, it follows from Lemma I-3.2 that

$$p_r u_{r1}^+ - q_r u_{r1}^- \leq I_r u_{r1} \leq q_r u_{r1}^+ - p_r u_{r1}^- \quad (1 \leq r \leq m)$$

(where $u^+ = u$ and $u^- = 0$ if $u \geq 0$, else $u^+ = 0$ and $u^- = |u|$).
Summing over r, we get

$$\sum_{r=1}^{m} \left(p_r u_{r1}^+ - q_r u_{r1}^- \right) \leq \sum_{r=1}^{m} I_r u_{r1} \leq \sum_{r=1}^{m} \left(q_r u_{r1}^+ - p_r u_{r1}^- \right).$$

This gives the lower and upper limits of K_1, so that the number of
values of K_1 is

$$\sum_{r=1}^{m} \left(q_r u_{r1}^+ - p_r u_{r1}^- \right) - \sum_{r=1}^{m} \left(p_r u_{r1}^+ - q_r u_{r1}^- \right) + 1$$

$$= \sum_{r=1}^{m} \left[q_r \left(u_{r1}^+ + u_{r1}^- \right) - p_r \left(u_{r1}^+ + u_{r1}^- \right) \right] + 1$$

$$= \sum_{r=1}^{m} (q_r - p_r)|u_{r1}| + 1.$$

□

Example 3.2 Let

$$\mathcal{D} = \begin{pmatrix} 3 & -2 \\ 0 & 4 \\ 2 & -3 \end{pmatrix}$$

denote the distance matrix of a double loop **L**. Consider two 2×2
unimodular matrices

$$\mathbf{U} = \begin{pmatrix} 1 & 2 \\ 1 & 1 \end{pmatrix} \quad \text{and} \quad \mathbf{V} = \begin{pmatrix} 2 & 1 \\ 1 & 1 \end{pmatrix}.$$

Form the products $\mathcal{D}\mathbf{U}$ and $\mathcal{D}\mathbf{V}$:

$$\mathcal{D}\mathbf{U} = \begin{pmatrix} 1 & 4 \\ 4 & 4 \\ -1 & 1 \end{pmatrix} \quad \text{and} \quad \mathcal{D}\mathbf{V} = \begin{pmatrix} 4 & 1 \\ 4 & 4 \\ 1 & -1 \end{pmatrix}.$$

Since $\mathcal{D}U$ has a (lexicographically) negative row, the transformation $\mathbf{L} \mapsto \mathbf{L_U}$ will not be valid. Since the rows of $\mathcal{D}V$ are all positive, the transformation $\mathbf{L} \mapsto \mathbf{L_V}$ is valid. The distance matrix of the program $\mathbf{L_V}$, which is equivalent to $\mathbf{L}$ (and which could be written as a double loop), is $\mathcal{D}V$.

The direction matrix of $\mathbf{L}$ is given by

$$\boldsymbol{\Delta} = \begin{pmatrix} 1 & -1 \\ 0 & 1 \end{pmatrix}.$$

Note that the direction matrix of $\mathbf{L_V}$ cannot be determined from $\boldsymbol{\Delta}$ and V alone. The distance vector $(3, -2)$ of $\mathbf{L}$ gives the direction vector $(1, -1)$, and it changes into the distance vector $(4, 1)$ of $\mathbf{L_V}$ whose sign is $(1, 1)$. The distance vector $(2, -3)$ of $\mathbf{L}$ also gives the direction vector $(1, -1)$, but it changes into the distance vector $(1, -1)$ of $\mathbf{L_V}$ whose sign is $(1, -1)$.

EXERCISES 3.2

1. Consider the loop nest $\mathbf{L} = (L_1, L_2)$:

   $L_1:$ **do** $I_1 = 0, 10$
   $L_2:$ **do** $I_2 = 0, 10$
                    $A(I_1, I_2) = A(I_1 - 1, I_2) + A(I_1, I_2 - 1) + A(I_1 - 2, I_2 + 1)$
          enddo
       enddo

   Find the transformed program $\mathbf{L_U}$, where U is a unimodular matrix given below. Explain why the transformed program is or is not equivalent to $\mathbf{L}$. In case of equivalence, show how the distance vectors change, and decide if the new inner loop can run in parallel. Draw the index space of the transformed program. [Hint: Invert U. Express I_1, I_2 in terms of K_1, K_2 from the relation $\mathbf{I} = \mathbf{KU}^{-1}$. Then, use the bounds on I_1, I_2 and Algorithm I-3.2 to compute the loop limits of the transformed program.]

   (a) $\mathbf{U} = \begin{pmatrix} 1 & 0 \\ 0 & 1 \end{pmatrix}$

   (b) $\mathbf{U} = \begin{pmatrix} 0 & 1 \\ 1 & 0 \end{pmatrix}$

(c) $\mathbf{U} = \begin{pmatrix} 1 & 1 \\ 1 & 0 \end{pmatrix}$

(d) $\mathbf{U} = \begin{pmatrix} 1 & 1 \\ 1 & 2 \end{pmatrix}$

(e) $\mathbf{U} = \begin{pmatrix} 2 & 3 \\ 3 & 4 \end{pmatrix}$

(f) $\mathbf{U} = \begin{pmatrix} 2 & 1 \\ 3 & 1 \end{pmatrix}$

(g) $\mathbf{U} = \begin{pmatrix} 1 & 1 \\ 16 & 15 \end{pmatrix}.$

2. Let $\mathbf{L_U}$ be equivalent to $\mathbf{L}$. Prove that $\mathbf{dU}$ is a uniform distance vector of $\mathbf{L_U}$ iff $\mathbf{d}$ is a uniform distance vector of $\mathbf{L}$.

3. Let $\mathcal{L}$ denote the set of all perfect nests $\mathbf{L}$ of a given length m (of the type considered in this book). Each $m \times m$ unimodular matrix $\mathbf{U}$ defines a mapping $\mathcal{T}_{\mathbf{U}} : \mathbf{L} \mapsto \mathbf{L_U}$ on $\mathcal{L}$. Prove that these mappings form a group under the product: $\mathcal{T}_{\mathbf{U}} \circ \mathcal{T}_{\mathbf{V}} = \mathcal{T}_{\mathbf{UV}}$.

3.3   Elementary Transformations

There are four basic types of elementary matrices: reversal, interchange, upper skewing, and lower skewing. Elementary matrices were studied in Section I-2.2; they are all unimodular. The unimodular transformation $\mathbf{L} \mapsto \mathbf{L_U}$ defined by a matrix $\mathbf{U}$ is

A *loop reversal* if $\mathbf{U}$ is a reversal matrix;
A *loop interchange* if $\mathbf{U}$ is an interchange matrix;
An *upper loop skewing* if $\mathbf{U}$ is an upper skewing matrix;
A *lower loop skewing* if $\mathbf{U}$ is a lower skewing matrix.

The first three transformations constitute the *elementary transformations*. They have certain 'simple' properties that a general transformation may not have. We do not give the name 'elementary' to the transformation defined by a lower skewing matrix, since it lacks any such special property.

A unimodular transformation can be constructed using elementary transformations as building blocks:

Theorem 3.4 *Any given unimodular transformation of a loop nest* **L** *can be accomplished by the successive application of a finite sequence of elementary transformations.*

PROOF. A unimodular matrix can be written as the product of a finite sequence of elementary matrices that are of type reversal, interchange, or upper skewing (Exercise I-2.4.5). The proof then follows from the associative property of unimodular transformations (Theorem 3.1(a)). □

To understand the elementary transformations better, we consider a rectangular double loop **L** of the form:

L_1 :   **do** $I_1 = p_1, q_1$
L_2 :   **do** $I_2 = p_2, q_2$
                $H(I_1, I_2)$
             enddo
          enddo

Having constant loop limits makes it easier to draw the index space, but otherwise, the shape of the index space has no significance in this discussion. The index space of **L** is shown in Figure 3.4. We will describe the elementary transformations in this space along the lines of Example 2.1.

The iterations of **L** are executed in the following way: process the columns $I_1 = p_1, I_1 = p_1 + 1, \ldots, I_1 = q_1$ from left to right, and execute the iterations on any given column from bottom up.

A distance vector of dependence is positive, so that it can never point from right to left (if nonvertical) or vertically downward. In Figure 3.4, we show four typical distance vectors: $(2, 1)$, $(2, 0)$, $(1, -2)$, and $(0, 1)$. They are labeled 1, 2, 3, and 4, and their signs are $(1, 1)$, $(1, 0)$, $(1, -1)$, and $(0, 1)$, respectively. (These are the four possible positive direction vectors in two dimensions.) The presence of any one of the vectors 1, 2, or 3 will indicate a dependence at level 1, and the presence of the vector 4 a dependence at level 2. The outer loop L_1 can execute in parallel iff there is no distance vector joining two distinct columns (i.e., no dependence at level 1). The

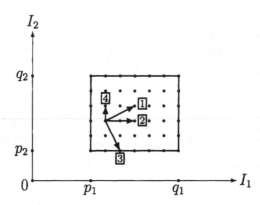

Figure 3.4: Index space with typical distance vectors.

inner loop L_2 can execute in parallel iff there is no vertical distance vector (i.e., no dependence at level 2).

The transformation defined by a unimodular matrix $\mathbf{U}$ will map $\mathbf{L}$ into a double loop $\mathbf{L_U}$ of the form:

$L_{U1}:$ **do** $K_1 = \alpha_1, \beta_1$
$L_{U2}:$ **do** $K_2 = \alpha_2(K_1), \beta_2(K_1)$
            $H(\mathbf{KU}^{-1})$
         enddo
      enddo

where $\mathbf{K} = \mathbf{IU}$. The index space of $\mathbf{L}$ is mapped into a parallelogram, which may be simply the reflection of the same rectangle across a line in a special case. If a transformation makes a distance vector negative (i.e., makes the vector point from right to left or in a vertically downward direction), then it is not valid. After a valid transformation, the changed directions of the distance vectors will determine if the outer or the inner loop in the transformed program can execute in parallel.

The elementary transformation of loop interchange was covered in Example 2.1 as a special case of loop permutation. We will consider here the other two elementary transformations: reversal (outer loop reversal and inner loop reversal) and upper skewing.

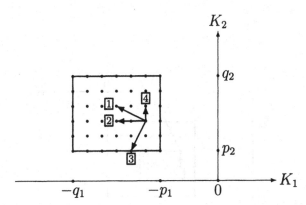

Figure 3.5: Index space after outer loop reversal.

Outer Loop Reversal. Take the reversal matrix

$$\mathbf{U} = \begin{pmatrix} -1 & 0 \\ 0 & 1 \end{pmatrix} \quad \text{whose inverse is} \quad \mathbf{U}^{-1} = \begin{pmatrix} -1 & 0 \\ 0 & 1 \end{pmatrix}.$$

This unimodular matrix transforms $\mathbf{L}$ into the double loop

$$
\begin{aligned}
L_{U1}: &\quad \textbf{do } K_1 = -q_1, -p_1 \\
L_{U2}: &\quad\quad \textbf{do } K_2 = p_2, q_2 \\
&\quad\quad\quad H(-K_1, K_2) \\
&\quad\quad \textbf{enddo} \\
&\quad \textbf{enddo}
\end{aligned}
$$

where the new index variables are given by $(K_1, K_2) = (-I_1, I_2)$. The index space of $\mathbf{L_U}$, shown in Figure 3.5, is the reflection of the index space of $\mathbf{L}$ across the vertical axis. The elements of the distance vectors 1–4 remain unchanged in absolute value; only directions of the vectors change. Outer loop reversal is valid iff there are no distance vectors of the types 1, 2, 3 in $\mathbf{L}$, that is, no dependence at level 1. In that case, the outer loop L_{U1} can execute in parallel. (The outer loop L_1 in (L_1, L_2) can also execute in parallel.) The level-2 dependences, if any, remain unchanged. The inner loop L_{U2} can execute in parallel iff there is no dependence in $\mathbf{L}$.

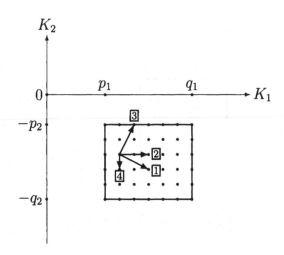

Figure 3.6: Index space after inner loop reversal.

Inner Loop Reversal. Consider the reversal matrix

$$\mathbf{U} = \begin{pmatrix} 1 & 0 \\ 0 & -1 \end{pmatrix} \text{ whose inverse is } \mathbf{U}^{-1} = \begin{pmatrix} 1 & 0 \\ 0 & -1 \end{pmatrix}.$$

This unimodular matrix transforms **L** into the double loop

$$
\begin{array}{ll}
L_{U1}: & \textbf{do } K_1 = p_1, q_1 \\
L_{U2}: & \quad \textbf{do } K_2 = -q_2, -p_2 \\
& \quad\quad H(K_1, -K_2) \\
& \quad \textbf{enddo} \\
& \textbf{enddo}
\end{array}
$$

where $(K_1, K_2) = (I_1, -I_2)$. The index space of $\mathbf{L_U}$, shown in Figure 3.6, is the reflection of the index space of **L** across the horizontal axis. The elements of the distance vectors 1–4 remain unchanged in absolute value; only directions of the vectors change. Inner loop reversal is valid iff there are no distance vectors of type 4 in **L**, that is, no dependence at level 2. In that case, the inner loop L_{U2} can execute in parallel. (The inner loop L_2 in (L_1, L_2) can also execute in parallel.) The level-1 dependences, if any, remain level-1 dependences. The outer loop L_{U1} can execute in parallel iff there is no dependence in **L**.

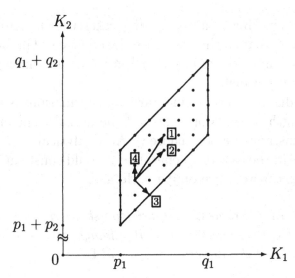

Figure 3.7: Index space after an upper loop skewing.

Upper Loop Skewing. Consider the upper skewing matrix

$$\mathbf{U} = \begin{pmatrix} 1 & 1 \\ 0 & 1 \end{pmatrix} \quad \text{whose inverse is} \quad \mathbf{U}^{-1} = \begin{pmatrix} 1 & -1 \\ 0 & 1 \end{pmatrix}.$$

This unimodular matrix transforms **L** into the double loop

$L_{U1}:$ **do** $K_1 = p_1, q_1$
$L_{U2}:$ **do** $K_2 = p_2 + K_1, q_2 + K_1$
           $H(K_1, K_2 - K_1)$
       enddo
     enddo

where the new index variables are given by $(K_1, K_2) = (I_1, I_1 + I_2)$. A distance vector (d_1, d_2) will change into the vector $(d_1, d_1 + d_2)$. Although the elements change, it is easy to see that a positive vector will always remain positive, so that the transformation is valid. The index space of $\mathbf{L_U}$ is displayed in Figure 3.7 which also shows the images of the vectors 1–4. Note that the level of a vector did not change.

Upper loop skewing is always valid (Exercise 1). Also, upper skewing does not change the level of a dependence. The outer (inner) loop in $\mathbf{L_U}$ can execute in parallel iff the outer (inner) loop in $\mathbf{L}$ can execute in parallel.

The above discussion on elementary transformations is independent of the length of the loop nest and the actual elements of the four types of distance vectors chosen. An analytical derivation of the conclusions in the case of a general nest would constitute a proof of the following theorem; we omit the details.

Theorem 3.5 *In a loop nest* $\mathbf{L}$*, upper loop skewing is always valid. The validity of a loop reversal or interchange can be determined from a knowledge of the direction matrix of* $\mathbf{L}$*.*

There is, however, a major difference in the way we can predict the change in a direction vector by a reversal or interchange on one hand, and an upper skewing on the other. Under a reversal or interchange, we would know exactly how a direction vector should change. For example, in a double loop (L_1, L_2), inner loop reversal would change a direction vector (σ_1, σ_2) into the direction vector $(\sigma_1, -\sigma_2)$, and a loop interchange would change (σ_1, σ_2) into (σ_2, σ_1). On the other hand, although an upper skewing is guaranteed to keep a positive vector positive, it may change a positive direction vector into a *different* positive direction vector.

Figure 3.8 shows the index space of the transformed program (L_{U1}, L_{U2}) where

$$\mathbf{U} = \begin{pmatrix} 1 & 0 \\ 1 & 1 \end{pmatrix}$$

is a lower skewing matrix. The particular distance vector of type 3 we used is changed into a vector that points from right to left, so that its presence would make the transformation invalid. On the other hand, if we use the vector $(2, -1)$ as our type 3 vector, then it would allow the transformation to be valid.

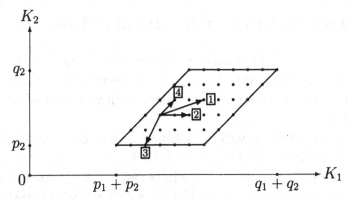

Figure 3.8: Index space after a lower loop skewing.

EXERCISES 3.3

1. Prove that upper loop skewing is always valid in a double loop. Extend this result to an arbitrary nest. Explain by an example how upper skewing changes a positive direction vector.

2. Consider the double loop $\mathbf{L} = (L_1, L_2)$ of this section and the elementary transformations: outer loop reversal, inner loop reversal, interchange, and upper skewing. Make a table showing the following items for each transformation:

    - The condition (in terms of dependence levels and/or direction vectors in $\mathbf{L}$) under which the transformation is valid;

    - The condition under which the outer loop L_{U1} can execute in parallel, assuming the transformation is valid;

    - The same item for the inner loop L_{U2};

    - The correlation, if any, between the fact that a loop in $\mathbf{L}$ can execute in parallel and that one or both loops in $\mathbf{L_U}$ can execute in parallel;

    - How the level of a dependence is changed by the transformation.

3. Consider a triple loop (L_1, L_2, L_3). For each elementary 3×3 matrix $\mathbf{U}$, find the form of the transformed program $\mathbf{L_U}$.

4. Generalize Exercise 2 to a triple loop.

3.4   Inner Loop Parallelization

We now come to the question of existence of a unimodular transformation satisfying a specified goal. In this section, the goal is inner loop parallelization; outer loop parallelization will be studied in the next section.

Given a loop nest L with a distance matrix $\mathcal{D}$, we want to find a valid unimodular transformation $L \mapsto L_U$ such that one or more innermost loops of L_U can execute in parallel. The problem reduces to finding a unimodular matrix U that satisfies a set of constraints determined by $\mathcal{D}$. We will show that for any $\mathcal{D}$, there always exists a unimodular matrix U such that the loops $L_{U2}, L_{U3}, \ldots, L_{Um}$ of the transformed program can execute in parallel. In fact, there are infinitely many such matrices. Although the number of loops that can execute in parallel is the same in each case, the iteration count of the outermost sequential loop, L_{U1}, may vary with the matrix. We then face an optimization problem: Of all possible matrices, choose one that will minimize the iteration count of L_{U1}. The index space of L then enters the picture.

A necessary and sufficient condition under which a loop in L_U can execute in parallel is given in the following lemma. This condition leads to the dependence-related constraints that the matrix U must satisfy for loop parallelization.

Lemma 3.6 *Consider a valid unimodular transformation $L \mapsto L_U$. A loop L_{Ur} in L_U can execute in parallel iff there is no distance vector d in L satisfying $dU \succ_r 0$.*

PROOF. A given loop L_{Ur} in L_U can execute in parallel iff there is no dependence carried by L_{Ur} (Lemma 1.1), that is, iff there is no dependence in L_U at level r. Distance vectors of L_U are of the form dU where d is a distance vector of L (Corollary 1 to Theorem 3.2). Having no dependence at level r in L_U is the same as having no distance vector in L_U with level r, that is, no distance vector d in L satisfying $dU \succ_r 0$. $\square$

The main result and algorithm of this section are explained informally in Example 3.3; their formal statements are given later.

Example 3.3 Consider a loop nest $\mathbf{L} = (L_1, L_2, L_3, L_4)$ and let its distance matrix be given by

$$\mathcal{D} = \begin{pmatrix} 0 & 0 & 0 & 2 \\ 0 & 3 & 1 & -2 \\ 0 & 4 & -6 & 0 \\ 1 & -5 & 3 & 1 \\ 2 & 1 & 0 & 0 \\ 3 & 0 & -2 & 1 \end{pmatrix}.$$

We want to find a 4×4 unimodular matrix $\mathbf{U}$ such that the program $\mathbf{L_U} = (L_{U1}, L_{U2}, L_{U3}, L_{U4})$ defined by $\mathbf{U}$ is equivalent to $\mathbf{L}$, and the loops L_{U2}, L_{U3}, L_{U4} can execute in parallel.

Since $\mathbf{L_U}$ is equivalent to $\mathbf{L}$, we must have $\mathbf{dU} \succ \mathbf{0}$ for each distance vector $\mathbf{d}$ of $\mathbf{L}$ (Theorem 3.2). Since there cannot be a dependence in $\mathbf{L_U}$ at the levels 2, 3, or 4, the following possibilities are ruled out (Lemma 3.6):

$$\mathbf{dU} \succ_2 \mathbf{0}, \mathbf{dU} \succ_3 \mathbf{0}, \mathbf{dU} \succ_4 \mathbf{0}.$$

Thus, we must have $\mathbf{dU} \succ_1 \mathbf{0}$ for each row of $\mathcal{D}$, that is, the elements of the first column of $\mathcal{D}\mathbf{U}$ must be all positive. The inequality $\mathbf{dU} \succ_1 \mathbf{0}$ is the same as $\mathbf{d} \cdot \mathbf{u}^1 > 0$, where $\mathbf{u}^1$ is the first column of $\mathbf{U}$. Since we are dealing with integers, this is equivalent to $\mathbf{d} \cdot \mathbf{u}^1 \geq 1$ for each row of $\mathcal{D}$.

To simplify notation, let us write $\mathbf{u}^1 = (u_1, u_2, u_3, u_4)$. Taking successively the rows of $\mathcal{D}$, we get the following six inequalities:

$$\left. \begin{array}{rrrrr} & & & 2u_4 & \geq 1 \\ & 3u_2 + & u_3 & - 2u_4 & \geq 1 \\ & 4u_2 - & 6u_3 & & \geq 1 \\ u_1 - & 5u_2 + & 3u_3 + & u_4 & \geq 1 \\ 2u_1 + & u_2 & & & \geq 1 \\ 3u_1 & & - 2u_3 + & u_4 & \geq 1. \end{array} \right\}$$

Put these inequalities into four groups as follows: The first group
consists of all inequalities $\mathbf{d} \cdot \mathbf{u}^1 \geq 1$ for $\mathbf{d} \succ_4 0$, that is, where $\mathbf{d}$ has
the form $(0, 0, 0, d_4)$ with $d_4 > 0$. In each member of this group, the
coefficients of u_1, u_2, u_3 are absent and that of u_4 is positive. The
second group consists of all inequalities $\mathbf{d} \cdot \mathbf{u}^1 \geq 1$ for $\mathbf{d} \succ_3 0$, so
that the coefficients of u_1, u_2 are absent and that of u_3 is positive in
each member of this group; and so on. It turns out that the second
group of inequalities is empty; the other three groups can be written
(after simplification) as:

$$u_4 \geq 1$$

$$\left.\begin{array}{rcl} u_2 & \geq & (1 - u_3 + 2u_4)/3 \\ u_2 & \geq & (1 + 6u_3)/4 \end{array}\right\}$$

$$\left.\begin{array}{rcl} u_1 & \geq & 1 + 5u_2 - 3u_3 - u_4 \\ u_1 & \geq & (1 - u_2)/2 \\ u_1 & \geq & (1 + 2u_3 - u_4)/3. \end{array}\right\}$$

For integer vectors (u_1, u_2, u_3, u_4), this system of inequalities can be
put in the form:

$$u_r \geq b_r(u_{r+1}, u_{r+2}, \ldots, u_m) \quad (1 \leq r \leq 4)$$

where

$$
\begin{aligned}
b_4 &= 1 \\
b_3(u_4) &= -\infty \\
b_2(u_3, u_4) &= \left\lceil \max\left(\frac{1 - u_3 + 2u_4}{3}, \frac{1 + 6u_3}{4}\right) \right\rceil \\
b_1(u_2, u_3, u_4) &= \left\lceil \max\left(1 + 5u_2 - 3u_3 - u_4, \frac{1 - u_2}{2}, \frac{1 + 2u_3 - u_4}{3}\right) \right\rceil.
\end{aligned}
$$

Since there are no upper bounds for the elements, it is clear that
there are infinitely many solutions to the system. If (u_1, u_2, u_3, u_4)
is a solution, then so is the vector $(u_1/g, u_2/g, u_3/g, u_4/g)$ where

$g = \gcd(u_1, u_2, u_3, u_4)$ (explain). By the method of Corollary 4
to Theorem I-3.4, we can find a unimodular matrix U whose first
column is $(u_1/g, u_2/g, u_3/g, u_4/g)$. This matrix satisfies the original
requirement that the first column of $\mathcal{D}U$ have all positive elements.

One particular solution is obtained by constructing the elements
u_4, u_3, u_2, u_1, sequentially in this order, such that the current element is always set to the smallest nonnegative integer satisfying
the corresponding lower bound. Thus, take $u_4 = 1$ and $u_3 = 0$.
Then we have $u_2 \geq b_2(0, 1) = 1$, and we choose $u_2 = 1$. For
$(u_2, u_3, u_4) = (1, 0, 1)$, we get $u_1 \geq b_1(1, 0, 1) = 5$, and we choose
$u_1 = 5$. The complete solution vector is $\mathbf{u}^1 = (5, 1, 0, 1)$. We could
use the method of Corollary 4 to Theorem I-3.4 to find a unimodular matrix with this vector as its first column. However, since the
fourth element u_4 is one, it is easy to construct such a matrix by
enlarging the 3×3 identity matrix $\mathcal{I}_3$. Note that the matrix

$$U = \begin{pmatrix} 5 & 1 & 0 & 0 \\ 1 & 0 & 1 & 0 \\ 0 & 0 & 0 & 1 \\ 1 & 0 & 0 & 0 \end{pmatrix}$$

is unimodular and that its first column is $\mathbf{u}^1$. We have extended $\mathcal{I}_3$
into a 4×4 matrix by adding $\mathbf{u}^1$ on the left as the first column and
using zeros to fill out the fourth row. (The 3×3 matrix obtained
by deleting the first column and fourth row of U is $\mathcal{I}_3$.) Note that
we have

$$\mathcal{D}U = \begin{pmatrix} 2 & 0 & 0 & 0 \\ 1 & 0 & 3 & 1 \\ 4 & 0 & 4 & -6 \\ 1 & 1 & -5 & 3 \\ 11 & 2 & 1 & 0 \\ 16 & 3 & 0 & -2 \end{pmatrix}$$

whose first column has all positive elements, as required.

We used the distance *matrix* $\mathcal{D}$ in the above example. However, it is more convenient notationally to use the *set* D of distance

vectors for the proof of the following theorem:

Theorem 3.7 *Given any loop nest* **L**, *there is a valid unimodular transformation* **L** $\mapsto$ **L**$_U$ *such that the loops* $L_{U2}, L_{U3}, \ldots, L_{Um}$ *of* **L**$_U$ *can execute in parallel.*

PROOF. Let D denote the set of distance vectors of **L**, and let

$$D_r = \{\mathbf{d} \in D : \mathbf{d} \succ_r \mathbf{0}\} \quad (1 \leq r \leq m).$$

If D is empty, then there is no dependence in **L** and all loops in it can execute in parallel. In this case, we simply take the identity matrix $\mathcal{I}_m$ for **U**. Assume then that D is nonempty. Since $D = D_1 \cup D_2 \cup \cdots \cup D_m$, at least one of the subsets D_r is nonempty.

As explained in the previous example, we are seeking a unimodular matrix **U** whose first column $\mathbf{u}^1$ satisfies $\mathbf{d} \cdot \mathbf{u}^1 \geq 1$ for all $\mathbf{d} \in D$. Writing $\mathbf{d} = (d_1, d_2, \ldots, d_m)$ and $\mathbf{u}^1 = (u_1, u_2, \ldots, u_m)$, we get the following system of inequalities:

$$d_1 u_1 + d_2 u_2 + \cdots + d_m u_m \geq 1 \quad (\mathbf{d} \in D). \quad (3.1)$$

Since a distance vector **d** in D_r satisfies $d_1 = d_2 = \cdots = d_{r-1} = 0$, we can break up the system (3.1) into a sequence of subsystems of the following type:

$$\left. \begin{array}{rll} d_m u_m & \geq 1 & (\mathbf{d} \in D_m) \\ d_{m-1} u_{m-1} + d_m u_m & \geq 1 & (\mathbf{d} \in D_{m-1}) \\ & \vdots & \\ d_1 u_1 + \cdots + d_{m-1} u_{m-1} + d_m u_m & \geq 1 & (\mathbf{d} \in D_1). \end{array} \right\}$$

Since $d_r > 0$ for $\mathbf{d} \in D_r$, we can rewrite this sequence as

$$\left. \begin{array}{rll} u_m & \geq 1 & (\mathbf{d} \in D_m) \\ u_{m-1} & \geq (1 - d_m u_m)/d_{m-1} & (\mathbf{d} \in D_{m-1}) \\ & \vdots & \\ u_1 & \geq (1 - d_2 u_2 - \cdots - d_m u_m)/d_1 & (\mathbf{d} \in D_1). \end{array} \right\} \quad (3.2)$$

If $D_r \neq \emptyset$, the subsystem for D_r gives a real lower bound for u_r; otherwise, the lower bound is $-\infty$. Since there are no upper bounds for the elements, it follows that there is an infinite set of integer vectors satisfying the system of constraints (3.2). Take any such vector $(u_1, u_2, \ldots, u_m)$, and let $g = \gcd(u_1, u_2, \ldots, u_m)$. Then $(u_1/g, u_2/g, \ldots, u_m/g)$ also satisfies (3.2). (Hint: Divide by g both sides of each inequality in the equivalent system (3.1).). By Corollary 4 to Theorem I-3.4, find a unimodular matrix $\mathbf{U}$ whose first column is $(u_1/g, u_2/g, \ldots, u_m/g)$. This matrix has the desired properties: $\mathbf{d} \cdot \mathbf{u}^1 \geq 1$ for $\mathbf{d} \in D$. $\square$

Let us now interpret Theorem 3.7 from a geometrical point of view. Consider the m-dimensional space $\mathbf{R}^m$ with coordinate axes $I_1, I_2, \ldots, I_m$. A nonzero vector $\mathbf{u} = (u_1, u_2, \ldots, u_m)$ and a constant c define a hyperplane whose equation is $\mathbf{u}\mathbf{I} = c$, that is,

$$u_1 I_1 + u_2 I_2 + \cdots + u_m I_m = c.$$

We may assume that $\gcd(u_1, u_2, \ldots, u_m) = 1$ without any loss of generality. In the two-dimensional space, a hyperplane is a line, and in the three-dimensional case, it is an ordinary plane. The same vector $\mathbf{u}$ and two integers p and q with $p \leq q$ can be used to define a sequence of parallel hyperplanes:

$$\mathbf{u}\mathbf{I} = p, \mathbf{u}\mathbf{I} = p + 1, \ldots, \mathbf{u}\mathbf{I} = q.$$

We say that this is a system of hyperplanes *in the direction* $\mathbf{u}$.

In the given loop nest $\mathbf{L}$, the index variable I_1 of the outermost loop L_1 runs from p_1 to q_1. Thus, the index space $\mathcal{R}$ of $\mathbf{L}$ is partitioned by a sequence of hyperplanes in the direction $(1, 0, 0, \ldots, 0)$:

$$I_1 = p_1, I_1 = p_1 + 1, \ldots, I_1 = q_1.$$

In the loop nest $\mathbf{L_U}$, the index variable K_1 of the outermost loop L_{U1} is given by $K_1 = \mathbf{I}\mathbf{u}^1 = \mathbf{u}^1 \cdot \mathbf{I}$, and it runs from α_1 to β_1, where

$$\alpha_1 = \min_{\mathbf{I} \in \mathcal{R}}(\mathbf{u}^1 \cdot \mathbf{I}) \quad \text{and} \quad \beta_1 = \max_{\mathbf{I} \in \mathcal{R}}(\mathbf{u}^1 \cdot \mathbf{I}).$$

Thus, the equivalent loop nest $\mathbf{L_U}$ is constructed by partitioning the index space of $\mathbf{L}$ by a sequence of hyperplanes in the direction of the vector $\mathbf{u}^1 = (u_1, u_2, \ldots, u_m)$:

$$\mathbf{u}^1 \cdot \mathbf{I} = \alpha_1, \mathbf{u}^1 \cdot \mathbf{I} = \alpha_1 + 1, \ldots, \mathbf{u}^1 \cdot \mathbf{I} = \beta_1.$$

A given index point $\mathbf{i}$ lies on the unique hyperplane in this sequence whose equation is $\mathbf{u}^1 \cdot \mathbf{I} = c(\mathbf{i})$ where $c(\mathbf{i}) = \mathbf{u}^1 \cdot \mathbf{i}$.

The new sequence of hyperplanes has an important property: If an iteration $H(\mathbf{j})$ depends on an iteration $H(\mathbf{i})$, then the hyperplane containing $\mathbf{j}$ comes after the hyperplane containing $\mathbf{i}$ in the sequence. This is easy to see since $\mathbf{j} - \mathbf{i}$ is some distance vector $\mathbf{d}$, and we have

$$c(\mathbf{j}) - c(\mathbf{i}) = \mathbf{u}^1 \cdot \mathbf{j} - \mathbf{u}^1 \cdot \mathbf{i} = \mathbf{u}^1 \cdot (\mathbf{j} - \mathbf{i}) = \mathbf{u}^1 \cdot \mathbf{d} = \mathbf{d}\mathbf{u}^1 > 0$$

by the construction of the matrix $\mathbf{U}$. The import of Theorem 3.7 is that a sequence of hyperplanes with this property exists. Given such a sequence, the iterations of $\mathbf{L}$ can be processed by taking the hyperplanes one by one in their prescribed order, and by executing in parallel all iterations corresponding to the index points on a given hyperplane.

As the proof of Theorem 3.7 shows, there are infinitely many hyperplane systems with this property. The ideal system is one for which the number of hyperplanes (i.e., the iteration count of the outermost loop L_{U1} of $\mathbf{L_U}$) is minimized. This leads to the following optimization problem:

Given a nest of m loops with an index space $\mathcal{R}$ and a set D of distance vectors $\mathbf{d} = (d_1, d_2, \ldots, d_m)$, find a vector $\mathbf{u}^1 = (u_1, u_2, \ldots, u_m)$ such that

1. $\gcd(u_1, u_2, \ldots, u_m) = 1$;

2. $d_1 u_1 + d_2 u_2 + \cdots + d_m u_m \geq 1$ $(\mathbf{d} \in D)$;

3. The value of the expression

$$\max_{\mathbf{I} \in \mathcal{R}}(\mathbf{u}^1 \cdot \mathbf{I}) - \min_{\mathbf{I} \in \mathcal{R}}(\mathbf{u}^1 \cdot \mathbf{I}) + 1$$

is minimized. (See Theorem 3.3.)

The first condition is implied by the other two; see Exercise 2. Condition (2) is equivalent to the system of inequalities (3.2). The expression in the last condition simplifies to (Corollary 1 to Theorem 3.3):

$$\sum_{r=1}^{m}(q_r - p_r)|u_{r1}| + 1$$

in the case of a rectangular loop nest. This optimization problem is beyond the scope of this book; we only point out that it can be easily solved in the case of a rectangular double loop (Exercise 7).

If the minimization clause is ignored, many algorithms can be easily designed for choosing a vector $(u_1, u_2, \ldots, u_m)$ satisfying Conditions (1) and (2). A vector $\mathbf{u}^1$ found this way would be independent of the index space $\mathcal{R}$. One such algorithm was suggested in [Lamp74], where the elements $u_m, u_{m-1}, \ldots, u_1$ are constructed from (3.2), sequentially in this order, such that the value of the current element is always set to the smallest nonnegative integer satisfying the corresponding constraint. In this algorithm, the first nonzero element has to be 1, so that $\gcd(u_1, u_2, \ldots, u_m)$ is guaranteed to be 1 (Exercise 3). Construction of a unimodular matrix $\mathbf{U}$ with $(u_1, u_2, \ldots, u_m)$ as its first column then becomes very easy: If

$$u_m = u_{m-1} = \cdots = u_{k+1} = 0 \quad \text{and} \quad u_k = 1,$$

then take

$$\mathbf{U} = \begin{pmatrix} u_1 & 1 & \cdots & 0 & 0 & \cdots & 0 \\ \vdots & \vdots & \ddots & \vdots & \vdots & \ddots & \vdots \\ u_{k-1} & 0 & \cdots & 1 & 0 & \cdots & 0 \\ 1 & 0 & \cdots & 0 & 0 & \cdots & 0 \\ 0 & 0 & \cdots & 0 & 1 & \cdots & 0 \\ \vdots & \vdots & \ddots & \vdots & \vdots & \ddots & \vdots \\ 0 & 0 & \cdots & 0 & 0 & \cdots & 1 \end{pmatrix} \tag{3.3}$$

such that the $(m-1) \times (m-1)$ matrix obtained by deleting column 1 and row k of $\mathbf{U}$ is the unit matrix $\mathcal{I}_{m-1}$.

Lamport's method was illustrated at the end of Example 3.3. We now formally state it in the form of an algorithm:

Algorithm 3.1 (Hyperplane Method) Given a nonempty finite set D of positive m-vectors $\mathbf{d} = (d_1, d_2, \ldots, d_m)$, this algorithm finds an $m \times m$ unimodular matrix $\mathbf{U}$ such that

$$\mathbf{dU} \succ_1 \mathbf{0} \quad (\mathbf{d} \in D).$$

1. [Find an m-vector $(u_1, u_2, \ldots, u_m)$ with nonnegative elements, such that $\gcd(u_1, u_2, \ldots, u_m) = 1$ and

$$d_1 u_1 + d_2 u_2 + \cdots + d_m u_m \geq 1 \quad (\mathbf{d} \in D).]$$

> **do** $r = 1, m, 1$
>   set $D_r \leftarrow \{\mathbf{d} \in D : \mathbf{d} \succ_r \mathbf{0}\}$
> **enddo**
> **do** $r = m, 1, -1$
>   **if** $D_r = \emptyset$
>   **then set** $u_r \leftarrow 0$
>   **else set**
>
> $$u_r \leftarrow \left\lceil \max_{\mathbf{d} \in D_r} \{(1 - d_{r+1} u_{r+1} - d_{r+2} u_{r+2} - \cdots - d_m u_m)/d_r\} \right\rceil^+$$
>
> **enddo**

2. [Find a unimodular matrix with first column $(u_1, u_2, \ldots, u_m)$.]

   Find k such that u_k is the first nonzero element in the sequence: $u_m, u_{m-1}, \ldots, u_1$.

   [Note that $u_k = 1$ (see Exercise 3).]

   Construct an $m \times m$ matrix $\mathbf{U}$ such that

   (a) The first column of $\mathbf{U}$ is $(u_1, u_2, \ldots, u_m)$;

   (b) The kth row of $\mathbf{U}$ is $(1, 0, 0, \ldots, 0)$;

   (c) The matrix obtained by deleting column 1 and row k of $\mathbf{U}$ is the identity matrix $\mathcal{I}_{m-1}$.   □

If $\gcd(u_1, u_2, \ldots, u_m) = 1$, then there exist infinitely many unimodular matrices $\mathbf{U}$ whose first column is $(u_1, u_2, \ldots, u_m)$. Changing from one such matrix to another changes only the inner $(m-1)$ loops of the nest $\mathbf{L_U}$. The outermost loop, that is the system of hyperplanes, is determined by the vector alone.

Example 3.4 Consider a double loop $\mathbf{L} = (L_1, L_2)$ with a nonempty set of distance vectors D. We have $D = D_1 \cup D_2$, where

$$
\begin{aligned}
D_1 &= \{(d_1, d_2) \in D : d_1 > 0\} \\
D_2 &= \{(d_1, d_2) \in D : d_1 = 0 \text{ and } d_2 > 0\}.
\end{aligned}
$$

Note that $D_1 = \emptyset$ means there is no dependence at level 1, and $D_2 = \emptyset$ means there is no dependence at level 2. The system of inequalities $\mathbf{du} > 0$ or $\mathbf{du} \geq 1$ reduces to

$$
\begin{aligned}
d_2 u_2 &\geq 1 \quad ((d_1, d_2) \in D_2) \\
d_1 u_1 + d_2 u_2 &\geq 1 \quad ((d_1, d_2) \in D_1).
\end{aligned}
$$

We list below the unimodular matrices that the hyperplane method will yield in the three different cases:

1. $D_1 \neq \emptyset$, $D_2 = \emptyset$. No transformation:

$$
\mathbf{U} = \begin{pmatrix} 1 & 0 \\ 0 & 1 \end{pmatrix}.
$$

2. $D_1 = \emptyset$, $D_2 \neq \emptyset$. Interchange loops:

$$
\mathbf{U} = \begin{pmatrix} 0 & 1 \\ 1 & 0 \end{pmatrix}.
$$

3. $D_1 \neq \emptyset$, $D_2 \neq \emptyset$. Skew and then interchange:

$$
\mathbf{U} = \begin{pmatrix} z & 1 \\ 1 & 0 \end{pmatrix} \quad \text{where} \quad z = \left\lceil \max_{(d_1, d_2) \in D_1} \{(1 - d_2)/d_1\} \right\rceil^+.
$$

Example 3.1 falls under Case 3. (A different matrix was used there.)

EXERCISES 3.4

1. In Example 3.3, take $u_4 = 2$ and find a unimodular matrix $\mathbf{U}$ with the desired properties.

2. Prove that if a vector $(u_1, u_2, \ldots, u_m)$ satisfies (3.1) and minimizes the expression
$$\max_{\mathbf{I} \in \mathcal{R}}(\mathbf{u}^1 \cdot \mathbf{I}) - \min_{\mathbf{I} \in \mathcal{R}}(\mathbf{u}^1 \cdot \mathbf{I}) + 1,$$
then $\gcd(u_1, u_2, \ldots, u_m) = 1$.

3. Prove that the first nonzero element in the sequence $u_m, u_{m-1}, \ldots, u_1$ in Algorithm 3.1 is always 1.

4. Let D denote the set of all distance vectors of dependence in a double loop. Find the unimodular matrix $\mathbf{U}$ that will be determined by the hyperplane method in each case given below:

   (a) $D = \emptyset$

   (b) $D = \{(0, 5), (0, 2)\}$

   (c) $D = \{(4, 3), (2, 0), (3, -6), (1, -12)\}$

   (d) $D = \{(0, 4), (1, 0)\}$

   (e) $D = \{(0, 3), (4, 2), (2, 0)\}$

   (f) $D = \{(0, 3), (1, 1)\}$

   (g) $D = \{(0, 1), (2, -3)\}$.

5. Given the distance matrix $\mathcal{D}$ of a loop nest $\mathbf{L} = (L_1, L_2, \ldots, L_m)$, by the hyperplane method, find a unimodular matrix $\mathbf{U}$ such that the nest $\mathbf{L_U} = (L_{U1}, L_{U2}, \ldots, L_{Um})$ is equivalent to $\mathbf{L}$ and the inner $(m-1)$ loops can execute in parallel:

   (a) $m = 3, \mathcal{D} = \begin{pmatrix} 1 & 0 & 0 \\ 0 & 1 & 0 \\ 0 & 0 & 1 \end{pmatrix}$

   (b) $m = 3, \mathcal{D} = \begin{pmatrix} 2 & 0 & 0 \\ 0 & 3 & 0 \\ 0 & 0 & 4 \end{pmatrix}$

   (c) $m = 3, \mathcal{D} = \begin{pmatrix} 2 & 4 & 6 \end{pmatrix}$

   (d) $m = 3, \mathcal{D} = \begin{pmatrix} 2 & 4 & 6 \\ 0 & 1 & -1 \end{pmatrix}$

(e) $m = 4$, $\mathcal{D} = \begin{pmatrix} 1 & -2 & -3 & -1 \\ 0 & 1 & -2 & -3 \\ 0 & 0 & 1 & -2 \end{pmatrix}$

(f) $m = 4$, $\mathcal{D} = \begin{pmatrix} 2 & -1 & -2 & 1 \\ 4 & 0 & 1 & 0 \\ 0 & 3 & 1 & -2 \\ 0 & 1 & -2 & 3 \\ 0 & 0 & 0 & 4 \\ 0 & 0 & 0 & 5 \end{pmatrix}$.

6. Show by an example that the hyperplane method does not always give the minimum number of hyperplanes.

7. Consider Example 3.4. Case 1 can be divided into two subcases based on whether there is a distance vector (d_1, d_2) such that $d_1 > 0$ and $d_2 < 0$. If there is no such distance vector, then we can interchange the loops. Assume now that the double loop is rectangular. Modify the hyperplane method in this case, so that we have the option of interchanging the loops if that would help in reducing the number of hyperplanes. Show that this modified algorithm is optimal in that it always gives the smallest number of hyperplanes. (See [Bane91].)

3.5 Outer Loop Parallelization

We start with our model loop nest **L** whose distance matrix is denoted by $\mathcal{D}$. In this section, we will study the existence of a valid unimodular transformation $\mathbf{L} \mapsto \mathbf{L_U}$ such that one or more outermost loops of $\mathbf{L_U}$ can execute in parallel.

The distance matrix of $\mathbf{L_U}$ is $\mathcal{D}U$. The first column of $\mathcal{D}U$ cannot have a negative element, since all rows of this matrix must be (lexicographically) positive. If this column has a positive element, then the outermost loop L_{U1} of $\mathbf{L_U}$ carries a dependence, and therefore it cannot execute in parallel. Thus, L_{U1} can execute in parallel iff the first column of the matrix $\mathcal{D}U$ is equal to the zero vector. Stretching this argument, we can see that the two outermost loops of $\mathbf{L_U}$ can execute in parallel iff the two leftmost columns of $\mathcal{D}U$ are zero, and likewise for any number of outermost loops. The problem then is to find a unimodular matrix $\mathbf{U}$, such that all rows of the product $\mathcal{D}\mathbf{U}$ are positive and one or more leftmost columns are zero.

The rank of a matrix is equal to the number of its linearly independent columns (which is the same as the number of its linearly independent rows). The matrix $\mathcal{D}\mathbf{U}$ has m columns, and therefore its rank is at most m. The rank is exactly m if all the columns are linearly independent. To have at least one zero column implies having a rank strictly less than m. Now rank$(\mathcal{D}\mathbf{U}) = $ rank$(\mathcal{D})$ since $\mathbf{U}$ is unimodular (Exercise I-2.4.6). Hence, a unimodular matrix $\mathbf{U}$ with the desired properties cannot exist if rank$(\mathcal{D}) = m$. On the other hand, we will show that if rank$(\mathcal{D}) < m$, then a unimodular matrix $\mathbf{U}$ exists, such that the transformation $\mathbf{L} \mapsto \mathbf{L_U}$ is valid and $[m - $ rank$(\mathcal{D})]$ outermost loops of $\mathbf{L_U}$ can execute in parallel. Before discussing the existence theorem and the algorithm that actually finds such a matrix, we will illustrate the process by an example:

Example 3.5 Consider a triple loop $\mathbf{L} = (L_1, L_2, L_3)$ with the distance matrix

$$\mathcal{D} = \begin{pmatrix} 6 & 4 & 2 \\ 0 & 1 & -1 \\ 1 & 0 & 1 \end{pmatrix}.$$

Let ρ denote the rank of $\mathcal{D}$. We want to find a 3×3 unimodular matrix $\mathbf{U}$, if possible, such that the loop nest $\mathbf{L_U} = (L_{U1}, L_{U2}, L_{U3})$ defined by $\mathbf{U}$ is equivalent to $\mathbf{L}$, and one or more outermost loops of $\mathbf{L_U}$ can execute in parallel. As explained above, such a matrix cannot exist if $\rho = 3$. We will compute ρ, and if $\rho < 3$, then we will find a 3×3 unimodular matrix $\mathbf{U}$, such that the rows of the product $\mathcal{D}\mathbf{U}$ are positive and its $(3 - \rho)$ leftmost columns are zero.

The transpose of $\mathcal{D}$ is given by

$$\mathcal{D}' = \begin{pmatrix} 6 & 0 & 1 \\ 4 & 1 & 0 \\ 2 & -1 & 1 \end{pmatrix}.$$

By Algorithm I-2.1, find two matrices

$$\mathbf{V} = \begin{pmatrix} 0 & 0 & 1 \\ 0 & 1 & -2 \\ 1 & -1 & -1 \end{pmatrix} \quad \text{and} \quad \mathbf{S} = \begin{pmatrix} 2 & -1 & 1 \\ 0 & 3 & -2 \\ 0 & 0 & 0 \end{pmatrix}$$

such that $\mathbf{V}$ is unimodular, $\mathbf{S}$ is echelon, and $\mathbf{V}\mathcal{D}' = \mathbf{S}$. This shows that

$$\rho = \text{rank}(\mathcal{D}) = \text{rank}(\mathcal{D}') = \text{rank}(\mathbf{S}) = 2 < 3,$$

so that a unimodular matrix with the desired properties may exist. Our strategy is to first find a 3×2 matrix $\mathbf{A}$ such that the first column of the product $\mathcal{D}\mathbf{A}$ is zero and the second column has positive elements.[3] Then, we will find a 3×3 unimodular matrix with similar properties.

The bottom row of $\mathbf{S}$ is zero. The relation $\mathbf{V}\mathcal{D}' = \mathbf{S}$ shows this zero row can be formed by multiplying the columns of $\mathcal{D}'$ with the third row of $\mathbf{V}$. Since the columns of $\mathcal{D}'$ are the distance vectors of $\mathbf{L}$, it follows that

$$\mathbf{d} \cdot (1, -1, -1) = 0 \qquad (3.4)$$

for each distance vector $\mathbf{d}$. We take $(1, -1, -1)'$ as the first column of $\mathbf{A}$.

Next, we need a vector $\mathbf{u}$ such that $\mathbf{du} > 0$, or equivalently, $\mathbf{du} \geq 1$ for each distance vector $\mathbf{d}$. The set of inequalities to be satisfied are:

$$\left. \begin{array}{rcrcrcl} 6u_1 & + & 4u_2 & + & 2u_3 & \geq & 1 \\ & & u_2 & - & u_3 & \geq & 1 \\ u_1 & & & + & u_3 & \geq & 1. \end{array} \right\}$$

By the first step of the Hyperplane Method (Algorithm 3.1), find a vector $\mathbf{u} = (1, 1, 0)$ such that

$$\mathbf{d} \cdot (1, 1, 0) > 0 \qquad (3.5)$$

---

[3] If the second column has all positive elements, then the rows of $\mathbf{A}$ are (lexicographically) positive, but the converse is not true. Thus, we are seeking an $\mathbf{A}$ with a stronger condition than needed. It is easier this way, and it has the additional advantage that there will be no dependence at level 3. We will return to this point later.

for each distance vector $\mathbf{d}$. We take $(1,1,0)'$ as the second column of $\mathbf{A}$. Thus, $\mathbf{A}$ is well-defined:

$$\mathbf{A} = \begin{pmatrix} 1 & 1 \\ -1 & 1 \\ -1 & 0 \end{pmatrix},$$

and equations (3.4) and (3.5) show that the first column of the product $\mathcal{D}\mathbf{A}$ is zero and the second column has positive elements. By Algorithm I-2.2, find two matrices

$$\mathbf{U} = \begin{pmatrix} -1 & 1 & 1 \\ 1 & 1 & 0 \\ 1 & 0 & 0 \end{pmatrix} \quad \text{and} \quad \mathbf{T} = \begin{pmatrix} -1 & 0 \\ 0 & 1 \\ 0 & 0 \end{pmatrix}$$

such that $\mathbf{U}$ is unimodular, $\mathbf{T}$ is echelon, and $\mathbf{A} = \mathbf{UT}$. This matrix $\mathbf{U}$ fits our description, since the product matrix

$$\mathcal{D}\mathbf{U} = \begin{pmatrix} 0 & 10 & 6 \\ 0 & 1 & 0 \\ 0 & 1 & 1 \end{pmatrix}$$

has positive rows and a leftmost zero column. It will be shown in the proof of the following theorem that the method for finding $\mathbf{U}$ illustrated in this example works in general.

For a given $m \times n$ matrix $\mathbf{A}$, the rows are usually denoted by $\mathbf{a}_1, \mathbf{a}_2, \ldots, \mathbf{a}_m$ and the columns by $\mathbf{a}^1, \mathbf{a}^2, \ldots, \mathbf{a}^n$. It often helps to write $\mathbf{A}$ in the following compact form:

$$\mathbf{A} = (\mathbf{a}^1, \mathbf{a}^2, \ldots, \mathbf{a}^n).$$

We will use these notations in the proof of Theorem 3.8 (the column notation has been used already).

Theorem 3.8 *Consider a nest $\mathbf{L}$ of m loops. Let $\mathcal{D}$ denote the distance matrix of $\mathbf{L}$ and ρ the rank of $\mathcal{D}$. If $\rho < m$, then there exists a valid unimodular transformation $\mathbf{L} \mapsto \mathbf{L_U}$ such that the outermost $(m - \rho)$ loops of $\mathbf{L_U}$ can execute in parallel.*

PROOF. To simplify notation, let us write $n = m - \rho$. As explained in the first part of this section, we are seeking an $m \times m$ unimodular matrix $\mathbf{U}$, such that the rows of the product matrix $\mathcal{D}\mathbf{U}$ are positive and the leftmost n columns are zero. We will first find an $m \times (n+1)$ matrix $\mathbf{A}$ whose columns $\mathbf{a}^1, \mathbf{a}^2, \ldots, \mathbf{a}^{n+1}$ satisfy the relations:

$$\mathbf{da}^1 = 0, \mathbf{da}^2 = 0, \ldots, \mathbf{da}^n = 0 \qquad (3.6)$$

and

$$\mathbf{da}^{n+1} > 0 \qquad (3.7)$$

for each distance vector $\mathbf{d}$ (i.e., for each row of $\mathcal{D}$). From $\mathbf{A}$, we will then derive an $m \times m$ unimodular matrix $\mathbf{U}$ whose leftmost $(n+1)$ columns satisfy similar relations:

$$\mathbf{du}^1 = 0, \mathbf{du}^2 = 0, \ldots, \mathbf{du}^n = 0 \qquad (3.8)$$

and

$$\mathbf{du}^{n+1} > 0 \qquad (3.9)$$

for each $\mathbf{d}$. Such a matrix $\mathbf{U}$ will satisfy all requirements.

To find ρ and the first n columns of $\mathbf{A}$, apply echelon reduction to the transpose $\mathcal{D}'$ of the distance matrix: By Algorithm I-2.1, find a unimodular matrix $\mathbf{V}$ and an echelon matrix $\mathbf{S}$, such that $\mathbf{V}\mathcal{D}' = \mathbf{S}$. The number of nonzero rows of $\mathbf{S}$ is the rank ρ of $\mathcal{D}$; the number of zero rows is $n = m - \rho$. Assume $\rho < m$ so that $\mathbf{S}$ has at least one zero row. The zero rows of $\mathbf{S}$ are the rows $\rho + 1, \rho + 2, \ldots, \rho + n \, (= m)$. For $1 \leq k \leq n$, row $(\rho+k)$ of $\mathbf{S}$ is formed by multiplying row $\mathbf{v}_{\rho+k}$ of $\mathbf{V}$ with the columns of $\mathcal{D}'$. Since the columns of $\mathcal{D}'$ are the distance vectors, we see that

$$\mathbf{dv}_{\rho+k} = \mathbf{v}_{\rho+k} \cdot \mathbf{d} = 0 \quad (1 \leq k \leq n)$$

for each distance vector $\mathbf{d}$. Set

$$\mathbf{a}^k \leftarrow \mathbf{v}_{\rho+k} \quad (1 \leq k \leq n). \qquad (3.10)$$

The conditions (3.6) are then satisfied.

To define the column $\mathbf{a}^{n+1}$ of $\mathbf{A}$, we apply the hyperplane method. By the first part of Algorithm 3.1, find an m-vector $\mathbf{u}$ such that $\mathbf{du} > 0$ for each distance vector $\mathbf{d}$. Set

$$\mathbf{a}^{n+1} \leftarrow \mathbf{u}. \qquad (3.11)$$

The matrix $\mathbf{A}$ is now well-defined, and its columns satisfy (3.6) and (3.7). By Algorithm I-2.2, find an $m \times m$ unimodular matrix $\mathbf{U}$ and an $m \times (n+1)$ echelon matrix

$$\mathbf{T} = \begin{pmatrix} t_{11} & t_{12} & t_{13} & \cdots & t_{1n} & t_{1(n+1)} \\ 0 & t_{22} & t_{23} & \cdots & t_{2n} & t_{2(n+1)} \\ 0 & 0 & t_{33} & \cdots & t_{3n} & t_{3(n+1)} \\ \vdots & \vdots & \vdots & \ddots & \vdots & \vdots \\ 0 & 0 & 0 & \cdots & t_{nn} & t_{n(n+1)} \\ 0 & 0 & 0 & \cdots & 0 & t_{(n+1)(n+1)} \\ 0 & 0 & 0 & \cdots & 0 & 0 \\ \vdots & \vdots & \vdots & \ddots & \vdots & \vdots \\ 0 & 0 & 0 & \cdots & 0 & 0 \end{pmatrix}$$

such that $\mathbf{A} = \mathbf{UT}$. Without any loss of generality, $\mathbf{T}$ may be chosen so that the diagonal element $t_{(n+1)(n+1)}$ is nonnegative.[4] We claim that this matrix $\mathbf{U}$ satisfies conditions (3.8) and (3.9).

Writing the relation $\mathbf{A} = \mathbf{UT}$ in the form

$$(\mathbf{a}^1, \mathbf{a}^2, \ldots, \mathbf{a}^{n+1}) = (\mathbf{u}^1, \mathbf{u}^2, \ldots, \mathbf{u}^{n+1}, \mathbf{u}^{n+2}, \ldots, \mathbf{u}^m) \cdot \mathbf{T},$$

we see that

$$\left. \begin{aligned} \mathbf{a}^1 &= t_{11}\mathbf{u}^1 \\ \mathbf{a}^2 &= t_{12}\mathbf{u}^1 + t_{22}\mathbf{u}^2 \\ &\vdots \\ \mathbf{a}^n &= t_{1n}\mathbf{u}^1 + t_{2n}\mathbf{u}^2 + \cdots + t_{nn}\mathbf{u}^n \end{aligned} \right\} \qquad (3.12)$$

---

[4]If this element is negative, then multiply both row $(n+1)$ of $\mathbf{T}$ and column $(n+1)$ of $\mathbf{U}$ by -1. Then, $\mathbf{U}$ is still unimodular, $\mathbf{T}$ is echelon, and the relation $\mathbf{A} = \mathbf{UT}$ still holds. The reason for this choice will become clear later.

and

$$\mathbf{a}^{n+1} = t_{1(n+1)}\mathbf{u}^1 + \cdots + t_{n(n+1)}\mathbf{u}^n + t_{(n+1)(n+1)}\mathbf{u}^{n+1}. \qquad (3.13)$$

To prove that conditions (3.8) hold, note that the diagonal elements $t_{11}, t_{22}, \ldots, t_{nn}$ of $\mathbf{T}$ have to be nonzero. This follows from the fact that the vectors $\mathbf{a}^1, \mathbf{a}^2, \ldots, \mathbf{a}^n$ are rows of a unimodular matrix (because of their definition (3.10)), and therefore must be linearly independent (why?). First, $t_{11} = 0$ implies $\mathbf{a}^1 = \mathbf{0}$, and therefore t_{11} must be nonzero. Then, $t_{22} = 0$ implies that $\mathbf{a}^1$ and $\mathbf{a}^2$ are linearly dependent, which means t_{22} must be nonzero; and so on. Multiplying the equations of (3.12) by any $\mathbf{d}$ and using (3.6), we get

$$\left. \begin{aligned} t_{11}(\mathbf{du}^1) &= 0 \\ t_{12}(\mathbf{du}^1) + t_{22}(\mathbf{du}^2) &= 0 \\ &\vdots \\ t_{1n}(\mathbf{du}^1) + t_{2n}(\mathbf{du}^2) + \cdots + t_{nn}(\mathbf{du}^n) &= 0. \end{aligned} \right\}$$

Since $t_{11}, t_{22}, \ldots, t_{nn}$ are all nonzero, this implies

$$\mathbf{du}^1 = \mathbf{du}^2 = \cdots = \mathbf{du}^n = 0$$

which is (3.8).

Finally, multiply (3.13) by any distance vector $\mathbf{d}$ to get

$$\mathbf{da}^{n+1} = t_{1(n+1)}(\mathbf{du}^1) + \cdots + t_{n(n+1)}(\mathbf{du}^n) + t_{(n+1)(n+1)}(\mathbf{du}^{n+1})$$

which reduces to

$$t_{(n+1)(n+1)}(\mathbf{du}^{n+1}) = \mathbf{da}^{n+1}$$

because of (3.8). Since $t_{(n+1)(n+1)} > 0$ by choice and $\mathbf{da}^{n+1} > 0$ by (3.7), we get $\mathbf{du}^{n+1} > 0$ which is (3.9). This completes the proof. $\quad\square$

As pointed out in Example 3.5, the matrix $\mathbf{U}$ constructed above satisfies a stronger condition than just having positive rows: column $(n + 1)$ has all positive elements. This brings the added advantage that there is no dependence in the transformed program $\mathbf{L_U}$ at the levels $n+2, n+3, \ldots, m$, that is, at the levels $m-\rho+2, m-\rho+3, \ldots, m$. Thus, all loops in $\mathbf{L_U}$ except $L_{U(m-\rho+1)}$ can execute in parallel.

We cannot get more than $(m-\rho)$ outermost parallel loops by a unimodular transformation:

Corollary 1 *If* $\mathbf{L} \mapsto \mathbf{L_U}$ *is a valid unimodular transformation such that k outermost loops of $\mathbf{L_U}$ can execute in parallel, then we have $k \leq m - \operatorname{rank}(\mathcal{D})$.*

PROOF. If k outermost loops of $\mathbf{L_U}$ can execute in parallel, then k leftmost columns of its distance matrix $\mathcal{D}\mathbf{U}$ are zero. That means $\mathcal{D}\mathbf{U}$ cannot have more than $(m-k)$ linearly independent columns, so that its rank is at most $(m-k)$. Hence, we have

$$\operatorname{rank}(\mathcal{D}) = \operatorname{rank}(\mathcal{D}\mathbf{U}) \leq m - k$$

which implies $k \leq m - \operatorname{rank}(\mathcal{D})$.   □

Algorithm 3.2 Given an $N \times m$ matrix $\mathcal{D}$ with positive rows, this algorithm finds the rank ρ of $\mathcal{D}$ and an $m \times m$ unimodular matrix $\mathbf{U}$, such that the product $\mathcal{D}\mathbf{U}$ has $(m-\rho)$ leftmost zero columns and all positive elements in its column $(m-\rho+1)$.

1. Compute the transpose $\mathcal{D}'$ of $\mathcal{D}$.
   [Its size is $m \times N$.]

2. By Algorithm I-2.1, find an $m \times m$ unimodular matrix $\mathbf{V}$ and an $m \times N$ echelon matrix $\mathbf{S}$ such that $\mathbf{V}\mathcal{D}' = \mathbf{S}$.

3. Set ρ to be the number of nonzero rows of $\mathbf{S}$ and n the number of zero rows.
   [Then $\rho = \operatorname{rank}(\mathbf{S}) = \operatorname{rank}(\mathcal{D}') = \operatorname{rank}(\mathcal{D})$, and $n = m - \rho$.]

4. By Algorithm 3.1, find an m-vector $\mathbf{u}$ such that $\mathbf{du} > 0$ for each row $\mathbf{d}$ of $\mathcal{D}$.

5. Construct an $m \times (n+1)$ integer matrix $\mathbf{A}$ by defining its columns as follows:

$$\mathbf{a}^k \leftarrow \mathbf{v}_{p+k} \quad (1 \le k \le n)$$
$$\mathbf{a}^{n+1} \leftarrow \mathbf{u}.$$

[Then, we have $\mathbf{da}^1 = \mathbf{da}^2 = \cdots = \mathbf{da}^n = 0$ and $\mathbf{da}^{n+1} > 0$, for each row $\mathbf{d}$ of $\mathcal{D}$.]

6. By Algorithm I-2.2, find an $m \times m$ unimodular matrix $\mathbf{U}$ and an $m \times (n+1)$ echelon matrix $\mathbf{T} = (t_{rk})$ such that $\mathbf{A} = \mathbf{UT}$.

If $t_{(n+1)(n+1)} < 0$, then multiply both row $(n+1)$ of $\mathbf{T}$ and column $(n+1)$ of $\mathbf{U}$ by -1.

[The matrix $\mathbf{U}$ satisfies $\mathbf{du}^1 = \mathbf{du}^2 = \cdots = \mathbf{du}^n = 0$ and $\mathbf{du}^{n+1} > 0$, for each row $\mathbf{d}$ of $\mathcal{D}$. This matrix has all the specified properties.] □

EXERCISES 3.5

1. In the proof of Theorem 3.8, show that $|t_{11}| = 1$.

2. Apply Algorithm 3.2 to the following matrices:

(a) $(\ 3 \quad 5 \ )$

(b) $\begin{pmatrix} 2 & 4 \\ 1 & -2 \\ 0 & 1 \end{pmatrix}$

(c) $\begin{pmatrix} 2 & -4 \\ 3 & -6 \\ 4 & -8 \end{pmatrix}$

(d) $\begin{pmatrix} 1 & 2 & 3 \\ 0 & 1 & -2 \\ 4 & -2 & 0 \end{pmatrix}$

(e) $\begin{pmatrix} 4 & -2 & 1 \\ 4 & 1 & -1 \\ 8 & 5 & -4 \end{pmatrix}.$

3.6   Computation of Loop Limits

The index space of **L** consists of all integer vectors in a polytope in
$\mathbf{R}^m$; it can be expressed as the set of integer m-vectors **I** such that

$$\left.\begin{array}{rcl} \mathbf{p}_0 & \leq & \mathbf{IP} \\ \mathbf{IQ} & \leq & \mathbf{q}_0 \end{array}\right\} \qquad (3.14)$$

where $\mathbf{p}_0$ is the lower limit vector, $\mathbf{q}_0$ the upper limit vector, **P** the
lower limit matrix, and **Q** the upper limit matrix of **L**. Consider the
transformation of **L** into the loop nest $\mathbf{L_U}$ with an $m \times m$ unimodular
matrix **U**. The index vectors **I** of **L** and **K** of $\mathbf{L_U}$ are connected by
the equation $\mathbf{K} = \mathbf{IU}$, so that $\mathbf{I} = \mathbf{KU}^{-1}$. Substituting for **I** in
(3.14) we see that the index space of $\mathbf{L_U}$ consists of all integer m-
vectors **K** satisfying

$$\left.\begin{array}{rcl} \mathbf{p}_0 & \leq & \mathbf{K}(\mathbf{U}^{-1}\mathbf{P}) \\ \mathbf{K}(\mathbf{U}^{-1}\mathbf{Q}) & \leq & \mathbf{q}_0. \end{array}\right\} \qquad (3.15)$$

By Fourier's elimination method (Algorithm I-3.2), we find a set of
$2m$ integer-valued functions $\alpha_r(K_1, \ldots, K_{r-1})$ and $\beta_r(K_1, \ldots, K_{r-1})$,
$1 \leq r \leq m$, such that this index space is described by the set of
inequalities:

$$\left.\begin{array}{rcccl} \alpha_1 & \leq & K_1 & \leq & \beta_1 \\ \alpha_2(K_1) & \leq & K_2 & \leq & \beta_2(K_1) \\ & & \vdots & & \\ \alpha_m(K_1, K_2, \ldots, K_{m-1}) & \leq & K_m & \leq & \beta_m(K_1, K_2, \ldots, K_{m-1}). \end{array}\right\}$$

These functions are the loop limits of the transformed nest $\mathbf{L_U}$.

Example 3.6 Consider a rectangular double loop $\mathbf{L} = (L_1, L_2)$:

L_1:   **do** $I_1 = p_1, q_1$
L_2:   **do** $I_2 = p_2, q_2$
                $H(I_1, I_2)$
            enddo
        enddo

Let us find the program $\mathbf{L_U}$ defined by the unimodular matrix

$$\mathbf{U} = \begin{pmatrix} 3 & 1 \\ 5 & 2 \end{pmatrix}.$$

The inverse of $\mathbf{U}$ is

$$\mathbf{U}^{-1} = \begin{pmatrix} 2 & -1 \\ -5 & 3 \end{pmatrix}.$$

The index variables K_1, K_2 of the transformed program and the index variables I_1, I_2 of the given program are related by the following equation:

$$(I_1, I_2) = (K_1, K_2) \cdot \mathbf{U}^{-1} = (2K_1 - 5K_2, -K_1 + 3K_2).$$

Since $p_1 \le I_1 \le q_1$ and $p_2 \le I_2 \le q_2$, we get the constraints:

$$\begin{aligned} p_1 &\le 2K_1 - 5K_2 \le q_1 \\ p_2 &\le -K_1 + 3K_2 \le q_2 \end{aligned}$$

or

$$\left.\begin{aligned} \tfrac{2}{5}K_1 - \tfrac{1}{5}q_1 &\le K_2 \le \tfrac{2}{5}K_1 - \tfrac{1}{5}p_1 \\ \tfrac{1}{3}K_1 + \tfrac{1}{3}p_2 &\le K_2 \le \tfrac{1}{3}K_1 + \tfrac{1}{3}q_2. \end{aligned}\right\} \tag{3.16}$$

Hence, for a given K_1, the range of K_2 is $\alpha_2(K_1) \le K_2 \le \beta_2(K_1)$, where

$$\alpha_2(K_1) = \left\lceil \max\left(\frac{2}{5}K_1 - \frac{1}{5}q_1, \frac{1}{3}K_1 + \frac{1}{3}p_2 \right) \right\rceil$$

$$\beta_2(K_1) = \left\lfloor \min\left(\frac{2}{5}K_1 - \frac{1}{5}p_1, \frac{1}{3}K_1 + \frac{1}{3}q_2 \right) \right\rfloor.$$

Eliminating K_2 from (3.16), we get

$$\frac{2}{5}K_1 - \frac{1}{5}q_1 \le \frac{1}{3}K_1 + \frac{1}{3}q_2$$

$$\frac{1}{3}K_1 + \frac{1}{3}p_2 \le \frac{2}{5}K_1 - \frac{1}{5}p_1,$$

so that

$$3p_1 + 5p_2 \leq K_1 \leq 3q_1 + 5q_2.$$

Thus, the transformed program defined by the unimodular matrix $\mathbf{U}$ can be represented by the double loop

L_{U1}:   **do** $K_1 = 3p_1 + 5p_2, 3q_1 + 5q_2$

L_{U2}:   **do** $K_2 = \alpha_2(K_1), \beta_2(K_1)$

$\qquad\qquad H(2K_1 - 5K_2, -K_1 + 3K_2)$

$\qquad\quad$ **enddo**

$\qquad$ **enddo**

Example 3.7 In this example, we will study how the triple loop

L_1:   **do** $I_1 = 3, 100$

L_2:   **do** $I_2 = -50, 78$

L_3:   **do** $I_3 = 21, 204$

$\qquad\qquad H(I_1, I_2, I_3)$

$\qquad\quad$ **enddo**

$\qquad\;$ **enddo**

$\qquad$ **enddo**

transforms under the transformation defined by the unimodular matrix

$$\mathbf{U} = \begin{pmatrix} 3 & 9 & 1 \\ -1 & -2 & 0 \\ 2 & 6 & 1 \end{pmatrix}.$$

First, we compute the inverse matrix:

$$\mathbf{U}^{-1} = \begin{pmatrix} -2 & -3 & 2 \\ 1 & 1 & -1 \\ -2 & 0 & 3 \end{pmatrix}.$$

The index variables K_1, K_2, K_3 of the transformed program and the index variables I_1, I_2, I_3 of the given program are related by the following equation:

$$\begin{aligned} (I_1, I_2, I_3) &= (K_1, K_2, K_3) \cdot \mathbf{U}^{-1} \\ &= (-2K_1 + K_2 - 2K_3, -3K_1 + K_2, 2K_1 - K_2 + 3K_3). \end{aligned}$$

Using the constraints on I_1, I_2, I_3, we see that K_1, K_2, K_3 must satisfy

$$\left.\begin{array}{rcccc} 3 & \leq & -2K_1 + K_2 - 2K_3 & \leq & 100 \\ -50 & \leq & -3K_1 + K_2 & \leq & 78 \\ 21 & \leq & 2K_1 - K_2 + 3K_3 & \leq & 204. \end{array}\right\} \tag{3.17}$$

Isolating K_3 we get

$$\left.\begin{array}{rcccc} -K_1 + \frac{1}{2}K_2 - 50 & \leq & K_3 & \leq & -K_1 + \frac{1}{2}K_2 - \frac{3}{2} \\ -\frac{2}{3}K_1 + \frac{1}{3}K_2 + 7 & \leq & K_3 & \leq & -\frac{2}{3}K_1 + \frac{1}{3}K_2 + 68, \end{array}\right\} \tag{3.18}$$

so that the range for K_3 is $\alpha_3(K_1, K_2) \leq K_3 \leq \beta_3(K_1, K_2)$, where

$$\alpha_3(K_1, K_2) = \left\lceil \max\left(-K_1 + \frac{1}{2}K_2 - 50, -\frac{2}{3}K_1 + \frac{1}{3}K_2 + 7\right) \right\rceil$$

$$\beta_3(K_1, K_2) = \left\lfloor \min\left(-K_1 + \frac{1}{2}K_2 - \frac{3}{2}, -\frac{2}{3}K_1 + \frac{1}{3}K_2 + 68\right) \right\rfloor.$$

After eliminating K_3 from (3.18), we get the inequalities:

$$-K_1 + \frac{1}{2}K_2 - 50 \leq -\frac{2}{3}K_1 + \frac{1}{3}K_2 + 68$$

$$-\frac{2}{3}K_1 + \frac{1}{3}K_2 + 7 \leq -K_1 + \frac{1}{2}K_2 - \frac{3}{2},$$

and we never used the inequalities

$$-50 \leq -3K_1 + K_2 \leq 78$$

in the original set (3.17). All these inequalities yield the range $\alpha_2(K_1) \leq K_2 \leq \beta_2(K_1)$, where

$$\begin{array}{rcl} \alpha_2(K_1) & = & \max(2K_1 + 51, 3K_1 - 50) \\ \beta_2(K_1) & = & \min(2K_1 + 708, 3K_1 + 78). \end{array}$$

Eliminating K_2, we get $-27 \leq K_1 \leq 758$ (details of computation have been omitted). Thus, the unimodular transformation defined by the matrix **U** will transform the nest (L_1, L_2, L_3) into the nest

L_{U1}:   **do** $K_1 = -27,758$

L_{U2}:   **do** $K_2 = \alpha_2(K_1), \beta_2(K_1)$

L_{U3}:   **do** $K_3 = \alpha_3(K_1, K_2), \beta_3(K_1, K_2)$

$\quad\quad\quad\quad H(-2K_1 + K_2 - 2K_3, -3K_1 + K_2, 2K_1 - K_2 + 3K_3)$

$\quad\quad\quad$ **enddo**

$\quad\quad$ **enddo**

$\quad$ **enddo**

In both examples discussed above, the loop nest was rectangular. If the nest **L** is not rectangular, the lower limit matrix **P** and/or the upper limit matrix **Q** are not equal to the identity matrix. The only difference in this case is that we need to compute the product $\mathbf{U}^{-1}\mathbf{P}$ and/or the product $\mathbf{U}^{-1}\mathbf{Q}$ to derive the inequalities involving $K_1, K_2, \ldots, K_m$ from (3.15). This is illustrated in some of the exercises of the section.

EXERCISES 3.6

1. Find the transformed program $\mathbf{L_U}$ of the double loop **L**:

L_1:   **do** $I_1 = p_1, q_1$

L_2:   **do** $I_2 = p_2, q_2$

$\quad\quad\quad H(I_1, I_2)$

$\quad\quad$ **enddo**

$\quad$ **enddo**

where

(a) $p_1 = 0, q_1 = 10, p_2 = I_1, q_2 = I_1 + 10$, and $\mathbf{U} = \begin{pmatrix} 2 & 3 \\ 3 & 4 \end{pmatrix}$

(b) $p_1 = 4, q_1 = 20, p_2 = 0, q_2 = 2I_1$, and $\mathbf{U} = \begin{pmatrix} -1 & 1 \\ 1 & -2 \end{pmatrix}$

(c) $p_1 = -184, q_1 = 70, p_2 = \lceil \max(5, 8 - I_1/2) \rceil$,

$\quad q_2 = \lfloor \min(100, 40 - I_1/2) \rfloor$, and $\mathbf{U} = \begin{pmatrix} 0 & 1 \\ 1 & 2 \end{pmatrix}$.

In each case, draw the perimeter of the index space of **L** and that of the index space of $\mathbf{L_U}$.

2. Find the transformed program $\mathbf{L_U}$ of the triple loop **L**:

L_1:   **do** $I_1 = p_1, q_1$
L_2:   **do** $I_2 = p_2, q_2$
L_3:   **do** $I_3 = p_3, q_3$
           $H(I_1, I_2, I_3)$
         enddo
      enddo
   enddo

where

(a) $p_1 = 1, q_1 = 100, p_2 = 1, q_2 = 100, p_3 = 1, q_3 = 100$, and

$$U = \begin{pmatrix} 1 & 0 & 3 \\ 0 & 1 & 0 \\ 0 & 0 & 1 \end{pmatrix}$$

(b) $p_1 = 0, q_1 = 200, p_2 = I_1, q_2 = I_1 + 50, p_3 = I_2, q_3 = I_2 + 100$, and

$$U = \begin{pmatrix} 2 & 1 & 1 \\ 1 & 1 & 0 \\ 2 & 1 & 2 \end{pmatrix}$$

(c) $p_1 = 1, q_1 = 100, p_2 = \max(I_1, 50), q_2 = 100, p_3 = \lceil I_2/2 \rceil$,
$q_3 = \min(I_1 + I_2, 100)$, and

$$U = \begin{pmatrix} -1 & 1 & 1 \\ 1 & 1 & 0 \\ 1 & 0 & 0 \end{pmatrix}.$$

3. Take a rectangular loop nest **L** and a unimodular matrix $U = (u_{rk})$. For any k in $1 \le k \le m$, the number of iterations of the loop L_{Uk} in L_U cannot exceed

$$\sum_{r=1}^{m} |u_{rk}|(q_r - p_r) + 1.$$

(See the part of Section 3.2 on loop limits.) Using this formula, find an upper bound on the number of iterations of an instance of the loop L_{U2} in Exercise 2(a). Repeat for L_{U3}.

4. Assume the loop nest **L** is regular where the lower limit matrix **P** and the upper limit matrix **Q** are unimodular (and, by definition, equal).

(a) Prove that there is a valid unimodular transformation $L \mapsto L_U$ such that L_U is rectangular.

(b) How are the limits of L_U related to the limits of **L**?

5. Using Algorithm 3.1 and the method of this section, transform each loop described below such that the inner loops in the transformed program can execute in parallel:

   (a) Loop limits given by Exercise 1(a) and distance vectors given by Exercise 3.4.4(c);

   (b) Loop limits given by Exercise 1(b) and distance vectors given by Exercise 3.4.4(g);

   (c) Loop limits given by Exercise 2(b) and distance vectors given by Exercise 3.4.5(d).

6. Using Algorithm 3.2 and the method of this section, transform each loop described below such that some outermost loops in the transformed program can execute in parallel:

   (a) Loop limits given by Exercise 1(a) and distance vectors given by Exercise 3.4.4(b);

   (b) Loop limits given by Exercise 2(a) and distance vectors given by Exercise 3.4.5(c);

   (c) Loop limits given by Exercise 2(c) and distance matrix given by Exercise 3.5.2(e).

Chapter 4

Remainder Transformations

4.1 Introduction

A unimodular transformation $\mathbf{I} \mapsto \mathbf{I}\mathbf{U}$ simply 'rotates' the coordinate axes (the I_r-axes). Such a rotation is effective in partitioning the dependence graph along hyperplanes or intersections of hyperplanes. In this chapter, we go one step further by examining more closely the relationship between two index points $\mathbf{i}$ and $\mathbf{j}$ when the iteration $H(\mathbf{j})$ depends on the iteration $H(\mathbf{i})$. For example, consider the double loop (L_1, L_2) of Example 1.4, with distance vectors $(1, 2)$ and $(2, 1)$. The distance vectors do not lie on a line; in fact, the rank of the distance matrix is 2. We cannot partition the dependence graph of $\mathbf{L}$ along lines to display vertical parallelism (Theorem 3.8). However, we did find by inspection the ideal vertical partition consisting of the weakly connected components (Figure 1.3), and it seems plausible that a reasonable vertical partition can be found by analytical methods. The key point here is that if two iterations $H(i_1, i_2)$ and $H(j_1, j_2)$ are weakly connected, then $(j_1 - i_1, j_2 - i_2)$ must be restricted somehow; it cannot be an arbitrary integer vector. By focusing on that restriction imposed by the distance matrix of the program, we can derive a vertical partition which is close to

113

the ideal one.

Let I denote any integer and b a positive integer. We can write I in the form $I = Y + Kb$, where $Y = I \bmod b$ and $K = \lfloor I/b \rfloor$. The part Kb is an integral multiple of b, and the part Y is the remainder when I is divided by b. This defines a one-to-one mapping $I \mapsto (Y, K)$ of $\mathbf{Z}$ into $\mathbf{Z}^2$. We can extend this to the case where $\mathbf{I}$ is an integer m-vector, and $\mathbf{S}$ a $\rho \times m$ echelon integer matrix with rank ρ and (lexicographically) positive rows.[1] A unique m-vector $\mathbf{Y}$ and a unique ρ-vector $\mathbf{K}$ may be defined such that $\mathbf{I} = \mathbf{Y} + \mathbf{KS}$. The part $\mathbf{KS}$ is the product of $\mathbf{S}$ and an integer vector, and the part $\mathbf{Y}$ can be considered to be the 'remainder' when $\mathbf{I}$ is 'divided' by the matrix $\mathbf{S}$. This defines a one-to-one mapping $\mathbf{I} \mapsto (\mathbf{Y}; \mathbf{K})$ of $\mathbf{Z}^m$ into $\mathbf{Z}^{m+\rho}$. We give the name *remainder transformation* to any loop transformation defined by a mapping (of the index space) of this type.

In Section 4.2, we describe remainder transformations of a single loop, and show how they can be used to find horizontal and vertical partitions of the dependence graph. The gcd transformation, a remainder transformation that finds a vertical partition for a general loop nest, is discussed in Section 4.3. A more general transformation for vertical parallelism, called echelon transformation, is studied in Section 4.4. In Chapter 5, we will use the single-loop results of Section 4.2 to derive horizontal partitions of a general loop nest.

4.2 Single-Loop Transformation

For $m = 1$, our model program is the single loop:

$L:$ **do** $I = p, q$
        $H(I)$
    enddo

where subscripts have been dropped. We will first explain the different cases of the remainder transformation by an example:

---

[1]These restrictions on $\mathbf{S}$ are needed for proper definitions.

Example 4.1 Consider the single loop:

L: **do** $I = 3, 18$
    S: $X(I) = X(I - 4) + X(I - 6)$
        enddo

The dependence graph of L is shown in Figure 4.1(a).[2] Take any positive integer b. Let $K = \lfloor I/b \rfloor$ and $Y = I \bmod b$, so that we have $I = bK + Y$ and $0 \leq Y \leq b - 1$. The range of (K, Y) is determined by the range of I, and there is a one-to-one correspondence between the values of I and the values of (K, Y) (in their respective ranges). Table 4.1 shows the values of (K, Y) corresponding to the values $3, 4, \ldots, 18$ of I, for three different values of b; it is used to find limits of loops considered below. Note that for any value of b, as I increases, so does (K, Y) in the lexicographic sense. Thus, executing the iterations of L in the increasing order of I is the same as executing them in the increasing order of (K, Y). This is true irrespective of the dependence structure of the loop L. The iterations of L do not change, nor does their execution order; they are only relabeled.

The value $b = 6$ is chosen arbitrarily; it has no special significance. Here, we have $I = 6K + Y$. The double loop $\mathbf{L_6}$:

    do $K = 0, 3$
       do $Y = \max(3 - 6K, 0), \min(18 - 6K, 5)$
          $X(6K + Y) = X(6K + Y - 4) + X(6K + Y - 6)$
       enddo
    enddo

consists of the iterations of L. Since the execution order of the iterations in $\mathbf{L_6}$ is the same as that in L, this double loop is equivalent to L. The dependence graph of $\mathbf{L_6}$ is shown in Figure 4.1(b). The K-loop cannot execute in parallel (direction vectors $(1, 0)$ and $(1, -1)$ are present); the Y-loop cannot execute in parallel (the direction

---

[2]To avoid crowding, we have shown only a few significant dependence edges in this and the subsequent dependence graphs for this example.

vector $(0, 1)$ is present); and the loops cannot be interchanged (the direction vector $(1, -1)$ is present).

The value $b = 4$ is the minimum of the two dependence distances of L. Here, we have $I = 4K + Y$. As before, the double loop $\mathbf{L_4}$:

do $K = 0, 4$
 do $Y = \max(3 - 4K, 0), \min(18 - 4K, 3)$
  $X(4K + Y) = X(4K + Y - 4) + X(4K + Y - 6)$
 enddo
enddo

is equivalent to L. The dependence graph of $\mathbf{L_4}$ is shown in Figure 4.1(c). The K-loop cannot execute in parallel (direction vectors $(1, 1)$, $(1, 0)$ and $(1, -1)$ are present), but the Y-loop can execute in parallel (the direction vector $(0, 1)$ is absent). The loops cannot be interchanged (the direction vector $(1, -1)$ is present). Thus, we can change the Y-loop into its corresponding **doall** loop.

The value $b = 2$ is the gcd of the two dependence distances of L. Here, we have $I = 2K + Y$. As before, the double loop $\mathbf{L_2}$:

do $K = 1, 9$
 do $Y = \max(3 - 2K, 0), \min(18 - 2K, 1)$
  $X(2K + Y) = X(2K + Y - 4) + X(2K + Y - 6)$
 enddo
enddo

is equivalent to L. The dependence graph of $\mathbf{L_2}$ is shown in Figure 4.1(d). The K-loop cannot execute in parallel (the direction vector $(1, 0)$ is present), but the Y-loop can execute in parallel (the direction vector $(0, 1)$ is absent). The loops can be interchanged (the direction vector $(1, -1)$ is absent). After the interchange, the outer loop (the Y-loop) still will not carry any dependence. Hence, L is equivalent to the mixed double loop:

doall $Y = 0, 1$
 do $K = \lceil (3 - Y)/2 \rceil, \lfloor (18 - Y)/2 \rfloor$
  $X(2K + Y) = X(2K + Y - 4) + X(2K + Y - 6)$
 enddo
enddoall

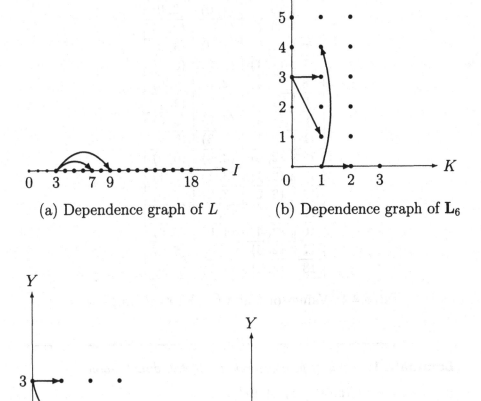

(a) Dependence graph of L

(b) Dependence graph of $\mathbf{L_6}$

(c) Dependence graph of $\mathbf{L_4}$

(d) Dependence graph of $\mathbf{L_2}$

Figure 4.1: Dependence graphs of the loop nests of Example 4.1.

I	(K, Y)		
	$b = 6$	$b = 4$	$b = 2$
3	(0, 3)	(0, 3)	(1, 1)
4	(0, 4)	(1, 0)	(2, 0)
5	(0, 5)	(1, 1)	(2, 1)
6	(1, 0)	(1, 2)	(3, 0)
7	(1, 1)	(1, 3)	(3, 1)
8	(1, 2)	(2, 0)	(4, 0)
9	(1, 3)	(2, 1)	(4, 1)
10	(1, 4)	(2, 2)	(5, 0)
11	(1, 5)	(2, 3)	(5, 1)
12	(2, 0)	(3, 0)	(6, 0)
13	(2, 1)	(3, 1)	(6, 1)
14	(2, 2)	(3, 2)	(7, 0)
15	(2, 3)	(3, 3)	(7, 1)
16	(2, 4)	(4, 0)	(8, 0)
17	(2, 5)	(4, 1)	(8, 1)
18	(3, 0)	(4, 2)	(9, 0)

Table 4.1: Values of I and (K, Y) in Example 4.1.

Lemma 4.1 *For any positive integer b, the double loop:*

L_1 :   **do** $K = \lceil (p - b + 1)/b \rceil, \lfloor q/b \rfloor$

L_2 :   **do** $Y = \max(p - bK, 0), \min(q - bK, b - 1)$

$\qquad\qquad H(bK + Y)$

$\qquad\quad$ **enddo**

$\qquad$ **enddo**

is equivalent to L.

PROOF. In terms of the index variable I of L, define two new integer variables K and Y by the equations:

$$K = \lfloor I/b \rfloor \qquad (4.1)$$

$$Y = I \bmod b. \qquad (4.2)$$

Then, we have

$$I = bK + Y \tag{4.3}$$

and

$$0 \leq Y \leq b - 1. \tag{4.4}$$

Since p and q are the lower and upper limits of L, the range of I is given by $p \leq I \leq q$. Substituting for I from (4.3), we get

$$p \leq bK + Y \leq q$$

or

$$p - bK \leq Y \leq q - bK.$$

These inequalities together with (4.4) yield the range for Y in terms of K:

$$\max(p - bK, 0) \leq Y \leq \min(q - bK, b - 1). \tag{4.5}$$

Eliminating Y, we get

$$\lceil (p - b + 1)/b \rceil \leq K \leq \lfloor q/b \rfloor. \tag{4.6}$$

For each value of I between p and q, there is a unique value of (K, Y) satisfying (4.6) and (4.5) such that $I = bK + Y$. Conversely, for each value of (K, Y) satisfying these inequalities, the value of $I = bK + Y$ lies between p and q. Since the loop limits of the nest (L_1, L_2) are given by (4.6) and (4.5), the set of iterations of it is the same as the set of iterations of L.

The execution order of iterations in (L_1, L_2) is exactly the same as that in L. To see this, consider any two distinct index values i and j of L. Let (k, y) denote the value of (K, Y) corresponding to the value i of I, and (l, z) the value corresponding to j. We need to show that $i < j$ iff $(k, y) \prec (l, z)$. It is enough to show that $i < j$ implies $(k, y) \prec (l, z)$ (explain). We have

$$
\begin{array}{rcll}
bk & \leq & bk + y & \text{(since } y \geq 0 \text{ from (4.4))} \\
   & = & i & \\
   & < & j & \text{(by assumption)} \\
   & = & bl + z & \\
   & < & bl + b & \text{(since } z < b \text{ by (4.4))}
\end{array}
$$

so that $k < l + 1$, that is, $k \leq l$. If $k < l$, then $(k, y) \prec (l, z)$. If $k = l$, then we have

$$y = i - bk = i - bl < j - bl = z$$

that is, $y < z$. In other words, $(k, y) \prec (l, z)$ holds in this case also.

The loop nest (L_1, L_2) simply relabels the iterations of L without changing their execution order. Hence, it is always equivalent to L irrespective of the dependence structure of the given loop.   □

Corollary 1 *Each distance vector of the loop nest (L_1, L_2) has one of the two forms:*

$$(\lfloor d/b \rfloor, d \bmod b) \quad or \quad (1 + \lfloor d/b \rfloor, -b + d \bmod b)$$

where d is a dependence distance of L. Conversely, if d is a distance of L, then at least one of the forms gives a distance vector of (L_1, L_2).

PROOF. Let (k, y) and (l, z) denote two index values of (L_1, L_2) such that the iteration $H(bl + z)$ depends on the iteration $H(bk + y)$. Let $i = bk + y$ and $j = bl + z$, so that in L, the iteration $H(j)$ depends on the iteration $H(i)$. Then, $d = j - i$ must be a dependence distance of L. We have

$$d = b(l - k) + (z - y). \tag{4.7}$$

Two cases arise. First, let $z \geq y$. Since $0 \leq y < b$ and $0 \leq z < b$, it follows that $0 \leq z - y < b$. Hence, we have

$$\left.\begin{aligned} l - k &= \lfloor d/b \rfloor \\ z - y &= d \bmod b. \end{aligned}\right\} \tag{4.8}$$

Next, let $z < y$. We can write (4.7) as

$$d = b(l - k - 1) + (b + z - y)$$

where $0 < b + z - y < b$. This means

$$\left.\begin{aligned} l - k - 1 &= \lfloor d/b \rfloor \\ b + z - y &= d \bmod b \end{aligned}\right\}$$

that is,

$$\left. \begin{array}{rcl} l - k & = & 1 + \lfloor d/b \rfloor \\ z - y & = & -b + d \bmod b. \end{array} \right\} \qquad (4.9)$$

Thus, each distance vector $(l - k, z - y)$ in (L_1, L_2) must have one of the two forms given by (4.8) and (4.9).

The second part of the corollary is proved similarly. □

The equivalent loop nest (L_1, L_2) will have more properties if the integer b is suitably restricted. First, we show that if b is small enough, then the inner loop L_2 can execute in parallel:

Theorem 4.2 *Suppose there are dependences in the loop L. If b is any positive integer less than or equal to each dependence distance, then the loop nest:*

$L_1 :$ **do** $K = \lceil (p - b + 1)/b \rceil, \lfloor q/b \rfloor$

$L_2 :$ **do** $Y = \max(p - bK, 0), \min(q - bK, b - 1)$

         $H(bK + Y)$

      enddo

   enddo

is equivalent to L and the inner loop L_2 can execute in parallel.

PROOF. Since b is a positive integer, the loop nest (L_1, L_2) is already equivalent to L by Lemma 4.1, and its distance vectors have the forms given in Corollary 1 to that lemma. We now have the extra condition that each distance d of L is bigger than or equal to b, so that $\lfloor d/b \rfloor \geq 1$. This means each distance vector (d_1, d_2) of (L_1, L_2) satisfies $d_1 > 0$. Since L_2 carries no dependence, it can execute in parallel (Lemma 1.1). □

Corollary 1 *The number of iterations of the K-loop in Theorem 4.2 is minimized if b is the minimum dependence distance of L.*

PROOF. The proof is simple and is left to the reader. □

If b divides each dependence distance, then the loops in the nest (L_1, L_2) can be interchanged, and then the outer loop in the transformed program can execute in parallel:

Theorem 4.3 *Suppose there are dependences in the loop L. If b is a positive integer that divides each dependence distance, then the loop nest:*

L_2 :   **do** $Y = 0, b - 1$

L_1 :   **do** $K = \lceil (p - Y)/b \rceil, \lfloor (q - Y)/b \rfloor$

                $H(Y + bK)$

          enddo

      enddo

is equivalent to L and the outer loop L_2 can execute in parallel. The dependence distances of (L_2, L_1) are of the form $(0, d/b)$ where d is a dependence distance of L.[3]

PROOF. Since b is a positive integer, the loop nest (L_1, L_2) of Lemma 4.1 is already equivalent to L, and its distance vectors have the forms given in Corollary 1 to that lemma. We now have the extra condition that each distance d of L is an integral multiple of b, so that $\lfloor d/b \rfloor = d/b$ and $d \bmod b = 0$. This means each dependence distance d of L gives the following distance vectors of (L_1, L_2): $(d/b, 0)$ and/or $(1 + d/b, -b)$. However, the second form can be ruled out (Exercise 3). So, each distance vector of (L_1, L_2) is of the form $(d/b, 0)$. As in Theorem 4.2, L_2 carries no dependence and hence can execute in parallel. In this case, we can go further: The loops can be interchanged since the direction vector $(1, -1)$ is absent. After the interchange, the distance vectors have the form $(0, d/b)$, so that now the outer loop L_2 can execute in parallel.

The loop limits after interchange can be found directly from the inequalities:

$$\left. \begin{array}{ccccc} 0 & \leq & Y & \leq & b - 1 \\ p & \leq & Y + bK & \leq & q. \end{array} \right\}$$

□

Corollary 1 *The number of iterations of the Y-loop in Theorem 4.3 is maximized if b is the gcd of all dependence distances of L.*

---

[3]To be consistent, we are using the notation L_1 for the K-loop and L_2 for the Y-loop.

PROOF. The proof is simple and is left to the reader. □

EXERCISES 4.2

1. In Example 4.1, take $b = 7$ and then $b = 3$. In each case, write down the equivalent loop nest, find all distance vectors, and draw the dependence graph. (The two nests will be denoted by $\mathbf{L}_7$ and $\mathbf{L}_3$ in our notation.)

2. Consider Corollary 1 to Lemma 4.1. Show that any given distance vector of (L_1, L_2) is uniform iff the corresponding distance d of L is uniform.

   Give an example such that

   (a) Only $(\lfloor d/b \rfloor, d \bmod b)$ is a distance vector;

   (b) Only $(1 + \lfloor d/b \rfloor, -b + d \bmod b)$ is a distance vector;

   (c) Both are distance vectors.

3. In the proof of Theorem 4.3, explain why $(1 + d/b, -b)$ cannot be a distance vector of (L_1, L_2).

4. For each of the loops given below, find two equivalent double loops as follows:

   - Take the minimum dependence distance for b and apply Theorem 4.2;

   - Take the gcd of all dependence distances and apply Theorem 4.3.

   (a) L: **do** $I = 7, 200$
   $$X(2I) = X(2I - 6) + X(2I - 12) + X(2I - 5)$$
   enddo

   (b) L: **do** $I = 50, 250$
   $$X(I - 3) = X(I + 5) + X(I + 9)$$
   enddo

   (c) L: **do** $I = 1, 100$
   $$X(I) = X(I + 4) + X(I + 5) + X(I + 6)$$
   enddo

4.3   GCD Transformation

In the previous section, we showed how to represent horizontal and vertical parallelism in a single loop by writing it in the form of an equivalent double loop. We now consider the model program **L**:

L_1:   **do** $I_1 = p_1, q_1$
L_2:   **do** $I_2 = p_2, q_2$

  ⋮   ⋮

L_m: **do** $I_m = p_m, q_m$
                 $H(I_1, I_2, \ldots, I_m)$
               enddo

           ⋮

             enddo
           enddo

with any number of loops. Theorem 4.2 will be used in the next chapter to help exploit horizontal parallelism in **L**. In this section, we will extend Theorem 4.3 to display vertical parallelism in the general program. We will use gcd's (as opposed to arbitrary divisors) to increase the amount of parallelism as much as possible (Corollary 1 to Theorem 4.3).

Let g_r denote the gcd of column r of the distance matrix $\mathcal{D}$ of **L**. The *gcd matrix* of **L** is the diagonal matrix:

$$\mathbf{G} = \begin{pmatrix} g_1 & 0 & \cdots & 0 \\ 0 & g_2 & \cdots & 0 \\ \vdots & \vdots & \ddots & \vdots \\ 0 & 0 & \cdots & g_m \end{pmatrix}.$$

Without any loss of generality, we may assume that $g_r > 0$ for each r in $1 \le r \le m$. If g_r is zero for some r, then column r of $\mathcal{D}$ is the zero vector, and therefore, the loop L_r can be moved outward to any position by a right circulation (Corollary 1 to Theorem 2.8). Thus, we can permute the loops of **L** to get an equivalent program consisting of an outer ring of loops L_r such that $g_r = 0$, and an inner core of loops L_r such that $g_r > 0$. Each loop in the outer ring can already execute in parallel; we focus on the inner nest of loops whose gcd matrix has strictly positive diagonal elements.

The index space $\mathcal{R}$ of $\mathbf{L}$ is a subset of $\mathbf{Z}^m$. Let $\mathbf{Y}$ and $\mathbf{K}$ denote any two m-vectors: $\mathbf{Y} = (Y_1, Y_2, \ldots, Y_m)$ and $\mathbf{K} = (K_1, K_2, \ldots, K_m)$. Define a mapping $\mathbf{I} \mapsto (\mathbf{Y}; \mathbf{K})$ of $\mathcal{R}$ into $\mathbf{Z}^{2m}$ by the equation:

$$\mathbf{I} = \mathbf{Y} + \mathbf{KG} \tag{4.10}$$

and the constraints:

$$0 \le Y_r \le g_r - 1 \quad (1 \le r \le m). \tag{4.11}$$

Lemma 4.4 *The mapping of $\mathcal{R}$ into $\mathbf{Z}^{2m}$ defined by (4.10) and (4.11) is well-defined and one-to-one.*

PROOF. The matrix equation (4.10) is equivalent to the system of m scalar equations:

$$I_r = Y_r + g_r K_r \quad (1 \le r \le m). \tag{4.12}$$

Note that (4.11) and (4.12) uniquely define $\mathbf{Y}$ and $\mathbf{K}$ in terms of $\mathbf{I}$:

$$Y_r = I_r \bmod g_r \tag{4.13}$$
$$K_r = \lfloor I_r / g_r \rfloor. \tag{4.14}$$

Also, for any given $\mathbf{Y}$ satisfying (4.11) and any given $\mathbf{K}$, there is only one $\mathbf{I}$ that is mapped to $(\mathbf{Y}; \mathbf{K})$, namely, the one given by (4.10). Hence, this mapping is one-to-one.   □

This mapping defines a new execution order for the iterations of $\mathbf{L}$. Let $\mathbf{L_G}$ denote the program consisting of the iterations of $\mathbf{L}$ such that they are executed in the increasing order of the vector:

$$(\mathbf{Y}; \mathbf{K}) = (Y_1, Y_2, \ldots, Y_m, K_1, K_2, \ldots, K_m).$$

The transformation $\mathbf{L} \mapsto \mathbf{L_G}$ is called the *gcd transformation* of $\mathbf{L}$. We can express the transformed program $\mathbf{L_G}$ as a nest of $2m$ loops. It is equivalent to $\mathbf{L}$, and the outermost m loops (the Y-loops) can execute in parallel:

Theorem 4.5 *Let* **G** *denote the gcd matrix of the loop nest* **L**. *If its main diagonal* $(g_1, g_2, \ldots, g_m)$ *has all positive elements, then the loop nest* **L$_\mathbf{G}$** :

> **do** $Y_1 = 0, g_1 - 1$
>
> $\vdots$
>
>   **do** $Y_m = 0, g_m - 1$
>   **do** $K_1 = \lceil (p'_1 - Y_1)/g_1 \rceil, \lfloor (q'_1 - Y_1)/g_1 \rfloor$
>
> $\vdots$
>
>   **do** $K_m = \lceil (p'_m - Y_m)/g_m \rceil, \lfloor (q'_m - Y_m)/g_m \rfloor$
> $H(Y_1 + g_1 K_1, Y_2 + g_2 K_2, \ldots, Y_m + g_m K_m)$
>
>   **enddo**
>
> $\vdots$
>
>   **enddo**
>   **enddo**
>
> $\vdots$
>
>   **enddo**

is equivalent to **L**, *where*

$$
\begin{aligned}
p'_r &= p_r(Y_1 + g_1 K_1, Y_2 + g_2 K_2, \ldots, Y_{r-1} + g_{r-1} K_{r-1}) \\
q'_r &= q_r(Y_1 + g_1 K_1, Y_2 + g_2 K_2, \ldots, Y_{r-1} + g_{r-1} K_{r-1}).
\end{aligned}
$$

Also, the outermost m *loops of* **L$_\mathbf{G}$** *can execute in parallel.*

PROOF. Define $2m$ variables $Y_1, Y_2, \ldots, Y_m, K_1, K_2, \ldots, K_m$ by the equation (4.12) and the constraints (4.11). Substituting from (4.12) in the inequalities (defining the bounds on the index variable I_r):

$$
p_r(I_1, I_2, \ldots, I_{r-1}) \le I_r \le q_r(I_1, I_2, \ldots, I_{r-1})
$$

we get the constraints:

$$
p'_r \le Y_r + g_r K_r \le q'_r
$$

or

$$
\lceil (p'_r - Y_r)/g_r \rceil \le K_r \le \lfloor (q'_r - Y_r)/g_r \rfloor \tag{4.15}
$$

for K_r. For each value of the index vector $\mathbf{I}$ of $\mathbf{L}$, there is a unique value of the vector $(\mathbf{Y}; \mathbf{K})$ satisfying (4.11) and (4.15). Conversely, for each value of $(\mathbf{Y}; \mathbf{K})$ satisfying (4.11) and (4.15), $\mathbf{I} = \mathbf{Y} + \mathbf{KG}$ gives an index value of $\mathbf{L}$. Thus, the loop nest $\mathbf{L_G}$ has the same set of iterations as the loop nest $\mathbf{L}$.

To prove the equivalence of $\mathbf{L_G}$ to $\mathbf{L}$, consider two iterations $H(\mathbf{i})$ and $H(\mathbf{j})$ of $\mathbf{L}$ such that $H(\mathbf{j})$ depends on $H(\mathbf{i})$. Then, $\mathbf{j} \succ \mathbf{i}$ and $\mathbf{j} - \mathbf{i}$ is a distance vector of $\mathbf{L}$. Let $(\mathbf{y}; \mathbf{k})$ denote the value of $(\mathbf{Y}; \mathbf{K})$ corresponding to the value $\mathbf{i}$ of $\mathbf{I}$, and $(\mathbf{z}; \mathbf{l})$ the value corresponding to $\mathbf{j}$. We will show that $\mathbf{z} = \mathbf{y}$ and $\mathbf{l} \succ \mathbf{k}$, implying $(\mathbf{z}; \mathbf{l}) \succ (\mathbf{y}; \mathbf{k})$, so that the iteration $H(\mathbf{z} + \mathbf{lG})$ or $H(\mathbf{j})$ will be executed after the iteration $H(\mathbf{y} + \mathbf{kG})$ or $H(\mathbf{i})$ in the loop nest $\mathbf{L_G}$.

Since $(j_1 - i_1, j_2 - i_2, \ldots, j_m - i_m)$ is a row of the distance matrix, $j_r - i_r$ is a multiple of g_r, that is, $j_r \bmod g_r = i_r \bmod g_r$, $1 \le r \le m$. Then, we have

$$z_r = j_r \bmod g_r = i_r \bmod g_r = y_r$$

for each r, so that $\mathbf{z} = \mathbf{y}$. Also,

$$
\begin{aligned}
l_r - k_r &= [g_r l_r - g_r k_r]/g_r \\
&= [(z_r + g_r l_r) - (y_r + g_r k_r)]/g_r \\
&= (j_r - i_r)/g_r.
\end{aligned}
$$

Since $(j_1 - i_1, j_2 - i_2, \ldots, j_m - i_m) \succ \mathbf{0}$ and $g_1, g_2, \ldots, g_m$ are positive, it follows that

$$((j_1 - i_1)/g_1, (j_2 - i_2)/g_2, \ldots, (j_m - i_m)/g_m) \succ \mathbf{0},$$

that is, $(l_1 - k_1, l_2 - k_2, \ldots, l_m - k_m) \succ \mathbf{0}$. Thus, $\mathbf{l} \succ \mathbf{k}$ which (together with $\mathbf{z} = \mathbf{y}$) proves the equivalence of $\mathbf{L_G}$ to $\mathbf{L}$.

Now, note that a typical distance vector of $\mathbf{L_G}$ has the form:

$$
\begin{aligned}
&(\mathbf{z}; \mathbf{l}) - (\mathbf{y}; \mathbf{k}) \\
&= (z_1 - y_1, z_2 - y_2, \ldots, z_m - y_m, l_1 - k_1, l_2 - k_2, \ldots, l_m - k_m) \\
&= (0, 0, \ldots, 0, (j_1 - i_1)/g_1, (j_2 - i_2)/g_2, \ldots, (j_m - i_m)/g_m) \\
&= (0, 0, \ldots, 0, d_1/g_1, d_2/g_2, \ldots, d_m/g_m)
\end{aligned}
$$

where $(d_1, d_2, \ldots, d_m)$ is a distance vector of **L**. This means the outermost m loops of $\mathbf{L_G}$ carry no dependence, and therefore they can execute in parallel (Lemma 1.1). $\square$

Corollary 1 *The nest of* **Y**-*loops of* $\mathbf{L_G}$ *has* $\det(\mathbf{G})$ *iterations.*

PROOF. The number of iterations of this nest is $\prod_{r=1}^{m} g_r$ which is equal to $\det(\mathbf{G})$. $\square$

Corollary 2 *The distance matrix of the nest of* **K**-*loops is* $\mathcal{D}\mathbf{G}^{-1}$.

PROOF. We showed in the proof of Theorem 4.5 that each distance vector $(\mathbf{z} - \mathbf{y}; \mathbf{l} - \mathbf{k})$ of the loop nest $\mathbf{L_G}$ has the form

$$(0, 0, \ldots, 0, d_1/g_1, d_2/g_2, \ldots, d_m/g_m)$$

where $(d_1, d_2, \ldots, d_m)$ is a distance vector of **L**. It can be shown similarly that the converse is also true: each distance vector of **L** yields a distance vector of $\mathbf{L_G}$ in this way. Thus, for a fixed iteration of the nest of **Y**-loops, the distance vectors of the nest of **K** loops are the vectors $(d_1/g_1, d_2/g_2, \ldots, d_m/g_m)$ or $\mathbf{dG}^{-1}$, where $\mathbf{d} = (d_1, d_2, \ldots, d_m)$ is a distance vector of **L**. Hence, the distance matrix of this nest can be written as $\mathcal{D}\mathbf{G}^{-1}$. $\square$

Example 4.2 Consider the double loop **L**:

L_1 :   **do** $I_1 = 1, 100$
L_2 :   **do** $I_2 = I_1, 2I_1 + 4$
                        $X(I_1, I_2) = X(I_1 - 2, I_2 - 3) + X(I_1, I_2 - 6)$
                    enddo
                enddo

Its distance matrix is given by

$$\mathcal{D} = \begin{pmatrix} 2 & 3 \\ 0 & 6 \end{pmatrix}.$$

The gcd of column 1 is $g_1 = 2$, and the gcd of column 2 is $g_2 = 3$. We introduce four new variables Y_1, Y_2, K_1, K_2 in terms of I_1, I_2 by the equation:

$$(I_1, I_2) = (Y_1, Y_2) + (K_1, K_2) \begin{pmatrix} 2 & 0 \\ 0 & 3 \end{pmatrix}$$

or

$$(I_1, I_2) = (Y_1 + 2K_1, Y_2 + 3K_2),$$

and the constraints:

$$0 \le Y_1 \le 1, 0 \le Y_2 \le 2.$$

By Theorem 4.5, the program:

doall $Y_1 = 0, 1$
doall $Y_2 = 0, 2$
        do $K_1 = \lceil (1 - Y_1)/2 \rceil, \lfloor (100 - Y_1)/2 \rfloor$
        do $K_2 = \lceil (Y_1 + 2K_1 - Y_2)/3 \rceil, \lfloor (2Y_1 + 4K_1 + 4 - Y_2)/3 \rfloor$
         $X(Y_1 + 2K_1, Y_2 + 3K_2) =$
                $X(Y_1 + 2K_1 - 2, Y_2 + 3K_2 - 3) +$
                $X(Y_1 + 2K_1, Y_2 + 3K_2 - 6)$
    enddo
    enddo
  enddoall
  enddoall

is equivalent to **L**. By Corollary 2, the distance matrix of the nest of **K**-loops is

$$\begin{pmatrix} 2 & 3 \\ 0 & 6 \end{pmatrix} \cdot \begin{pmatrix} 2 & 0 \\ 0 & 3 \end{pmatrix}^{-1} = \begin{pmatrix} 1 & 1 \\ 0 & 2 \end{pmatrix}.$$

In the next example, we have the case where not every g_r is positive. It is handled by moving outward the loops L_r with $g_r = 0$, and then looking at those loops for which $g_r > 0$.

Example 4.3 Consider the triple loop **L**:

L_1 :   **do** $I_1 = 1, 100$
L_2 :   **do** $I_2 = 1, 100$
L_3 :   **do** $I_3 = 1, 100$
                 $X(I_1, I_2, I_3) = X(I_1 - 4, I_2 - 3, I_3) +$
                             $X(I_1 - 6, I_2 + 9, I_3)$
             enddo
          enddo
       enddo

whose distance matrix is

$$\begin{pmatrix} 4 & 3 & 0 \\ 6 & -9 & 0 \end{pmatrix}.$$

The gcd of the third column is zero. Note that the permutation $(L_1, L_2, L_3) \mapsto (L_3, L_1, L_2)$ is valid. After this permutation, we get the equivalent loop nest:

L_3 :   **do** $I_3 = 1, 100$
L_1 :   **do** $I_1 = 1, 100$
L_2 :   **do** $I_2 = 1, 100$
                 $X(I_1, I_2, I_3) = X(I_1 - 4, I_2 - 3, I_3) +$
                             $X(I_1 - 6, I_2 + 9, I_3)$
             enddo
          enddo
       enddo

The new distance matrix is

$$\begin{pmatrix} 0 & 4 & 3 \\ 0 & 6 & -9 \end{pmatrix}.$$

Since the outermost loop in the nest (L_3, L_1, L_2) carries no dependence, it can execute in parallel.

Consider the inner loop nest (L_1, L_2) with distance vector (I_1, I_2) and distance matrix:

$$\begin{pmatrix} 4 & 3 \\ 6 & -9 \end{pmatrix}.$$

Apply Theorem 4.5 to this nest. The gcd of the first column of the distance matrix is $g_1 = \gcd(4, 6) = 2$, and the gcd of the second column is $g_2 = \gcd(3, -9) = 3$. The variables I_1, I_2 are replaced by new variables Y_1, Y_2, K_1, K_2, where

$$(I_1, I_2) = (Y_1, Y_2) + (K_1, K_2) \begin{pmatrix} 2 & 0 \\ 0 & 3 \end{pmatrix} = (Y_1 + 2K_1, Y_2 + 3K_2)$$

and
$$0 \le Y_1 \le 1, \, 0 \le Y_2 \le 2.$$

Transforming (L_1, L_2) by Theorem 4.5 and changing the I_3-loop to its corresponding **doall** loop, we get the following program equivalent to the given triple loop (L_1, L_2, L_3):

doall $I_3 = 1, 100$
    doall $Y_1 = 0, 1$
    doall $Y_2 = 0, 2$
        do $K_1 = \lceil(1 - Y_1)/2\rceil, \lfloor(100 - Y_1)/2\rfloor$
        do $K_2 = \lceil(1 - Y_2)/3\rceil, \lfloor(100 - Y_2)/3\rfloor$
            $X(Y_1 + 2K_1, Y_2 + 3K_2, I_3) =$
                $X(Y_1 + 2K_1 - 4, Y_2 + 3K_2 - 3, I_3) +$
                $X(Y_1 + 2K_1 - 6, Y_2 + 3K_2 + 9, I_3)$
        enddo
        enddo
    enddoall
    enddoall
enddoall

We will now outline two other slightly different approaches to the problem of vanishing gcd's; they are ultimately equivalent to the method described in the above example.

We may transform separately each loop L_r such that $g_r > 0$ using Theorem 4.3, and then use loop permutation to push outward all loops that have zero columns in the distance matrix. Take any loop L_r such that $g_r > 0$. As in Theorem 4.3, introduce two new variables Y_r and K_r by $I_r = Y_r + g_r K_r$ and $0 \leq Y_r \leq g_r - 1$. Replace the loop L_r by a nest (L_{r2}, L_{r1}) with index vector (Y_r, K_r), where Y_r has the range

$$0 \leq Y_r \leq g_r - 1,$$

and K_r the range

$$\lceil (p_r - Y_r)/g_r \rceil \leq K_r \leq \lfloor (q_r - Y_r)/g_r \rfloor.$$

Replace I_r by the expression $Y_r + g_r K_r$ throughout the current state of the program. Then the transformed nest of $m + 1$ loops:

$$(L_1, L_2, \ldots, L_{r-1}, L_{r2}, L_{r1}, L_{r+1}, \ldots, L_m)$$

is equivalent to $\mathbf{L}$. Its distance vectors are of the form

$$(d_1, d_2, \ldots, d_{r-1}, 0, d_r/g_r, d_{r+1}, \ldots, d_m)$$

where $(d_1, d_2, \ldots, d_m)$ is a distance vector of $\mathbf{L}$. The proof is similar to the proof of Theorem 4.3.[4]

Process the loops $L_1, L_2, \ldots, L_m$ one by one as described above, based on whether the corresponding gcd g_r is positive. Let $\tilde{\mathbf{L}}$ denote the final loop nest. The number of loops in it is clearly $(m+n)$ where n is the number of nonzero columns of $\mathcal{D}$. Let $\tilde{\mathcal{D}}$ denote the distance matrix of $\tilde{\mathbf{L}}$; it has $(m+n)$ columns of which m are equal to the zero vector. Move the m loops of $\tilde{\mathbf{L}}$ corresponding to the zero columns of $\tilde{\mathcal{D}}$ outward over the remaining loops. This permutation is valid (Corollary 1 to Theorem 2.8). After the permutation, each of these loops can execute in parallel (Lemma 1.1). Thus, we finally get an equivalent nest with an outer ring of m **doall** loops and a core of n **do** loops.

In another approach, we could generalize the gcd transformation by modifying the conditions (4.11) and (4.12) to accommodate the possibility that one or more g_r may be zero. The main problem now

---

[4]The only major difference now is that each d_r is not necessarily positive, while all dependence distances in the single loop case were positive. This, however, causes no problems.

is that (4.12) cannot define a K_r if the corresponding g_r is zero. We take $K_r = 0$ in this case and agree that the K_r-loop in the final program will be deleted. Also, $g_r = 0$ implies $Y_r = I_r$, so that the limits of the Y_r-loop have to be found by the usual elimination process during loop permutation.

To avoid confusion, we will restrict the gcd transformation to a loop nest such that each gcd g_r is positive, and use loop permutation along with the gcd transformation to handle more general loop nests as illustrated in Example 4.3.

EXERCISES 4.3

1. Prove that $\mathbf{dG}^{-1}$ is a uniform distance vector of $\mathbf{L_G}$ iff $\mathbf{d}$ is a uniform distance vector of $\mathbf{L}$.

2. For each loop nest given below, use the method of this section to find an equivalent mixed loop nest with an outermost ring of **doall** loops. Also, find the distance matrix of the inner nest of **do** loops.

   (a)   **do** $I_1 = 1, 100$
         do $I_2 = I_1, 100$
            $X(I_1, I_2) = X(I_1 - 4, I_2 - 6) + X(I_1 + 8, I_2 - 8)$
         enddo
       enddo

   (b)   **do** $I_1 = 1, 100$
         do $I_2 = 1, I_1$
            $X(I_1, I_2) = X(I_1 - 2, I_2 - 3) + X(I_1 - 1, I_2 - 6)$
         enddo
       enddo

   (c)   **do** $I_1 = 1, 100$
         do $I_2 = 2I_1, 100$
            do $I_3 = 1, 100$
               $X(I_1, I_2, I_3) = X(I_1 - 2, I_2, I_3 - 3) +$
                           $X(I_1 - 4, I_2, I_3 - 6) +$
                           $X(I_1 - 2, I_2, I_3 + 3)$
            enddo
         enddo
       enddo

3. In Theorem 4.5, would we gain anything by applying the theorem again to the nest of **K**-loops? Explain.

4.4   Echelon Transformation

In this section, we will study a remainder transformation that separates index points more carefully than the gcd transformation, and produces more vertical parallelism in general.

Let N denote the number of distance vectors in the loop nest **L**. Apply Algorithm I-2.2 to the $N \times m$ distance matrix $\mathcal{D}$ to find an $N \times N$ unimodular matrix **V** and an $N \times m$ echelon matrix $\mathbf{S} = (s_{tr})$, such that

$$\mathcal{D} = \mathbf{VS}. \qquad (4.16)$$

Let ρ denote the number of nonzero rows of **S**, so that

$$\rho = \mathrm{rank}(\mathcal{D}) = \mathrm{rank}(\mathbf{S}). \qquad (4.17)$$

For $1 \le t \le \rho$, let $s_{t\ell_t}$ denote the leading element of row t. Without any loss of generality, we may assume that all these leading elements are positive (why?), that is, the nonzero rows of **S** are (lexicographically) positive. Let $\hat{\mathbf{S}}$ denote the $\rho \times m$ submatrix of **S** consisting of the nonzero rows, and $\hat{\mathbf{V}}$ the $N \times \rho$ submatrix of **V** consisting of the leftmost ρ columns. Then, $\mathcal{D}$ can be written in the form:

$$\mathcal{D} = \hat{\mathbf{V}}\hat{\mathbf{S}}. \qquad (4.18)$$

Any row of $\hat{\mathbf{V}}$ postmultiplied by $\hat{\mathbf{S}}$ gives a row of $\mathcal{D}$. Since the rows of $\mathcal{D}$ are positive, the following lemma implies that so are the rows of $\hat{\mathbf{V}}$.

Lemma 4.6 *Let*

$$\mathbf{d} = \mathbf{v}\hat{\mathbf{S}}$$

where **d** *is an m-vector,* **v** *is a ρ-vector, and* $\hat{\mathbf{S}} = (s_{tr})$ *is a $\rho \times m$ echelon matrix with rank ρ and (lexicographically) positive rows. Then,* **v** *is positive iff* **d** *is positive, and* **v** *is zero iff* **d** *is zero.*

PROOF.   For $1 \le t \le \rho$, let ℓ_t denote the column of the leading element of row t. By hypothesis, these elements are all positive. Let

$\mathbf{d} = (d_1, d_2, \ldots, d_m)$ and $\mathbf{v} = (v_1, v_2, \ldots, v_\rho)$. We will indicate how to prove by induction that $\mathbf{d} \succ \mathbf{0}$ implies $\mathbf{v} \succ \mathbf{0}$. Other implications can be established similarly.

The equation giving d_r is

$$d_r = v_1 s_{1r} + v_2 s_{2r} + \cdots + v_\rho s_{\rho r} \quad (1 \leq r \leq m).$$

For $1 \leq r < \ell_1$, column r of $\hat{\mathbf{S}}$ is zero, so that $d_r = 0$. Then, we have $d_{\ell_1} = v_1 s_{1\ell_1}$. If $d_{\ell_1} > 0$, then $v_1 > 0$, so that $\mathbf{v} \succ \mathbf{0}$. Assume $d_{\ell_1} = 0$ which implies $v_1 = 0$. For $\ell_1 < r < \ell_2$, column r of $\hat{\mathbf{S}}$ has zeroes in rows 2 through ρ, so that $d_r = 0$. Then, d_{ℓ_2} is given by $d_{\ell_2} = v_2 s_{2\ell_2}$. If $d_{\ell_2} > 0$, then $v_2 > 0$, so that $\mathbf{v} \succ \mathbf{0}$. Assume $d_{\ell_2} = 0$ which implies $v_2 = 0$; and continue this process. Since the leading element of $\mathbf{d}$ is positive, we will eventually come to a positive leading element for $\mathbf{v}$. □

Let $\mathbf{Y}$ denote an m-vector and $\mathbf{K}$ a ρ-vector: $\mathbf{Y} = (Y_1, Y_2, \ldots, Y_m)$ and $\mathbf{K} = (K_1, K_2, \ldots, K_\rho)$. The echelon decomposition $\mathcal{D} = \mathbf{VS}$ of the distance matrix leads to a mapping $\mathbf{I} \mapsto (\mathbf{Y}; \mathbf{K})$ of the index space $\mathcal{R}$ of $\mathbf{L}$ into $\mathbf{Z}^{m+\rho}$. It is defined by the equation:

$$\mathbf{I} = \mathbf{Y} + \mathbf{K}\hat{\mathbf{S}} \tag{4.19}$$

and the constraints:

$$0 \leq Y_{\ell_t} \leq s_{t\ell_t} - 1 \quad (1 \leq t \leq \rho). \tag{4.20}$$

Lemma 4.7 *The mapping $\mathbf{I} \mapsto (\mathbf{Y}; \mathbf{K})$ of the index space $\mathcal{R}$ into $\mathbf{Z}^{m+\rho}$ defined by (4.19) and (4.20) is well-defined and one-to-one.*

PROOF. The leading element of row 1 of $\hat{\mathbf{S}}$ is $s_{1\ell_1}$. The scalar equation contained in (4.19) corresponding to column ℓ_1 of $\hat{\mathbf{S}}$ is

$$I_{\ell_1} = Y_{\ell_1} + s_{1\ell_1} K_1.$$

Since

$$0 \leq Y_{\ell_1} \leq s_{1\ell_1} - 1$$

by (4.20), we get

$$K_1 = \lfloor I_{\ell_1}/s_{1\ell_1} \rfloor.$$

The scalar equation contained in (4.19) corresponding to column ℓ_2 of $\hat{\mathbf{S}}$ is

$$I_{\ell_2} = Y_{\ell_2} + s_{1\ell_2}K_1 + s_{2\ell_2}K_2$$

or

$$I_{\ell_2} - s_{1\ell_2}K_1 = Y_{\ell_2} + s_{2\ell_2}K_2.$$

Since

$$0 \le Y_{\ell_2} \le s_{2\ell_2} - 1$$

by (4.20), we get

$$K_2 = \lfloor (I_{\ell_2} - s_{1\ell_2}K_1)/s_{2\ell_2} \rfloor.$$

Continuing this process, we can find sequentially unique expressions for the elements of the vector $\mathbf{K}$ in terms of the elements of $\mathbf{I}$; the elements of $\mathbf{Y}$ do not appear in these expressions.

Once $\mathbf{K}$ has been completely determined, the vector $\mathbf{Y}$ is found from the equation: $\mathbf{Y} = \mathbf{I} - \mathbf{K}\hat{\mathbf{S}}$, and it is unique. Thus, the mapping of the lemma is well-defined.

Also, for any given $\mathbf{Y}$ satisfying (4.20) and any given $\mathbf{K}$, there is only one $\mathbf{I}$ that is mapped to $(\mathbf{Y}; \mathbf{K})$, namely, the one given by (4.19). Hence, the mapping of the lemma is one-to-one.   □

This one-to-one mapping $\mathbf{I} \mapsto (\mathbf{Y}; \mathbf{K})$ of $\mathcal{R}$ discussed above defines a new execution order for the iterations of $\mathbf{L}$. Let $\mathbf{L_S}$ denote the program consisting of the iterations of $\mathbf{L}$ such that they are executed in the increasing order of the vector:

$$(\mathbf{Y}; \mathbf{K}) = (Y_1, Y_2, \ldots, Y_m, K_1, K_2, \ldots, K_\rho).$$

Theorem 4.8 *The program* $\mathbf{L_S}$ *can be expressed as a nest of* $(m + \rho)$ *loops. It is equivalent to* $\mathbf{L}$, *and the* m *outermost loops (the* $\mathbf{Y}$-*loops) can execute in parallel.*

PROOF. The index vector $\mathbf{I}$ of $\mathbf{L}$ satisfies the following constraints:

$$\left. \begin{array}{rcl} \mathbf{p_0} & \leq & \mathbf{IP} \\ \mathbf{IQ} & \leq & \mathbf{q_0.} \end{array} \right\} \qquad (4.21)$$

Substituting from (4.19), we get

$$\left. \begin{array}{rcl} \mathbf{p_0} & \leq & \mathbf{YP} + \mathbf{K}(\hat{\mathbf{S}}\mathbf{P}) \\ \mathbf{YQ} + \mathbf{K}(\hat{\mathbf{S}}\mathbf{Q}) & \leq & \mathbf{q_0.} \end{array} \right\} \qquad (4.22)$$

From the system of inequalities consisting of (4.20) and (4.22), eliminate the variables:

$$K_\rho, K_{\rho-1}, \ldots, K_1, Y_m, Y_{m-1}, \ldots, Y_1$$

(in this order) by Fourier Elimination (Algorithm I-3.2) to get bounds of the form:

$$\begin{array}{rcccl} \alpha_1 & \leq & Y_1 & \leq & \beta_1 \\ \alpha_2(Y_1) & \leq & Y_2 & \leq & \beta_2(Y_1) \\ & & \vdots & & \\ \alpha_m(Y_1, Y_2, \ldots, Y_{m-1}) & \leq & Y_m & \leq & \beta_m(Y_1, Y_2, \ldots, Y_{m-1}) \\ \alpha_{m+1}(\mathbf{Y}) & \leq & K_1 & \leq & \beta_{m+1}(\mathbf{Y}) \\ \alpha_{m+2}(\mathbf{Y}, K_1) & \leq & K_2 & \leq & \beta_{m+2}(\mathbf{Y}, K_1) \\ & & \vdots & & \\ \alpha_{m+\rho}(\mathbf{Y}, K_1, K_2, \ldots, K_{\rho-1}) & \leq & K_\rho & \leq & \beta_{m+\rho}(\mathbf{Y}, K_1, K_2, \ldots, K_{\rho-1}). \end{array}$$

For each value of $\mathbf{I}$ satisfying (4.21), there is a unique value of $(\mathbf{Y}; \mathbf{K})$ satisfying these constraints, and conversely. The nest of $(m + \rho)$ loops with index vector

$$(\mathbf{Y}; \mathbf{K}) = (Y_1, Y_2, \ldots, Y_m, K_1, K_2, \ldots, K_\rho)$$

and limits

$$\alpha_1, \beta_1, \alpha_2, \beta_2, \ldots, \alpha_{m+\rho}, \beta_{m+\rho}$$

has the same set of iterations as $\mathbf{L}$, and there the iterations are executed in the increasing order of $(\mathbf{Y}; \mathbf{K})$. Thus, the program $\mathbf{L_S}$ can be represented as this nest of loops.

To prove the equivalence of $\mathbf{L_S}$ to $\mathbf{L}$, consider two iterations $H(\mathbf{i})$ and $H(\mathbf{j})$ of $\mathbf{L}$ such that $H(\mathbf{j})$ depends on $H(\mathbf{i})$. Let $(\mathbf{y}; \mathbf{k})$ denote the value of $(\mathbf{Y}; \mathbf{K})$ corresponding to the value $\mathbf{i}$ of $\mathbf{I}$, and $(\mathbf{z}; \mathbf{l})$ the value corresponding to $\mathbf{j}$. Since $\mathbf{d} = \mathbf{j} - \mathbf{i}$ is a distance vector of $\mathbf{L}$, it follows from the relation $\mathcal{D} = \hat{\mathbf{V}}\hat{\mathbf{S}}$ that $\mathbf{d} = \mathbf{v}_a\hat{\mathbf{S}}$ for some row $\mathbf{v}_a$ of $\hat{\mathbf{V}}$. We have

$$
\begin{aligned}
\mathbf{j} &= \mathbf{i} + \mathbf{d} \\
&= \mathbf{y} + \mathbf{k}\hat{\mathbf{S}} + \mathbf{v}_a\hat{\mathbf{S}} \\
&= \mathbf{y} + (\mathbf{k} + \mathbf{v}_a)\hat{\mathbf{S}}.
\end{aligned}
$$

Since $\mathbf{y}$ satisfies (4.20), $(\mathbf{y}; \mathbf{k} + \mathbf{v}_a)$ is the image of $\mathbf{j}$ under the mapping of Lemma 4.7. But the image of $\mathbf{j}$ is also $(\mathbf{z}, \mathbf{l})$, by assumption. Since this mapping is well-defined, it follows that

$$
\begin{aligned}
\mathbf{z} &= \mathbf{y} & (4.23) \\
\mathbf{l} - \mathbf{k} &= \mathbf{v}_a. & (4.24)
\end{aligned}
$$

Then,

$$
(\mathbf{z}; \mathbf{l}) - (\mathbf{y}; \mathbf{k}) = (\mathbf{z} - \mathbf{y}; \mathbf{l} - \mathbf{k}) = (\mathbf{0}; \mathbf{v}_a)
$$

is positive, since $\mathbf{v}_a$ is positive by Lemma 4.6. Hence, the iteration $H(\mathbf{z} + \mathbf{l}\hat{\mathbf{S}})$ or $H(\mathbf{j})$ will be executed after the iteration $H(\mathbf{y} + \mathbf{k}\hat{\mathbf{S}})$ or $H(\mathbf{i})$ in the loop nest $\mathbf{L_S}$. In other words, $\mathbf{L_S}$ is equivalent to $\mathbf{L}$.

It is clear that any distance vector of $\mathbf{L_S}$ is of the form $(\mathbf{0}; \mathbf{v}_a)$. Since the outermost m loops of $\mathbf{L_S}$ carry no dependence, they can execute in parallel (Lemma 1.1). □

Corollary 1 *The distance matrix of the nest of $\mathbf{K}$-loops is $\hat{\mathbf{V}}$.*

PROOF. We showed in the proof of the above theorem that each distance vector $(\mathbf{z} - \mathbf{y}; \mathbf{l} - \mathbf{k})$ of the loop nest $\mathbf{L_S}$ has the form $(\mathbf{0}; \mathbf{v}_a)$ where $\mathbf{v}_a$ is a row of $\hat{\mathbf{V}}$. It can be shown similarly that each row $\mathbf{v}_a$ of $\hat{\mathbf{V}}$ gives a distance vector $(\mathbf{0}; \mathbf{v}_a)$ of $\mathbf{L_S}$. Thus, the rows of $\hat{\mathbf{V}}$ constitute the distance vectors of the nest of $\mathbf{K}$-loops in $\mathbf{L_S}$. □

Corollary 2 *If $\rho = m$, then the number of iterations of the nest of* **Y**-*loops in* $\mathbf{L_S}$ *is* $|\det(\mathcal{D})|$, *and the distance matrix of the nest of* **K**-*loops is* $\mathbf{V}$.

PROOF. The proof is simple and is left to the reader. □

Let $\mathbf{L'_S}$ denote the mixed loop nest after the **Y**-loops in $\mathbf{L_S}$ have been changed into their corresponding **doall** loops. Take any two index values $(\mathbf{y}; \mathbf{k})$ and $(\mathbf{z}; \mathbf{l})$ in $\mathbf{L'_S}$. The iteration $H(\mathbf{y} + \mathbf{k}\hat{\mathbf{S}})$ will execute before the iteration $H(\mathbf{z} + \mathbf{l}\hat{\mathbf{S}})$, iff $\mathbf{y} = \mathbf{z}$ and $\mathbf{k} \prec \mathbf{l}$. The following corollary shows that the execution order of iterations in $\mathbf{L'_S}$ is independent of the particular echelon decomposition $\mathcal{D} = \mathbf{VS}$ of $\mathcal{D}$ used.

Corollary 3 *Consider any two distinct iterations $H(\mathbf{i})$ and $H(\mathbf{j})$ of* **L**. *In* $\mathbf{L'_S}$, $H(\mathbf{i})$ *will execute before* $H(\mathbf{j})$, *iff*

$$\mathbf{j} - \mathbf{i} = \mathbf{e}\mathcal{D}$$

for some integer vector $\mathbf{e}$ *and* $\mathbf{i} \prec \mathbf{j}$.

PROOF. Let $(\mathbf{y}; \mathbf{k})$ denote the value of $(\mathbf{Y}; \mathbf{K})$ corresponding to $\mathbf{i}$ and $(\mathbf{z}; \mathbf{l})$ the value corresponding to $\mathbf{j}$, so that

$$\mathbf{i} = \mathbf{y} + \mathbf{k}\hat{\mathbf{S}} \quad \text{and} \quad \mathbf{j} = \mathbf{z} + \mathbf{l}\hat{\mathbf{S}}.$$

The 'if' Part: Let $\mathbf{j} - \mathbf{i} = \mathbf{e}\mathcal{D}$ and $\mathbf{i} \prec \mathbf{j}$. We have

$$
\begin{aligned}
\mathbf{j} - \mathbf{i} &= \mathbf{e}\mathcal{D} \\
&= \mathbf{e}\hat{\mathbf{V}}\hat{\mathbf{S}} \quad &\text{(by (4.18))} \\
&= \mathbf{f}\hat{\mathbf{S}} \quad &\text{where } \mathbf{f} = \mathbf{e}\hat{\mathbf{V}}.
\end{aligned}
$$

Since $\mathbf{j} - \mathbf{i} \succ \mathbf{0}$ and the rows of $\hat{\mathbf{S}}$ are positive, Lemma 4.6 implies that $\mathbf{f} \succ \mathbf{0}$. Also, as in the proof of Theorem 4.8, we can show that

$$
\begin{aligned}
\mathbf{z} &= \mathbf{y} \\
\mathbf{l} - \mathbf{k} &= \mathbf{f}.
\end{aligned}
$$

Then, since $\mathbf{y} = \mathbf{z}$ and $\mathbf{k} \prec \mathbf{l}$, the iteration $H(\mathbf{y} + \mathbf{k}\hat{\mathbf{S}})$ or $H(\mathbf{i})$ will execute before the iteration $H(\mathbf{z} + \mathbf{l}\hat{\mathbf{S}})$ or $H(\mathbf{j})$ in $\mathbf{L}'_{\mathbf{S}}$.

The 'only if' Part: Suppose that the iteration $H(\mathbf{i})$ or $H(\mathbf{y}+\mathbf{k}\hat{\mathbf{S}})$ will execute before the iteration $H(\mathbf{j})$ or $H(\mathbf{z}+\mathbf{l}\hat{\mathbf{S}})$ in $\mathbf{L}'_{\mathbf{S}}$. Then, we have $\mathbf{y} = \mathbf{z}$ and $\mathbf{k} \prec \mathbf{l}$. This implies

$$
\begin{aligned}
\mathbf{j} - \mathbf{i} &= (\mathbf{z} + \mathbf{l}\hat{\mathbf{S}}) - (\mathbf{y} + \mathbf{k}\hat{\mathbf{S}}) \\
&= (\mathbf{l} - \mathbf{k}) \cdot \hat{\mathbf{S}} \\
&= (\mathbf{l} - \mathbf{k}; \mathbf{0}) \cdot \mathbf{S} && \text{(where } \mathbf{0} \text{ has } (N - \rho) \text{ elements)} \\
&= (\mathbf{l} - \mathbf{k}; \mathbf{0}) \cdot \mathbf{V}^{-1}\mathcal{D} && \text{(by (4.16))} \\
&= \mathbf{e}\mathcal{D}
\end{aligned}
$$

where $\mathbf{e}$ is an integer m-vector. (Since $\mathbf{V}$ is unimodular, $\mathbf{V}^{-1}$ is an integer matrix.)   □

The loop nest $\mathbf{L}'_{\mathbf{S}}$ has the same set of iterations as that of $\mathbf{L}$, and the execution order of iterations in it is independent of the particular echelon decomposition $\mathcal{D} = \mathbf{VS}$ of $\mathcal{D}$ used. (The distance matrix of the nest of $\mathbf{K}$-loops depends on the choice of $\mathbf{V}$.) Thus, there is a unique program $\mathbf{L}'$ that can be represented by a loop nest of the form $\mathbf{L}'_{\mathbf{S}}$, where $\mathbf{S}$ is any echelon matrix (whose nonzero rows are positive) derived from $\mathcal{D}$. The transformation $\mathbf{L} \mapsto \mathbf{L}'$ is called the *echelon transformation* of the loop nest $\mathbf{L}$.

The major steps in getting to the echelon transformation are summarized below:

Algorithm 4.1 (Echelon Transformation) For a nest $\mathbf{L}$ of m **do** loops, this algorithm finds an equivalent loop nest representing the echelon transformation. We assume as given: the lower limit matrix $\mathbf{P}$, the lower limit vector $\mathbf{p}_0$, the upper limit matrix $\mathbf{Q}$, the upper limit vector $\mathbf{q}_0$, the body $H(\mathbf{I})$ in terms of the index vector $\mathbf{I}$, and the $N \times m$ distance matrix $\mathcal{D}$. We will find the rank ρ of $\mathcal{D}$, and a nest $\mathbf{L}'_{\mathbf{S}}$ (equivalent to $\mathbf{L}$) consisting of an outer nest of m **doall** loops with index variables $Y_1, Y_2, \ldots, Y_m$, and an inner nest of ρ **do** loops with index variables $K_1, K_2, \ldots, K_\rho$. Let $\mathbf{Y} = (Y_1, Y_2, \ldots, Y_m)$ and $\mathbf{K} = (K_1, K_2, \ldots, K_\rho)$. We will also find the distance matrix of the nest of $\mathbf{K}$-loops.

1. By Algorithm I-2.2 (Modified Echelon Reduction algorithm), find an $N \times N$ unimodular matrix $\mathbf{V}$ and an $N \times m$ echelon matrix $\mathbf{S} = (s_{tr})$, such that $\mathcal{D} = \mathbf{VS}$.

2. Set ρ to be the number of nonzero rows of $\mathbf{S}$.

   [We have $\mathrm{rank}(\mathbf{S}) = \mathrm{rank}(\mathcal{D}) = \rho$.]

3. For $1 \leq t \leq \rho$, if row t of $\mathbf{S}$ is (lexicographically) negative, then multiply it by -1, and also multiply column t of $\mathbf{V}$ by -1.

   [All nonzero rows of $\mathbf{S}$ are now positive.]

4. Find the leading elements $s_{1\ell_1}, s_{2\ell_2}, \ldots, s_{\rho\ell_\rho}$ of the nonzero rows of $\mathbf{S}$.

   [These leading elements are all positive.]

5. Find the $\rho \times m$ submatrix $\hat{\mathbf{S}}$ of $\mathbf{S}$ consisting of its nonzero rows (the topmost ρ rows), and the $N \times \rho$ submatrix $\hat{\mathbf{V}}$ of $\mathbf{V}$ consisting of its leftmost ρ columns.

6. Take $H(\mathbf{Y} + \mathbf{K}\hat{\mathbf{S}})$ to be the body of $\mathbf{L}'_{\mathbf{S}}$.

7. By Algorithm I-3.2 (Fourier elimination), find the lower and upper limits of the variables:

$$Y_1, Y_2, \ldots, Y_m, K_1, K_2, \ldots, K_\rho,$$

by eliminating them in the reverse order from the inequalities:

$$\left. \begin{array}{rcl} \mathbf{p_0} & \leq & (\mathbf{Y} + \mathbf{K}\hat{\mathbf{S}})\mathbf{P} \\ (\mathbf{Y} + \mathbf{K}\hat{\mathbf{S}})\mathbf{Q} & \leq & \mathbf{q_0} \end{array} \right\}$$

and

$$0 \leq Y_{\ell_t} \leq s_{t\ell_t} - 1 \quad (1 \leq t \leq \rho).$$

8. Take the submatrix $\hat{\mathbf{V}}$ of $\mathbf{V}$ as the distance matrix of the nest of $\mathbf{K}$-loops in $\mathbf{L}'_{\mathbf{S}}$.

Example 4.4 Consider again the double loop **L** of Example 4.2:

$$\begin{aligned}
&\textbf{do } I_1 = 1, 100\\
&\quad \textbf{do } I_2 = I_1, 2I_1 + 4\\
&\qquad X(I_1, I_2) = X(I_1 - 2, I_2 - 3) + X(I_1, I_2 - 6)\\
&\quad \textbf{enddo}\\
&\textbf{enddo}
\end{aligned}$$

We will find the echelon transformation by Algorithm 4.1, and show that it can capture more vertical parallelism in a given program than the gcd transformation. The distance matrix

$$\mathcal{D} = \begin{pmatrix} 2 & 3 \\ 0 & 6 \end{pmatrix}$$

is already an echelon matrix with positive rows, and the rank is 2. Define a mapping $(I_1, I_2) \mapsto (Y_1, Y_2, K_1, K_2)$ of the index space of **L** into $\mathbf{Z}^4$ by the equation:

$$(I_1, I_2) = (Y_1, Y_2) + (K_1, K_2) \cdot \begin{pmatrix} 2 & 3 \\ 0 & 6 \end{pmatrix}$$

or

$$(I_1, I_2) = (Y_1 + 2K_1, Y_2 + 3K_1 + 6K_2), \tag{4.25}$$

and the constraints:

$$\left. \begin{aligned} 0 \le Y_1 \le 1\\ 0 \le Y_2 \le 5. \end{aligned} \right\} \tag{4.26}$$

The index variables I_1 and I_2 satisfy the constraints:

$$\left. \begin{aligned} 1 \;\le\; &I_1 \;\le\; 100\\ I_1 \;\le\; &I_2 \;\le\; 2I_1 + 4. \end{aligned} \right\}$$

Substituting from (4.25), we get

$$\left. \begin{aligned} 1 \;\le\; \quad Y_1 + 2K_1 \quad &\le\; 100\\ Y_1 + 2K_1 \;\le\; Y_2 + 3K_1 + 6K_2 &\le\; 2Y_1 + 4K_1 + 4. \end{aligned} \right\} \tag{4.27}$$

Eliminate the variables K_2, K_1, Y_2, Y_1 (in this order) from the system of inequalities (4.26) and (4.27) to derive the following set of bounds:

$$\left.\begin{array}{ccccc}
0 & \leq & Y_1 & \leq & 1 \\
0 & \leq & Y_2 & \leq & 5 \\
\lceil (1 - Y_1)/2 \rceil & \leq & K_1 & \leq & \lfloor (100 - Y_1)/2 \rfloor \\
\lceil (Y_1 - Y_2 - K_1)/6 \rceil & \leq & K_2 & \leq & \lfloor (2Y_1 - Y_2 + K_1 + 4)/6 \rfloor.
\end{array}\right\}$$

The mixed loop nest $\mathbf{L_S'}$:

> **doall** $Y_1 = 0, 1$
> **doall** $Y_2 = 0, 5$
>   **do** $K_1 = \lceil (1 - Y_1)/2 \rceil, \lfloor (100 - Y_1)/2 \rfloor$
>   **do** $K_2 = \lceil (Y_1 - Y_2 - K_1)/6 \rceil, \lfloor (2Y_1 - Y_2 + K_1 + 4)/6 \rfloor$
> $X(Y_1 + 2K_1, Y_2 + 3K_1 + 6K_2)$
> $= X(Y_1 + 2K_1 - 2, Y_2 + 3K_1 + 6K_2 - 3) +$
> $X(Y_1 + 2K_1, Y_2 + 3K_1 + 6K_2 - 6)$
>   **enddo**
>   **enddo**
> **enddoall**
> **enddoall**

is equivalent to **L**. This program represents a vertical partition with 12 members, while the program obtained by the gcd transformation in Example 4.2 represented one with 6 members.

We did not have to find an echelon decomposition of $\mathcal{D}$ explicitly, since $\mathcal{D}$ was echelon to start with. The echelon decomposition here is:

$$\begin{pmatrix} 2 & 3 \\ 0 & 6 \end{pmatrix} = \begin{pmatrix} 1 & 0 \\ 0 & 1 \end{pmatrix} \cdot \begin{pmatrix} 2 & 3 \\ 0 & 6 \end{pmatrix}.$$

The unimodular matrix $\mathbf{V}$ in this case is the 2×2 identity matrix $\mathcal{I}_2$. Thus, the distance matrix of the nest of **K**-loops in the above mixed loop nest is $\mathcal{I}_2$ (Corollary 2 to Theorem 4.8).

Example 4.5 Consider the triple loop **L**:

L_1 :   **do** $I_1 = 1, 100$
L_2 :   **do** $I_2 = 1, 200$
L_3 :   **do** $I_3 = I_1, 300$
$$X(I_1, I_2, I_3) = X(I_1 - 1, I_2 - 3, I_3) +$$
$$X(I_1 - 2, I_2 - 10, I_3) +$$
$$X(I_1 - 1, I_2 + 1, I_3)$$
            enddo
         enddo
      enddo

whose distance matrix is

$$\mathcal{D} = \begin{pmatrix} 1 & 3 & 0 \\ 2 & 10 & 0 \\ 1 & -1 & 0 \end{pmatrix}.$$

By Algorithm I-2.2, we find two matrices

$$\mathbf{V} = \begin{pmatrix} 1 & 1 & 0 \\ 2 & 3 & 1 \\ 1 & 0 & 0 \end{pmatrix} \quad \text{and} \quad \mathbf{S} = \begin{pmatrix} 1 & -1 & 0 \\ 0 & 4 & 0 \\ 0 & 0 & 0 \end{pmatrix},$$

such that $\mathbf{V}$ is unimodular, $\mathbf{S}$ is echelon, and $\mathcal{D} = \mathbf{VS}$. The leading elements of nonzero rows of $\mathbf{S}$ are positive. It is clear that

$$\rho = \text{rank}(\mathcal{D}) = \text{rank}(\mathbf{S}) = 2.$$

The submatrix $\hat{\mathbf{S}}$ of $\mathbf{S}$ consisting of its nonzero rows is given by

$$\hat{\mathbf{S}} = \begin{pmatrix} 1 & -1 & 0 \\ 0 & 4 & 0 \end{pmatrix}.$$

Define a mapping $(I_1, I_2, I_3) \mapsto (Y_1, Y_2, Y_3, K_1, K_2)$ of the index space of **L** into $\mathbf{Z}^5$ by the equation:

$$(I_1, I_2, I_3) = (Y_1, Y_2, Y_3) + (K_1, K_2) \cdot \begin{pmatrix} 1 & -1 & 0 \\ 0 & 4 & 0 \end{pmatrix} \tag{4.28}$$

and the constraints:

$$0 \leq Y_1 \leq 0 \quad \text{and} \quad 0 \leq Y_2 \leq 3. \tag{4.29}$$

Equation (4.28) is equivalent to the system:

$$\left.\begin{array}{rcl} I_1 & = & Y_1 + K_1 \\ I_2 & = & Y_2 - K_1 + 4K_2 \\ I_3 & = & Y_3. \end{array}\right\} \tag{4.30}$$

Substituting for I_1, I_2, I_3 from (4.30) into the constraints defining the loop limits of **L**, we get the following set of inequalities:

$$\left.\begin{array}{ccccc} 1 & \leq & Y_1 + K_1 & \leq & 100 \\ 1 & \leq & Y_2 - K_1 + 4K_2 & \leq & 200 \\ Y_1 + K_1 & \leq & Y_3 & \leq & 300. \end{array}\right\} \tag{4.31}$$

Eliminate the variables K_2, K_1, Y_3, Y_2, Y_1 from (4.29) and (4.31):

$$\left.\begin{array}{ccccc} \lceil (1 - Y_2 + K_1)/4 \rceil & \leq & K_2 & \leq & \lfloor (200 - Y_2 + K_1)/4 \rfloor \\ 1 - Y_1 & \leq & K_1 & \leq & \min(100 - Y_1, Y_3 - Y_1) \\ 1 & \leq & Y_3 & \leq & 300 \\ 0 & \leq & Y_2 & \leq & 3 \\ 0 & \leq & Y_1 & \leq & 0. \end{array}\right\}$$

Using the fact that $Y_1 = 0$, we simplify expressions and get the following program equivalent to **L** according to Algorithm 4.1:

```
doall Y₂ = 0, 3
doall Y₃ = 1, 300
      do K₁ = 1, min(100, Y₃)
      do K₂ = ⌈(1 − Y₂ + K₁)/4⌉, ⌊(200 − Y₂ + K₁)/4⌋
      X(K₁, Y₂ − K₁ + 4K₂, Y₃) =
              X(K₁ − 1, Y₂ − K₁ + 4K₂ − 3, Y₃) +
              X(K₁ − 2, Y₂ − K₁ + 4K₂ − 10, Y₃) +
              X(K₁ − 1, Y₂ − K₁ + 4K₂ + 1, Y₃)
      enddo
      enddo
enddoall
enddoall
```

The distance matrix of the nest of **K**-loops is the submatrix consisting of the two leftmost columns of **V**, that is, the matrix:

$$\mathbf{V} = \begin{pmatrix} 1 & 1 \\ 2 & 3 \\ 1 & 0 \end{pmatrix}.$$

EXERCISES 4.4

1. Prove that a distance vector $\mathbf{v}_a$ of the nest of **K**-loops is uniform iff the corresponding distance vector $\mathbf{v}_a\hat{\mathbf{S}}$ of **L** is uniform (see Corollary 1 to Theorem 4.8).

2. Apply Algorithm 4.1 to the loop nest of Example 4.3.

3. Apply Algorithm 4.1 to the loop nests of Exercise 4.3.2.

4. Suppose we apply Theorem 4.8 to a nest of loops to get an equivalent program consisting of an outermost ring of **doall** loops and a core of **do** loops. Would we gain anything by applying the theorem again to this inner nest of **do**-loops? Explain.

For this chapter, we were influenced by the research of David Padua [Padu79] and that of Erik D'Hollander [D'Hol92]. The idea of breaking up the index vector into two parts using a special form of the distance matrix came from D'Hollander, as did the concept of the linear partition to be covered in Chapter 5. Important work related to the material of this chapter has been done by Constantine Polychronopoulos [Poly88], Jih-Kwon Peir & Ron Cytron [PeCy89], Weijia Shang & Jose Fortes ([ShFo88], [ShFo91]), and others.

Chapter 5

Program Partitioning

5.1 Introduction

In Section 1.5, we talked briefly about two kinds of parallelism: horizontal and vertical, and the two types of partitions of the dependence graph that correspond to them. A vertical partition is represented by a mixed loop nest with an outer ring of **doall** loops, and a horizontal partition is represented by a mixed loop nest with two parts: an outer ring of **do** loops and an inner core of **doall** loops. In Chapters 2–4, we studied various loop transformations, and showed how they can be used to find equivalent programs with innermost or outermost parallel loops. Thus, we have already developed methods to display horizontal and vertical parallelism in a given loop nest. The aim of this chapter is to put these results in proper perspective. We will look at a partition separately from the loop nests that can represent it. It then becomes easier to compare different partitions of a given type, and understand how they are situated between the worst and the best partitions from the point of view of parallelization.

We will study vertical partitions in Section 5.2, and horizontal partitions in Section 5.3. The two partitions will be combined in Section 5.4.

147

5.2   Vertical Partitions

Let $\mathcal{R}$ denote the index space of the loop nest **L** and $\mathcal{D}$ its distance matrix. Let there be N distance vectors of **L**, so that $\mathcal{D}$ is an $N \times m$ matrix. A partition of the dependence graph of **L** is *vertical* if two iterations $H(\mathbf{i})$ and $H(\mathbf{j})$ belong to the same member of the partition whenever they are weakly connected. Lemma 5.1 stated below follows immediately from the definition:

Lemma 5.1 *Any partition of the dependence graph coarser than a vertical partition is itself vertical.*

The finer a vertical partition is, the more members it has, and the better it is from the point of view of parallelization. The coarsest (i.e., the worst) vertical partition is obviously the trivial partition with a single member: the entire dependence graph. The finest (i.e., the best) vertical partition is the weak partition, the one consisting of the weakly connected components of the dependence graph (see Section I-1.4):

Theorem 5.2 *The weak partition of the dependence graph of the loop nest* **L** *is the finest vertical partition.*

PROOF. Since two weakly connected iterations must belong to the same weakly connected component, the weak partition is vertical. Now, take any arbitrary vertical partition of the dependence graph of **L**, and take any weakly connected component of the graph. Any two distinct iterations in the component are weakly connected, and therefore must belong to the same member of the other partition, since that partition is vertical. Hence, the weakly connected component is totally included in one member of the partition. This means the weak partition is finer than any vertical partition.   □

The following corollary is an immediate consequence of the above theorem; we omit the proof.

Corollary 1 *Any member of an arbitrary vertical partition of the dependence graph of* **L** *is the union of one or more weakly connected components of the graph.*

A vertical partition defines an execution order for the iterations of **L** in a natural way: An iteration $H(\mathbf{i})$ is executed before another iteration $H(\mathbf{j})$ if both iterations belong to the same member of the partition and $\mathbf{i} \prec \mathbf{j}$. Such an execution order is clearly valid since if $H(\mathbf{j})$ depends on $H(\mathbf{i})$, then the two iterations are weakly connected and $\mathbf{i} \prec \mathbf{j}$. Given a vertical partition, we want to find a loop nest equivalent to **L**, whose execution order is the same as that of the partition. This is referred to as *implementing* the vertical partition. The implementation displays *vertical parallelism* in the program.

The weak partition, the ideal vertical partition, is hard to implement since it depends very closely on the index space. The methods developed in this book let us implement other vertical partitions that are defined independently of the index space.

It is convenient to define a partition by its corresponding equivalence relation (Section I-1.2). Consider the relation between iterations of **L** defined by the requirement that $H(\mathbf{i})$ and $H(\mathbf{j})$ be related if $\mathbf{j} - \mathbf{i} = \mathbf{e}D$ for some integer vector $\mathbf{e}$. Clearly, it is an equivalence relation. The partition of the dependence graph consisting of the equivalence classes of this relation will be called the *linear partition.*

Theorem 5.3 *The linear partition is vertical.*

PROOF. Because of Lemma 5.1, we need only show that the linear partition is coarser than the weak partition, that is, any two weakly connected iterations must belong to the same member of the linear partition.

Let $H(\mathbf{i})$ and $H(\mathbf{j})$ denote two weakly connected iterations. Then, there is a sequence of index points $\mathbf{i}_0, \mathbf{i}_1, \ldots, \mathbf{i}_n$ such that $\mathbf{i}_0 = \mathbf{i}$, $\mathbf{i}_n = \mathbf{j}$, and either $H(\mathbf{i}_k)$ depends on $H(\mathbf{i}_{k-1})$ or $H(\mathbf{i}_{k-1})$ depends on $H(\mathbf{i}_k)$ for $1 \le k \le n$. This means for each k there is a row $\mathbf{d}_t$ of $\mathcal{D}$ (which is a distance vector of **L**), such that $\mathbf{i}_k - \mathbf{i}_{k-1} = \pm \mathbf{d}_t$. We can write

$$
\begin{aligned}
\mathbf{j} - \mathbf{i} &= \mathbf{i}_n - \mathbf{i}_0 \\
&= (\mathbf{i}_1 - \mathbf{i}_0) + (\mathbf{i}_2 - \mathbf{i}_1) + \cdots + (\mathbf{i}_n - \mathbf{i}_{n-1}) \\
&= e_1 \mathbf{d}_1 + e_2 \mathbf{d}_2 + \cdots + e_N \mathbf{d}_N
\end{aligned}
$$

for some integers $e_1, e_2, \ldots, e_N$.[1] Setting $\mathbf{e} = (e_1, e_2, \ldots, e_N)$, we get $\mathbf{j} - \mathbf{i} = \mathbf{e}\mathcal{D}$. $\qquad\qquad\qquad\qquad\qquad\qquad\qquad\qquad\qquad\quad$ □

The linear partition is a coarser vertical partition than the weak partition. That the two partitions are different in general is clear from the dependence graph of Example 1.4.[2] There, we have

$$
(0,4) - (0,1) = (2,-1) \begin{pmatrix} 1 & 2 \\ 2 & 1 \end{pmatrix},
$$

but the iterations $H(0,1)$ and $H(0,4)$ are not weakly connected. Note that if $\mathcal{R}$ were all of $\mathbf{Z}^m$, then the linear and weak partitions would be identical, since then we could retrace the proof of Theorem 5.3 backwards. In that case, for any given index point $\mathbf{i}_k$ and any distance vector $\mathbf{d}_t$, the points $\mathbf{i}_k + \mathbf{d}_t$ and $\mathbf{i}_k - \mathbf{d}_t$ would be in the index space.

Corollary 3 to Theorem 4.8 shows that the mixed loop nest $\mathbf{L}'_{\mathbf{S}}$ obtained by Algorithm 4.1 has the execution order of the linear partition. We state this fact formally as a theorem:

Theorem 5.4 *The linear partition can be implemented by the echelon transformation.*

Next, define a relation between iterations of $\mathbf{L}$ by the requirement that $H(\mathbf{i})$ and $H(\mathbf{j})$ be related if $\mathbf{j} - \mathbf{i} = \mathbf{f}G$ for some integer m-vector $\mathbf{f}$, where G is the gcd matrix defined in Section 4.3. Clearly,

---

[1] Take all terms of the form $\pm\mathbf{d}_1$. Adding them up, we get an expression of the form $e_1\mathbf{d}_1$. If there are no such terms, take $e_1 = 0$. Then, take all terms of the form $\pm\mathbf{d}_2$, and so on.

[2] Note that if two partitions are identical, then each is finer or coarser than the other. Thus, the fact that one partition is coarser than another partition does not necessarily imply that they are distinct.

it is an equivalence relation. The partition of the dependence graph consisting of the equivalence classes of this relation is called the *gcd partition*.

Theorem 5.5 *The gcd partition is a vertical partition coarser than the linear partition.*

PROOF. Because of Lemma 5.1, it suffices to prove that if two iterations lie in the same member of the linear partition, then they must lie in the same member of the gcd partition.

Let $H(\mathbf{i})$ and $H(\mathbf{j})$ denote iterations that belong to the same member of the linear partition. By definition, there is an integer N-vector $\mathbf{e}$ such that

$$\mathbf{j} - \mathbf{i} = \mathbf{e}\mathcal{D}. \qquad (5.1)$$

We can write

$$\mathcal{D} = \begin{pmatrix} d'_{11} & d'_{12} & \cdots & d'_{1m} \\ d'_{21} & d'_{22} & \cdots & d'_{2m} \\ \vdots & \vdots & \ddots & \vdots \\ d'_{N1} & d'_{N2} & \cdots & d'_{Nm} \end{pmatrix} \cdot \begin{pmatrix} g_1 & 0 & \cdots & 0 \\ 0 & g_2 & \cdots & 0 \\ \vdots & \vdots & \ddots & \vdots \\ 0 & 0 & \cdots & g_m \end{pmatrix}$$

where

$$d'_{tr} = \begin{cases} d_{tr}/g_r & \text{if } g_r > 0 \\ 0 & \text{if } g_r = 0, \end{cases} \qquad (1 \le t \le N, 1 \le r \le m)$$

are integers. Hence, we can write

$$\mathbf{j} - \mathbf{i} = \mathbf{f}\mathbf{G}$$

where $\mathbf{f}$ is an integer m-vector. Thus, $H(\mathbf{i})$ and $H(\mathbf{j})$ belong to the same member of the gcd partition. □

The linear and gcd partitions are different in general; see Examples 4.2 and 4.4. Under certain conditions, the two partitions are identical (Exercise 1).

The execution order defined by the gcd partition is as follows: For two iterations $H(\mathbf{i})$ and $H(\mathbf{j})$ of $\mathbf{L}$, $H(\mathbf{i})$ is executed before $H(\mathbf{j})$ if $\mathbf{i} \prec \mathbf{j}$, and $i_r \bmod g_r = j_r \bmod g_r$ for each r.[3] The gcd partition can be implemented using loop permutation and the gcd transformation as explained in Section 4.3 (see Example 4.3).

We can define yet another vertical partition by the following equivalence relation in the set of iterations of $\mathbf{L}$: Two iterations $H(\mathbf{i})$ and $H(\mathbf{j})$ are related if $\mathbf{j} - \mathbf{i} = \mathbf{x}\mathcal{D}$ for some *real* N-vector $\mathbf{x}$. We give the name *real linear partition* to the partition defined by this equivalence relation, to distinguish it from the linear partition defined earlier. The following result is obvious:

Theorem 5.6 *The real linear partition is a vertical partition coarser than the linear partition.*

If $\operatorname{rank}(\mathcal{D}) = m$, then the rows of $\mathcal{D}$ span $\mathbf{Z}^m$, so that any m-vector can be written as a real linear combination of these rows. The real linear partition of the dependence graph becomes trivial in this case: there is only one member, namely, the whole graph. If $\operatorname{rank}(\mathcal{D}) < m$, then the real linear partition can be implemented by a unimodular transformation:

Theorem 5.7 *If $\operatorname{rank}(\mathcal{D}) < m$, then we can find an equivalent program $\mathbf{L}'$ by a unimodular transformation, such that the execution order of iterations (of $\mathbf{L}$) in $\mathbf{L}'$ is the same as that defined by the real linear partition of the dependence graph of $\mathbf{L}$.*

PROOF. Let $\rho = \operatorname{rank}(\mathcal{D})$. As shown in the proof of Theorem 3.8, there exists a unimodular matrix $\mathbf{U}$ such that the leftmost $(m - \rho)$ columns of $\mathcal{D}\mathbf{U}$ are zero and the transformation $\mathbf{L} \mapsto \mathbf{L}_\mathbf{U}$ is valid. The index vector of $\mathbf{L}_\mathbf{U}$ is $\mathbf{K} = \mathbf{I}\mathbf{U}$. The outermost $(m - \rho)$ loops of $\mathbf{L}_\mathbf{U}$ can execute in parallel. Let $\mathbf{L}'$ denote the mixed loop nest obtained from $\mathbf{L}_\mathbf{U}$ by changing those loops into their corresponding **doall** loops. In $\mathbf{L}'$, an iteration $H(\mathbf{i})$ is executed before an iteration $H(\mathbf{j})$, iff the first $(m - \rho)$ elements of $\mathbf{i}\mathbf{U}$ and $\mathbf{j}\mathbf{U}$ are equal and $\mathbf{i} \prec \mathbf{j}$.

---

[3]By definition, $x \bmod 0 = x$, so that $i_r = j_r$ when $g_r = 0$.

Let **i** and **j** denote any two index points of **L**. First, assume that the iteration $H(\mathbf{i})$ is executed before the iteration $H(\mathbf{j})$ in the execution order defined by the real linear partition. Then, there exists a real vector **x** such that $\mathbf{j} - \mathbf{i} = \mathbf{x}\mathcal{D}$, and $\mathbf{i} \prec \mathbf{j}$. We have $(\mathbf{j} - \mathbf{i})\mathbf{U} = \mathbf{x} \cdot \mathcal{D}\mathbf{U}$. Since the leftmost $(m - \rho)$ columns of $\mathcal{D}\mathbf{U}$ are zero, the leftmost $(m - \rho)$ elements of the vector $(\mathbf{j} - \mathbf{i})\mathbf{U}$ are zero, that is, the index points $\mathbf{iU}$ and $\mathbf{jU}$ have the first $(m - \rho)$ elements equal. Since $\mathbf{i} \prec \mathbf{j}$ also holds, the iteration $H(\mathbf{i})$ is executed before the iteration $H(\mathbf{j})$ in $\mathbf{L}'$.

Next, suppose that the iteration $H(\mathbf{i})$ is executed before the iteration $H(\mathbf{j})$ in $\mathbf{L}'$. Then, the leftmost $(m - \rho)$ elements of the vector $(\mathbf{j} - \mathbf{i})\mathbf{U}$ are zero, and $\mathbf{i} \prec \mathbf{j}$. We have

$$(\mathbf{j} - \mathbf{i}) \cdot \mathbf{u}^r = 0 \quad (1 \leq r \leq m - \rho)$$

where $\mathbf{u}^1, \mathbf{u}^2, \ldots, \mathbf{u}^{m-\rho}$ are the leftmost $(m-\rho)$ columns of **U**. These columns are linearly independent and they span a subspace of rank $(m - \rho)$. The subspace consisting of all vectors orthogonal to these columns has rank ρ. The rows of $\mathcal{D}$ belong to this orthogonal subspace, and they generate it since $\mathrm{rank}(\mathcal{D}) = \rho$. Since $\mathbf{j} - \mathbf{i}$ also belongs to this subspace, we can express $\mathbf{j} - \mathbf{i}$ as a real linear combination of the rows of $\mathcal{D}$. Thus, there is a real vector **x** such that $\mathbf{j} - \mathbf{i} = \mathbf{x}\mathcal{D}$. Since $\mathbf{i} \prec \mathbf{j}$ also holds, $H(\mathbf{i})$ is executed before $H(\mathbf{j})$ in the execution order defined by the real linear partition. $\square$

In general, the real linear partition is not finer or coarser than the gcd partition:

Example 5.1 The distance matrix of the loop nest **L**:

```
L₁ :        do I₁ = 1, 100
L₂ :          do I₂ = 1, 100
L₃ :            do I₃ = 1, 100
   H(I) :          X(I₁, I₂, I₃) = X(I₁ − 2, I₂ − 6, I₃ − 2) +
                                    X(I₁, I₂ − 3, I₃ − 3)
               enddo
             enddo
           enddo
```

is

$$\mathcal{D} = \begin{pmatrix} 2 & 6 & 2 \\ 0 & 3 & 3 \end{pmatrix}.$$

The gcd matrix is given by

$$\mathbf{G} = \begin{pmatrix} 2 & 0 & 0 \\ 0 & 3 & 0 \\ 0 & 0 & 1 \end{pmatrix}.$$

The iterations $H(\mathbf{i})$ and $H(\mathbf{j})$ for $\mathbf{i} = (1,1,1)$ and $\mathbf{j} = (3,4,2)$ lie in the same member of the gcd partition, since

$$\mathbf{j} - \mathbf{i} = (2,3,1) = (1,1,1) \cdot \begin{pmatrix} 2 & 0 & 0 \\ 0 & 3 & 0 \\ 0 & 0 & 1 \end{pmatrix} = (1,1,1) \cdot \mathbf{G}.$$

Now, the system of equations

$$\mathbf{j} - \mathbf{i} = (x_1, x_2) \cdot \mathcal{D}$$

that is, the system

$$(2,3,1) = (x_1, x_2) \cdot \begin{pmatrix} 2 & 6 & 2 \\ 0 & 3 & 3 \end{pmatrix}$$

has no real solution. This means the iterations $H(\mathbf{i})$ and $H(\mathbf{j})$ do not lie in the same member of the real linear partition. Hence, the gcd partition is not finer than the real linear partition.

Next, consider the iterations $H(\mathbf{i})$ and $H(\mathbf{j})$ where $\mathbf{i} = (1,1,1)$ and $\mathbf{j} = (2,5,3)$. Since

$$\mathbf{j} - \mathbf{i} = (1,4,2) = (1/2, 1/3) \cdot \begin{pmatrix} 2 & 6 & 2 \\ 0 & 3 & 3 \end{pmatrix} = (1/2, 1/3) \cdot \mathcal{D}$$

the iterations belong to the same member of the real linear partition. However, the system of equations

$$\mathbf{j} - \mathbf{i} = (e_1, e_2, e_3) \cdot \mathbf{G}$$

that is, the system

$$(1, 4, 2) = (e_1, e_2, e_3) \cdot \begin{pmatrix} 2 & 0 & 0 \\ 0 & 3 & 0 \\ 0 & 0 & 1 \end{pmatrix}$$

has no integer solution. This means the iterations $H(\mathbf{i})$ and $H(\mathbf{j})$ do not lie in the same member of the gcd partition. Hence, the real linear partition is not finer than the gcd partition.

Finally, we consider vertical partitions that can be implemented by loop permutations alone. If the distance matrix $\mathcal{D}$ has one or more zero columns, then we can define a partition of the dependence graph of **L** by the following equivalence relation: Two iterations $H(\mathbf{i})$ and $H(\mathbf{j})$ are related if $i_r = j_r$ whenever column r of $\mathcal{D}$ is zero. This is a vertical partition coarser than the gcd partition (Exercise 3), and can be implemented by a loop permutation (Corollary 1 to Theorem 2.8).

EXERCISES 5.2

1. Find condition(s) under which the gcd partition is identical to the linear partition.

2. Find condition(s) under which the real linear partition is identical to the linear partition. Give an example where they are different.

3. Let the distance matrix $\mathcal{D}$ have one or more zero columns. Consider the vertical partition defined by the following equivalence relation: Two iterations $H(\mathbf{i})$ and $H(\mathbf{j})$ are related if $i_r = j_r$ whenever column r of $\mathcal{D}$ is zero. Show that this is a vertical partition coarser than the gcd partition.

4. For the loop nest of Example 5.1, find three equivalent mixed loop nests that implement the three vertical partitions: linear, gcd, real linear. Find the same for the the inner nest of **do** loops that you get in each case. Should we continue this process forever?

5.3   Horizontal Partitions

A *horizontal partition* of the dependence graph of $\mathbf{L}$ is a partition
into a sequence of antichains $\{\mathcal{H}_0, \mathcal{H}_1, \ldots, \mathcal{H}_n\}$ such that no iteration in an antichain depends on any iteration in a previous antichain,
that is, $H(\mathbf{i}) \in \mathcal{H}_k$, $H(\mathbf{j}) \in \mathcal{H}_l$, and $H(\mathbf{j})$ depends on $H(\mathbf{i})$ imply
$k < l$. From the point of view of parallelization, the worst horizontal
partitions are those with single-element antichains (where $(n+1)$ is
the total number of iterations of $\mathbf{L}$). These are the finest partitions.
The best horizontal partitions are those for which $(n+1)$ is equal
to the length of the longest chain in the dependence graph. The
coarsest partition in this group is the one consisting of maximal
antichains as described in Theorem I-1.1.

We find horizontal partitions of the dependence graph by 'slic-
ing up' the index space in certain directions. The 'thickness' of a
slice (which is an antichain) will depend on the particular direction
chosen. A precise description of this process is given below:

An m-vector $\mathbf{u} = (u_1, u_2, \ldots, u_m)$ is a *valid wavefront direction*
for $\mathbf{L}$ if $\gcd(u_1, u_2, \ldots, u_m) = 1$ and

$$\mathbf{du} > 0 \quad (\mathbf{d} \in D).$$

We saw in Section 3.4 that valid wavefront directions always exist.
The scalar products $\mathbf{du}$ of distance vectors with $\mathbf{u}$ are the *dependence distances* of $\mathbf{L}$ *along* $\mathbf{u}$. The *minimum dependence distance
along* $\mathbf{u}$ is denoted by $b(\mathbf{u})$ and is defined by

$$b(\mathbf{u}) = \min_{\mathbf{d} \in D} \mathbf{du}.$$

Note that $b(\mathbf{u}) > 0$ for each valid wavefront direction $\mathbf{u}$.

Iterations $H(\mathbf{I})$ of $\mathbf{L}$ can be grouped into antichains based on
the value of $\mathbf{Iu}$:

Theorem 5.8 *Let* $\mathbf{u}$ *denote a valid wavefront direction for the loop
nest* $\mathbf{L}$. *Let* $b(\mathbf{u})$ *denote the minimum dependence distance of* $\mathbf{L}$

along **u**, *and let*

$$p(\mathbf{u}) = \min_{\mathbf{I} \in \mathcal{R}} \mathbf{Iu}, \quad q(\mathbf{u}) = \max_{\mathbf{I} \in \mathcal{R}} \mathbf{Iu}, \quad n(\mathbf{u}) = \left| \frac{q(\mathbf{u}) - p(\mathbf{u})}{b(\mathbf{u})} \right|.$$

Then, the sequence $\{\mathcal{H}_0, \mathcal{H}_1, \ldots, \mathcal{H}_n\}$ *forms a horizontal partition of the dependence graph of* **L**, *where*

$$\mathcal{H}_K = \{H(\mathbf{I}) : \mathbf{I} \in \mathcal{R}, \, p + bK \le \mathbf{Iu} < p + b(K+1)\}$$

for $0 \le K \le n$.

PROOF. The scalar product **Iu** lies in the range $p \le \mathbf{Iu} \le q$. Partition the set $\{p, p+1, \ldots, q\}$ into a sequence of consecutive intervals each having b integers (the last interval may have fewer than b). The number of such intervals is $n+1$, and the intervals are:

$$\{p, p+1, \ldots, p+b-1\}$$
$$\{p+b, p+b+1, \ldots, p+2b-1\}$$
$$\vdots$$
$$\{p+bn, p+bn+1, \ldots, \min(p+b(n+1)-1, q)\}.$$

If the value of **Iu** is one of the integers p through $(p+b-1)$, then $H(\mathbf{I})$ lies in the set $\mathcal{H}_0$; if the value of **Iu** is one of the integers $(p+b)$ through $(p+2b-1)$, then $H(\mathbf{I})$ lies in the set $\mathcal{H}_1$; and so on. It is clear then that these sets $\mathcal{H}_K$ form a partition of the dependence graph. For a given **I**, the iteration $H(\mathbf{I})$ lies in the unique subset $\mathcal{H}_K$ where

$$p + bK \le \mathbf{Iu} < p + b(K+1),$$

that is,

$$K = \lfloor (\mathbf{Iu} - p)/b \rfloor. \tag{5.2}$$

To prove that the partition $\{\mathcal{H}_0, \mathcal{H}_1, \ldots, \mathcal{H}_n\}$ of the dependence graph is horizontal, take two iterations $H(\mathbf{i})$ and $H(\mathbf{j})$ such that

$H(\mathbf{j})$ depends on $H(\mathbf{i})$. Let $H(\mathbf{i}) \in \mathcal{H}_k$ and $H(\mathbf{j}) \in \mathcal{H}_l$. We will show that $k < l$. Indeed, we have

$$
\begin{aligned}
k &= \lfloor (\mathbf{iu} - p)/b \rfloor \\
&\leq (\mathbf{iu} - p)/b \\
&= (\mathbf{ju} - p)/b - (\mathbf{ju} - \mathbf{iu})/b \\
&< \lfloor (\mathbf{ju} - p)/b \rfloor + 1 - (\mathbf{ju} - \mathbf{iu})/b \\
&= l - [(\mathbf{ju} - \mathbf{iu})/b - 1] \\
&\leq l
\end{aligned}
$$

since

$$
0 < b(\mathbf{u}) = \min_{\mathbf{d} \in D} \mathbf{dU} \leq (\mathbf{j} - \mathbf{i})\mathbf{u} = \mathbf{ju} - \mathbf{iu}
$$

so that $(\mathbf{ju} - \mathbf{iu})/b \geq 1$.   □

We say that the horizontal partition $\{\mathcal{H}_0, \mathcal{H}_1, \ldots, \mathcal{H}_n\}$ *corresponds* to the wavefront direction $\mathbf{u}$. The proofs of the following corollaries are straightforward and are left to the reader:

Corollary 1 *The number of members of the horizontal partition of Theorem 5.8 is*

$$
n(\mathbf{u}) + 1 = \left\lfloor (\max_{\mathbf{I} \in \mathcal{R}} \mathbf{Iu} - \min_{\mathbf{I} \in \mathcal{R}} \mathbf{Iu})/(\min_{\mathbf{d} \in D} \mathbf{du}) \right\rfloor + 1.
$$

Corollary 2 *If $\mathbf{u}$ is a valid wavefront direction for $\mathbf{L}$, then the length of any chain of iterations in the dependence graph of $\mathbf{L}$ cannot exceed $n(\mathbf{u}) + 1$.*

Suppose we have found a valid wavefront direction $\mathbf{u}$ that minimizes $n(\mathbf{u})$. Then, the corresponding partition $\{\mathcal{H}_0, \mathcal{H}_1, \ldots, \mathcal{H}_n\}$ of the dependence graph is very 'close' to being an ideal horizontal partition. To see this, let $\mathbf{d}_0$ denote a distance vector such that

$$
b \equiv b(\mathbf{u}) = \min_{\mathbf{d} \in D} \mathbf{du} = \mathbf{d}_0 \mathbf{u}.
$$

Let $H(\mathbf{i}_0)$ denote an iteration in $\mathcal{H}_0$. Define a sequence of points $\{\mathbf{i}_k : 1 \leq k \leq n\}$ by

$$\mathbf{i}_k = \mathbf{i}_{k-1} + \mathbf{d}_0 \quad (1 \leq k \leq n).$$

Then, we have

$$\mathbf{i}_k \cdot \mathbf{u} = \mathbf{i}_{k-1} \cdot \mathbf{u} + \mathbf{d}_0 \cdot \mathbf{u} = \mathbf{i}_{k-1} \cdot \mathbf{u} + b$$

so that

$$\lfloor (\mathbf{i}_k \cdot \mathbf{u} - p)/b \rfloor = \lfloor (\mathbf{i}_{k-1} \cdot \mathbf{u} - p)/b \rfloor + 1. \tag{5.3}$$

Since $\mathbf{i}_0 \in \mathcal{H}_0$, we have $\lfloor (\mathbf{i}_0 \cdot \mathbf{u} - p)/b \rfloor = 0$ by (5.2). It follows from the recurrence relation (5.3) that

$$\lfloor (\mathbf{i}_k \cdot \mathbf{u} - p)/b \rfloor = k \quad (1 \leq k \leq n).$$

Thus, if the index space $\mathcal{R}$ of $\mathbf{L}$ were large enough to hold the points $\mathbf{i}_0, \mathbf{i}_1, \ldots, \mathbf{i}_n$, then the iteration $H(\mathbf{i}_k)$ would belong to the subset $\mathcal{H}_k$ and $H(\mathbf{i}_k)$ would depend on $H(\mathbf{i}_{k-1})$, $1 \leq k \leq n$. Then, $H(\mathbf{i}_0), H(\mathbf{i}_1), \ldots, H(\mathbf{i}_n)$ would be a chain in the dependence graph. In other words, $n+1$ would be the length of the longest chain in the dependence graph (in view of Corollary 2), and hence the horizontal partition $\{\mathcal{H}_k : 0 \leq k \leq n\}$ would be one of the best.

A horizontal partition $\{\mathcal{H}_0, \mathcal{H}_1, \ldots, \mathcal{H}_N\}$ defines a valid execution order for the iterations of $\mathbf{L}$ in a natural way: An iteration $H(\mathbf{i})$ is executed before an iteration $H(\mathbf{j})$, iff $H(\mathbf{i}) \in \mathcal{H}_k$ and $H(\mathbf{j}) \in \mathcal{H}_l$ where $k < l$. Once a suitable wavefront direction has been found, implementation of the corresponding horizontal partition is quite easy ('implementation' is defined as in the previous section):

Algorithm 5.1 Given a nest $\mathbf{L}$ of m **do** loops and a valid wavefront direction $\mathbf{u}$ for $\mathbf{L}$, this algorithm finds an equivalent mixed nest $\mathbf{L}'$ of $(m + 1)$ loops, such that the outermost loop is a **do** loop, the m innermost loops are **doall** loops, and the execution order of $\mathbf{L}'$ is the same as that defined by the horizontal partition corresponding to $\mathbf{u}$. Let $\mathbf{I}$ denote the index vector and $\mathcal{D}$ the distance matrix of $\mathbf{L}$.

1. Using Algorithm I-2.2, find an $m \times m$ unimodular matrix $\mathbf{U}$ whose first column is $\mathbf{u}$ (see Corollary 4 to Theorem I-3.4).

2. As explained in Section 3.6, find the loop nest $\mathbf{L_U}$ defined by the unimodular matrix $\mathbf{U}$.

   [The first column of the distance matrix $\mathcal{D}\mathbf{U}$ of $\mathbf{L_U}$ consists of the scalar products $\mathbf{du}$ where $\mathbf{d}$ is a distance vector of $\mathbf{L}$. This column has all positive elements since $\mathbf{u}$ is a valid wavefront direction. Thus, $\mathbf{L_U}$ is equivalent to $\mathbf{L}$ and its $(m-1)$ inner loops can execute in parallel.]

3. By Theorem 4.2, replace the K_1-loop by a double loop with index vector (K, Y) such that the Y-loop can execute in parallel.

4. Change the loops with index variables $Y, K_2, K_3, \ldots, K_m$ into their corresponding **doall** loops. Denote the resulting program by $\mathbf{L'}$.

The next question is "How do we find a valid wavefront direction for a given loop nest?" One way is to look for a loop L_ℓ in the nest such that column ℓ of the distance matrix $\mathcal{D}$ has only positive elements (i.e., the ℓth element of each distance vector is positive). Let b_ℓ denote the minimum of all these elements. We can take

$$\mathbf{u} = (\underbrace{0, 0, \ldots, 0}_{\ell-1}, 1, 0, \ldots, 0)$$

as a valid wavefront direction. Algorithm 5.1 can be simplified in this case, as explained below:

Since column ℓ of the direction matrix $\mathbf{\Delta}$ of $\mathbf{L}$ has all 1's, we can move the loop L_ℓ outward to the outermost position by a right circulation (Corollary 1 to Theorem 2.8). In the transformed program

$$(L_\ell, L_1, L_2, \ldots, L_{\ell-1}, L_{\ell+1}, \ldots, L_m),$$

the inner $(m-1)$ loops carry no dependence, and therefore they can all execute in parallel (Lemma 1.1). The transformed program is now considered to be a single loop L_ℓ whose body is the loop nest

$$(L_1, L_2, \ldots, L_{\ell-1}, L_{\ell+1}, \ldots, L_m),$$

and whose minimum dependence distance is b_ℓ. We apply Theorem 4.2 to this loop to create a nest of two loops $(L_{\ell1}, L_{\ell2})$ where the inner loop $L_{\ell2}$ can execute in parallel. We now have an equivalent nest

$$(L_{\ell1}, L_{\ell2}, L_1, L_2, \ldots, L_{\ell-1}, L_{\ell+1}, \ldots, L_m)$$

of $(m+1)$ loops where the inner m loops can all execute in parallel.

If there are two or more loops that would qualify to be our L_ℓ, then we will choose the one that would minimize the iteration count of the outermost sequential loop in the final transformed program.

This process is explained below by an example:

Example 5.2 The distance matrix of the loop nest **L**:

$L_1 :$ **do** $I_1 = 1, 100$
$L_2 :$ **do** $I_2 = 1, 100$
$L_3 :$ **do** $I_3 = 1, 100$
    $H(\mathbf{I}) :$ $X(I_1, I_2, I_3) = X(I_1 - 1, I_2 + 1, I_3 - 4) +$
                                $X(I_1, I_2 - 1, I_3 - 2)$
      enddo
    enddo
  enddo

is

$$\mathcal{D} = \begin{pmatrix} 1 & -1 & 4 \\ 0 & 1 & 2 \end{pmatrix}.$$

Column 3 of $\mathcal{D}$ has all positive entries. The right circulation that brings L_3 to the outermost position is valid, so that **L** is equivalent to the loop nest:

L_3 :   **do** $I_3 = 1, 100$
L_1 :   **do** $I_1 = 1, 100$
L_2 :   **do** $I_2 = 1, 100$
      $H(\mathbf{I})$: $X(I_1, I_2, I_3) = X(I_1 - 1, I_2 + 1, I_3 - 4) +$
                                    $X(I_1, I_2 - 1, I_3 - 2)$
            enddo
          enddo
        enddo

The distance matrix of this loop nest is

$$\begin{pmatrix} 4 & 1 & -1 \\ 2 & 0 & 1 \end{pmatrix}.$$

Since the two inner loops carry no dependence, they can execute in parallel. The minimum dependence distance for the outermost loop is $b = 2$. Apply Theorem 4.2 to this loop. We replace I_3 by two new variables Y and K where $I_3 = Y + 2K$. The following equivalent program results:

   do $K = 0, 50$
      do $Y = \max(1 - 2K, 0), \min(100 - 2K, 1)$
L_1 :   **do** $I_1 = 1, 100$
L_2 :   **do** $I_2 = 1, 100$
                $X(I_1, I_2, Y + 2K) = X(I_1 - 1, I_2 + 1, Y + 2K - 4) +$
                                    $X(I_1, I_2 - 1, Y + 2K - 2)$
          enddo
        enddo
      enddo
    enddo

The distance matrix of this loop nest is

$$\begin{pmatrix} 2 & 0 & 1 & -1 \\ 1 & 0 & 0 & 1 \end{pmatrix}$$

(explain). Here, the three inner loops can execute in parallel, so that the given program is equivalent to the loop nest:

> **do** $K = 0, 50$
>> **doall** $Y = \max(1 - 2K, 0), \min(100 - 2K, 1)$
> L_1 :   **doall** $I_1 = 1, 100$
> L_2 :   **doall** $I_2 = 1, 100$
>>>> $X(I_1, I_2, Y + 2K) =$
>>>>> $X(I_1 - 1, I_2 + 1, Y + 2K - 4) +$
>>>>> $X(I_1, I_2 - 1, Y + 2K - 2)$
>>> **enddoall**
>> **enddoall**
> **enddoall**
> **enddo**

When we do not have a column of $\mathcal{D}$ with all positive elements, we can always apply a unimodular transformation to create such a column (Algorithm 3.1). As shown in Theorem 3.7, there are infinitely many valid wavefront directions each of which will lead to a horizontal partition. The number of members of the partition will depend on the choice of the wavefront direction.

EXERCISES 5.3

1. Take the double loop of Example 3.1. Clearly, the wavefront direction $\mathbf{u} = (1, 1)$ gives the best horizontal partition. Can you find another double loop with the same body for which the wavefront direction $(2, 1)$ will give a better horizontal partition (i.e., with fewer antichains) than $(1, 1)$?

2. Consider the program of Example 5.1. Implement a horizontal partition by Algorithm 5.1 with the following choice for a valid wavefront direction $\mathbf{u}$:

   (a) Take $\mathbf{u} = (0, 1, 0)$;

   (b) Take $\mathbf{u} = (0, 0, 1)$;

   (c) Find $\mathbf{u}$ by Algorithm 3.1.

   Compare the three equivalent loop nests.

3. Using Algorithms 3.1 and 5.1, implement a horizontal partition for the loop nest of Example 5.2. Is this partition better or worse than the horizontal partition obtained in the example?

5.4   Vertical and Horizontal Parallelism

To find both vertical and horizontal parallelism in a given loop nest
L, we first apply the echelon transformation to get an equivalent
loop nest with an outermost nest of **doall** loops and a core of **do**
loops (Algorithm 4.1). Then, we find a valid wavefront direction by
the Hyperplane method (Algorithm 3.1) for that inner nest of **do**
loops. Next, we transform this nest by Algorithm 5.1. The ultimate
result is an equivalent mixed loop nest with an outermost nest of
doall loops, then a **do** loop, and then an inner core of **doall** loops.

Less expensive algorithms can be easily designed that avoid the
echelon transformation, but use other transformations used in the
book (Exercise 1). The trade-off is a possible loss of parallelism.

EXERCISES 5.4

1. Describe ways to display both vertical and horizontal parallelism in a
   given loop nest when you can use all the algorithms in this book except
   echelon transformation.

2. Find both vertical and horizontal parallelism in the loop nests of Exercise 4.3.2 by using Algorithms 4.1, 3.1, and 5.1 as described in this
   section.

5.5   Suggested Reading

The literature on loop transformations is vast. The bibliography
in this book is only a small subset of it, even though we have included some references not explicitly referred to in the text. Mike
Wolfe's thesis is a good introduction to the pioneering work at the
University of Illinois, and so is Randy Allen's thesis to the research at Rice. One should follow the research done at the Center for Supercomputing Research and Development (mainly by the
groups of David Padua and Constantine Polychronopoulos), Rice
University (Ken Kennedy's department), Oregon Graduate Insti-
tute (Michael Wolfe's group), Stanford University (Monica Lam's
group), Ecole des Mines de Paris (François Irigoin's group), State

University of Ghent, Belgium (Erik D'Hollander), Purdue University (Jose Fortes), Cornell University (Keshav Pingali's group), University of California at Irvine (Alex Nicolau's group), and the works of Michael Burke, Ron Cytron, Jeanne Ferrante at IBM Yorktown Heights. Again, this is not a comprehensive list.

Bibliography

[AlKe84]   John R. Allen & Ken Kennedy. Automatic Loop Inter-
             change. *Proceedings of the SIGPLAN '84 Symposium on
             Compiler Construction*, Montreal, Canada, June 17-22,
             1984. pp. 233–246. Available as *SIGPLAN Notices*, vol.
             19, no. 6. June 1984.

[AlKe87]   John R. Allen & Ken Kennedy. Automatic Translation
             of Fortran Programs to Vector Form. *ACM Transac-
             tions on Programming Languages and Systems*, vol. **9**,
             no. 4, pp. 491–542. October 1987.

[Alle83]   John R. Allen. Dependence Analysis for Subscripted
             Variables and its Application to Program Transforma-
             tions. *PhD Thesis*. Dept. of Mathematical Sciences,
             Rice University, Houston, Texas. April 1983. Avail-
             able as *Document 83-14916* from University Microfilms,
             Ann Arbor, Michigan.

[Bane88a]   Utpal Banerjee. *Dependence Analysis for Supercom-
             puting*. Kluwer Academic Publishers, Norwell, Mas-
             sachusetts. 1988.

[Bane90]   Utpal Banerjee. A Theory of Loop Permutations. In
             *Proceedings of the Second Workshop on Languages and
             Compilers for Parallel Computing*, Urbana, Illinois, Au-
             gust 1989. Available as *Languages and Compilers for
             Parallel Computing* (eds. D. Gelernter, A. Nicolau & D.

Padua). pp. 54–74. The MIT Press, Cambridge, Massachusetts. 1990.

[Bane91]   Utpal Banerjee. Unimodular Transformations of Double Loops. In *Proceedings of the Third Workshop on Languages and Compilers for Parallel Computing*, Irvine, California, August 1–3, 1990. Available as *Advances in Languages and Compilers for Parallel Computing* (eds. A. Nicolau, D. Gelernter, T. Gross & D. Padua). pp. 192–219. The MIT Press, Cambridge, Massachusetts. 1991.

[Bane93]   Utpal Banerjee. *Loop Transformations for Restructuring Compilers—The Foundations*. Kluwer Academic Publishers, Norwell, Massachusetts. 1993.

[BCKT79]   Utpal Banerjee, Shyh-Ching Chen, David J. Kuck & Ross A. Towle. Time and Parallel Processor Bounds for Fortran-Like Loops. *IEEE Transactions on Computers*, vol. **C-28**, no. 9, pp. 660–670. September 1979.

[BENP93]   Utpal Banerjee, Rudolf Eigenmann, Alexandru Nicolau & David A. Padua. Automatic Program Parallelization. *Proceedings of the IEEE*, vol. **81**, no. 2, pp. 211–243. February 1993.

[D'Hol89]   Erik H. D'Hollander. Partitioning and Labeling of Index Sets in Do Loops with Constant Dependence Vectors. *Proceedings of the 1989 International Conference on Parallel Processing, vol. II: Software*, St. Charles, Illinois, August 8–12, 1989. pp. 139–144. Pennsylvania State University Press, University Park, Pennsylvania. August 1989.

[D'Hol92]   Erik H. D'Hollander. Partitioning and Labeling of Loops by Unimodular Transformations. *IEEE Trans-*

actions on Parallel and Distributed Systems, vol. **3**, no. 4, pp. 465–476. July 1992.

[Dowl90] Michael L. Dowling. Optimal Code Parallelization using Unimodular Transformations. *Parallel Computing*, vol. **16**, pp. 157–171, 1990.

[Even79] Shimon Even. *Graph Algorithms*. Computer Science Press, Rockville, Maryland. 1979.

[Gibb85] Alan Gibbons. *Algorithmic Graph Theory*. Cambridge University Press, New York, New York. 1985.

[Halm65] Paul R. Halmos. *Naive Set Theory*. D. Van Nostrand, Princeton, New Jersey. 1965.

[HaPo90] Mohammad Haghighat & Constantine D. Polychronopoulos. Symbolic Dependence Analysis for High-Performance Parallelizing Compilers. In *Proceedings of the Third Workshop on Languages and Compilers for Parallel Computing*, Irvine, California, August 1–3, 1990. Available as *Advances in Languages and Compilers for Parallel Computing* (eds. A. Nicolau, D. Gelernter, T. Gross & D. Padua). The MIT Press, Cambridge, Massachusetts. pp. 310–330. 1991.

[IrTr89] François Irigoin & Rémi Triolet. Dependence Approximation and Global Parallel Code Generation for Nested Loops. In *Parallel and Distributed Algorithms*, (eds. M. Cosnard et al.). Elsivier (North-Holland), New York, New York. pp. 297–308. 1989.

[Knut73] Donald E. Knuth. *The Art of Computer Programming, Volume 1/ Fundamental Algorithms*, Second Edition. Addison-Wesley, Reading, Massachusetts. 1973.

[Knut81]   Donald E. Knuth. *The Art of Computer Programming, Volume 2: Seminumerical Algorithms*, Second Edition. Addison-Wesley, Reading, Massachusetts. 1981.

[Lamp74]   L. Lamport. The Parallel Execution of DO Loops. *Communications of the ACM*, vol. **17**, no. 2, pp. 83–93. February, 1974.

[MaBi88]   Saunders MacLane & Garrett Birkhoff. *Algebra*, Third Edition. Chelsea Publishing Co., New York, New York. 1988.

[Padu79]   David A. Padua. Multiprocessors: Discussion of some Theoretical and Practical Problems. *PhD Thesis. Report 79-990*. Dept. of Computer Science, University of Illinois at Urbana-Champaign, Urbana, Illinois. November 1979.

[PaWo86]   David A. Padua & Michael J. Wolfe. Advanced Compiler Optimizations for Supercomputers. *Communications of the ACM*, vol. **29**, no. 12, pp. 1184–1201. December 1986.

[PeCy89]   J.-K. Peir & R. Cytron. Minimum Distance: A Method for Partitioning Recurrences for Multiprocessors. *IEEE Transactions on Computers*, vol. **C-38**, no. 8, pp. 1203–1211. August 1989.

[PoBa87]   Constantine D. Polychronopoulos & Utpal Banerjee. Processor Allocation for Horizontal and Vertical Parallelism and Related Speedup Bounds. *IEEE Transactions on Computers*, vol. **C-36**, no. 4, pp. 410–420. April 1987.

[Poly88]   Constantine D. Polychronopoulos. Compiler Optimizations for Enhancing Parallelism and their impact on Architecture Design. *IEEE Transactions on Computers*, vol. **C-37**, no. 8, pp. 991–1004. August 1988.

[Prat76]   R. E. Prather. *Discrete Mathematical Structures for Computer Science.* Houghton Mifflin Co., Boston, Massachusetts. 1976.   .

[Schr87]   Alexander Schrijver. *Theory of Linear and Integer Programming.* John Wiley & Sons, New York, New York. 1987.

[ShFo88]   Weijia Shang & Jose A. B. Fortes. Independent Partitioning of Algorithms with Uniform Dependences. *Proceedings of the 1988 International Conference on Parallel Processing, vol. II: Software*, St. Charles, Illinois, August 15–19, 1988. pp. 26–33. Pennsylvania State University Press, University Park, Pennsylvania. August 1988.

[ShFo91]   Weijia Shang & Jose A. B. Fortes. Time Optimal Linear Schedules for Algorithms with Uniform Dependences. *IEEE Transactions on Computers*, vol. **40**, no. 6, pp. 723–742. June 1991.

[WoLa91a]   Michael E. Wolf & Monica S. Lam. An Algorithmic Approach to Compound Loop Transformations. In *Proceedings of the Third Workshop on Languages and Compilers for Parallel Computing*, Irvine, California, August 1–3, 1990. Available as *Advances in Languages and Compilers for Parallel Computing* (eds. A. Nicolau, D. Gelernter, T. Gross & D. Padua). pp. 243–259. The MIT Press, Cambridge, Massachusetts. 1991.

[WoLa91b]   Michael E. Wolf & Monica S. Lam. A Loop Transformation Theory and an Algorithm to maximize Parallelism. *IEEE Transactions on Parallel and Distributed Systems*, vol. **2**, no. 4, pp. 452–471. October 1991.

[Wolf82]   Michael J. Wolfe. Optimizing Compilers for Supercomputers. *PhD Thesis, Report 82-1105*, Dept. of Computer

Science, University of Illinois at Urbana-Champaign, Urbana, Illinois. October 1982. Available as Center for Supercomputing Research & Development *Report 329*, and as *Document 83-03027* from University Microfilms, Ann Arbor, Michigan.

[Wolf86a]   Michael J. Wolfe. Loop Skewing: The Wavefront Method Revisited. *International Journal of Parallel Programming*, vol. **15**, no. 4, pp. 279–293. August 1986.

[Wolf86b]   Michael J. Wolfe. Advanced Loop Interchanging. *Proceedings of the 1986 International Conference on Parallel Processing*, St. Charles, Illinois, August 19–22, 1986. pp. 536–543. IEEE Computer Society Press, Los Angeles, California. 1986.

[Wolf89]   Michael J. Wolfe. *Optimizing Supercompilers for Supercomputers*. The MIT Press, Cambridge, Massachusetts. 1989.

Index